William John Abbot

Blue Jackets of '61

A history of the navy in the war of secession

William John Abbot

Blue Jackets of '61
A history of the navy in the war of secession

ISBN/EAN: 9783744747882

Printed in Europe, USA, Canada, Australia, Japan

Cover: Foto ©ninafisch / pixelio.de

More available books at **www.hansebooks.com**

A HISTORY OF THE NAVY IN THE WAR OF SECESSION

BY

WILLIS J. ABBOT

WITH ILLUSTRATIONS

PRINCIPALLY BY W. C. JACKSON

NEW YORK
DODD, MEAD, AND COMPANY
1887

CONTENTS.

CHAPTER I.
                                                                                                    PAGE

THE OPENING OF THE CONFLICT. — THE NAVIES OF THE CONTESTANTS. — DIX'S FAMOUS DESPATCH. — THE RIVER-GUNBOATS 1

CHAPTER II.
FORT SUMTER BOMBARDED. — ATTEMPT OF THE "STAR OF THE WEST" TO RE-ENFORCE ANDERSON. — THE NAVAL EXPEDITION TO FORT SUMTER. — THE RESCUE OF THE FRIGATE "CONSTITUTION." — BURNING THE NORFOLK NAVY-YARD 10

CHAPTER III.
DIFFICULTIES OF THE CONFEDERATES IN GETTING A NAVY. — EXPLOIT OF THE "FRENCH LADY." — NAVAL SKIRMISHING ON THE POTOMAC. — THE CRUISE OF THE "SUMTER," 25

CHAPTER IV.
THE POTOMAC FLOTILLA. — CAPTURE OF ALEXANDRIA. — ACTIONS AT MATTHIAS POINT. — BOMBARDMENT OF THE HATTERAS FORTS 37

CHAPTER V.
THE "TRENT" AFFAIR. — OPERATIONS IN ALBEMARLE AND PAMLICO SOUNDS. — DESTRUCTION OF THE CONFEDERATE FLEET 53

CONTENTS.

CHAPTER VI.

REDUCTION OF NEWBERN. — EXPLOITS OF LIEUT. CUSHING. — DESTRUCTION OF THE RAM "ALBEMARLE" 70

CHAPTER VII.

THE BLOCKADE-RUNNERS. — NASSAU AND WILMINGTON. — WORK OF THE CRUISERS. . 90

CHAPTER VIII.

DUPONT'S EXPEDITION TO HILTON HEAD AND PORT ROYAL. — THE FIERY CIRCLE . . 114

CHAPTER IX.

THE FIRST IRON-CLAD VESSELS IN HISTORY. — THE "MERRIMAC" SINKS THE "CUMBERLAND," AND DESTROYS THE "CONGRESS." — DUEL BETWEEN THE "MONITOR" AND "MERRIMAC" 129

CHAPTER X.

THE NAVY IN THE INLAND WATERS. — THE MISSISSIPPI SQUADRON. — SWEEPING THE TENNESSEE RIVER 155

CHAPTER XI.

FAMOUS CONFEDERATE PRIVATEERS, — THE "ALABAMA," THE "SHENANDOAH," THE "NASHVILLE" 180

CHAPTER XII.

WORK OF THE GULF SQUADRON. — THE FIGHT AT THE PASSES OF THE MISSISSIPPI. — DESTRUCTION OF THE SCHOONER "JUDAH." — THE BLOCKADE OF GALVESTON, AND CAPTURE OF THE "HARRIET LANE" 206

CHAPTER XIII.

THE CAPTURE OF NEW ORLEANS. — FARRAGUT'S FLEET PASSES FORT ST. PHILIP AND FORT JACKSON 219

CHAPTER XIV.

Along the Mississippi. — Forts Jackson and St. Philip surrender. — The Battle at St. Charles. — The Ram "Arkansas." — Bombardment and Capture of Port Hudson 243

CHAPTER XV.

On to Vicksburg. — Bombardment of the Confederate Stronghold. — Porter's Cruise in the Forests 254

CHAPTER XVI.

Vicksburg surrenders, and the Mississippi is opened. — Naval Events along the Gulf Coast 279

CHAPTER XVII.

Operations about Charleston. — The Bombardment, the Siege, and the Capture, 293

CHAPTER XVIII.

The Battle of Mobile Bay 303

CHAPTER XIX.

The Fall of Fort Fisher. — The Navy ends its Work 313

ILLUSTRATIONS.

	PAGE
Sinking of the "Alabama"	*Frontispiece*
The "Hartford," Farragut's Flagship	2
Departure of a Naval Expedition from Port Royal	4
Fort Moultrie	11
Anderson's Command occupying Fort Sumter	12
Major Robert Anderson	14
Fort Sumter under Fire	16
Destruction of Norfolk Navy-Yard	22
The "French Lady"	27
Blockading the Mouth of the Mississippi	31
Flag of the Confederacy	38
Naval Patrol on the Potomac	44
The Fleet off Hatteras	48
Attack on the Hatteras Forts	50
Shores of Albemarle Sound	57
Contrabands escaping to Fleet	63
Flag of South Carolina	73
Destruction of the "Albemarle"	87
Nassau: the Haunt of Blockade-Runners	94
Cotton Ships at Nassau	96
Blockade-Runner in North Carolina Sounds	101
Pursuing a Blockade-Runner	105
Fortress Monroe	118
DuPont's Expedition off Cape Hatteras	120

ILLUSTRATIONS.

	PAGE
THE OPENING GUN	124
THE FIGHT AT HILTON HEAD	126
"MERRIMAC" AND "CUMBERLAND"	141
BATTLE OF THE "MONITOR" AND "MERRIMAC"	147
HANDLING A GUN	150
A RIVER GUNBOAT	158
MORTAR-BOATS AT ISLAND NO. 10	171
LOOTING A PRIZE	185
RESCUE OF CAPT. SEMMES	195
THE END OF A PRIVATEER	198
THE "NASHVILLE" BURNING A PRIZE	200
"SHENANDOAH" BURNING WHALERS	204
FORT PENSACOLA	209
DESTRUCTION OF THE SCHOONER "JUDAH"	211
CAPTURE OF THE "HARRIET LANE"	216
LEVEE AT NEW ORLEANS BEFORE THE WAR	221
FIRE-RAFT AT FORTS OF THE MISSISSIPPI	227
BREAKING THE CHAIN	231
RAM "TENNESSEE" AT MOBILE BAY	233
NEW ORLEANS ON APPROACH OF FLEET	239
THE "ARKANSAS" UNDER FIRE	250
PORTER'S FLOTILLA ON THE RED RIVER	264
DUMMY GUNBOAT PASSING FORTS ON THE MISSISSIPPI	272
PASSING THE VICKSBURG BATTERIES	277
MANNING THE YARDS	283
BAILEY'S DAM ON THE RED RIVER	288
CUTTING OUT A BLOCKADE-RUNNER	296
CHARLESTON BOMBARDED	299
WAR-SHIPS OFF CHARLESTON HARBOR	301
FIGHT AT MOBILE BAY	310
CHARGE OF SAILORS AT FORT FISHER	316

BLUE-JACKETS OF '61.

CHAPTER I.

THE OPENING OF THE CONFLICT. — THE NAVIES OF THE CONTESTANTS. — DIX'S FAMOUS DESPATCH. — THE RIVER GUNBOATS.

THE story of the naval operations of the civil war is a record of wonderful energy and inventive skill in improvising and building war-vessels, vigilance and courage in handling them, and desperate bravery and dash displayed by officers and seamen in the great engagements in which vessels of either side took part. Yet of the immense body of literature dealing with the war, the greater part is given to telling the story of the great armies of the North and South. The details of the great land battles are familiar to many who have but a vague idea of the service done by the "blue jackets" of the North, and the daring deeds performed by the navies of both sides.

When the first mutterings of the storm of war began to be heard, the United States Government had at its disposal sixty-nine vessels-of-war, of which twenty-seven were laid up for repairs, or, sailors would say, "out of commission." Of the forty-two vessels in commission, twenty-six were absent on missions to the East Indies, the African coast, and other distant quarters of the globe. Long months must elapse before the most hasty orders could reach them. Many were sailing-vessels, and must consume many months of precious time before they could reach the shores of the

THE "HARTFORD," FARRAGUT'S FLAGSHIP.

United States. Indeed, though on the inauguration of President Lincoln on March 4, 1861, all these vessels were immediately recalled, not one arrived before the middle of June, and many were delayed until late in the following winter. Of the vessels at home, many were old-fashioned sailing-frigates; beautiful with their towering masts and clouds of snowy canvas, but almost useless in that day when steam had become known as the only means of propelling vessels-of-war.

In officers and men the navy was almost as deficient as in vessels. A long peace had filled the lists of officers with old men past that age in which may be expected the alertness and energy that must be possessed by Jack afloat. The lower grades were filled by boyish officers from the Naval Academy, who had never seen a gun fired in anger. The service was becoming rusty from long idleness.

Such was the condition of the navy of the United States when Abraham Lincoln was made President. Four years later the navy of the United States consisted of six hundred and seventy-one vessels. No nation of the world had such a naval power. The stern lessons of the great war had taught shipbuilders that wooden ships were a thing of the past. The little "Monitor" had by one afternoon's battle proved to all the sovereigns of Europe that their massive ships were useless. And all this had been done by a people grappling in deadly strife with an enemy in their very dwellings. The world's history contains no more wonderful story of energy and invention.

When President Lincoln began his term of office, he appointed Gideon Welles of Connecticut Secretary of the Navy. South Carolina had seceded from the Union. Mississippi, Georgia, Florida, Alabama, and Louisiana had followed South Carolina. Anderson, with a handful of United States troops, was holding Fort Sumter, expecting every minute to see the puff of smoke from the distant casement of Fort Moultrie, and hear the shriek of the shell that should announce the opening of the attack. At Washington, politicians were intriguing. The loyalty of no man could be regarded as certain. Officers of the army and navy were daily resigning, and hastening to put themselves under the command of their various States. In the South all was activity. In the North the popular desire for a compromise hampered the authorities so that no decided stand against the spread of the rebellion could be made. The new Secretary of the Navy found himself face to face with the certainty of a long and bloody war, yet had under his command a navy hardly adequate for times

DEPARTURE OF A NAVAL EXPEDITION FROM PORT ROYAL.

of peace. To add to his perplexity, many of the oldest and most skilful officers in the navy resigned, saying that their duty to their States was greater than to the United States as a whole. A few revenue officers even went so far as to deliver to the State authorities the vessels of which they were in command. One commander, a Georgian, bringing his ship back from foreign waters, hesitated long whether to take it to the navy-yard at New York, or to deliver it to the Southern leaders. He finally decided to obey orders, and the ship remained with the United States. Some days afterward the commander told his lieutenant of his hesitation. "We all saw it," said the younger officer; "and had you turned the ship's prow towards Charleston, you would have been instantly put in irons."

The surrender of another naval vessel called forth that famous despatch from John A. Dix that will ever be linked with his name. The United States revenue cutter "McClelland" was lying at New Orleans, under the command of Capt. Breshwood. The revenue service is distinct from the regular navy, and is under the general command of the Secretary of the Treasury. John A. Dix, then Secretary of the Treasury, suspected that Capt. Breshwood was about to surrender his vessel to the Confederates, and sent an agent to order him to take the vessel to New York. Breshwood refused, and instantly Dix sent the despatch: "Tell Lieut. Caldwell to arrest Capt. Breshwood, assume command of the cutter, and obey the order through you. If Capt. Breshwood, after arrest, undertakes to interfere with the command of the cutter, tell Lieut. Caldwell to consider him as a mutineer, and treat him accordingly. *If any man attempts to haul down the American flag, shoot him on the spot.*" This despatch was intercepted by the Confederates, and the cutter was surrendered. But Dix's determined words reverberated through the North, and thrilled all hearts with the hope that the time for delay was past, and that the growing rebellion would be put down with a firm hand.

So at the opening of the war we find the North with a navy consisting of but a few old-fashioned ships, few sailors, officers everywhere resigning, and a general feeling of distrust of brother officers in all grades.

The condition of the South as regards the navy was even worse. The

Southern States had never done any great amount of ship-building. The people were almost all engaged in farming. The crops of cotton and sugar that they raised were shipped in vessels built in Maine, and manned by sailors from the sea-faring villages of New England. At the time the war broke out, there was hardly a ship-yard in the confines of the Confederacy A few vessels were gained by the treachery of United States officers. The capture of the Norfolk navy-yard brought them large quantities of naval stores, and by wonderful activity a few vessels were built for service on inland sounds and rivers. But at no time could the Confederacy have been said to have a navy; and, keeping this fact in view, the record the Confederates made with two or three vessels is most wonderful. In war-vessels for service on that wonderful net-work of rivers that make up the water-ways of the Mississippi Valley, the South was not so deficient as in ships of the sea-going class. The long, crescent-shaped levee at New Orleans is lined throughout certain seasons of the year by towering river-steamers which ply up and down the Mississippi and connecting streams, taking from the plantations huge loads of cotton, sugar, and rice, and carrying to the planters those supplies which can only be furnished by the markets of a great city. The appearance of one of these towering river transports as she comes sailing down the turbid stream of the great Father of Waters, laden to the water's edge with brown bales of cotton, and emitting from her lofty, red crowned smoke-stacks dense clouds of pitchy black smoke, is most wonderful. Unlike ocean-steamers, the river-steamer carries her load upon her deck. Built to penetrate far towards the head-waters of rivers and bayous that in summer become mere shallow ditches, these steamers have a very light draught. Many of them, whose tiers of white cabins tower sixty or seventy feet into the air, have but three feet of hull beneath the river's surface. The first deck, when the vessel is but lightly loaded, stands perhaps two feet out of water. Above this, carried on rows of posts twenty feet high, comes the first cabin. All between is open to the air on either side; so that, as one of the huge river-monsters passes at night, the watcher on the bank can see the stalwart, black, half-naked bodies of the negro stokers, bending before the glowing furnace doors, and throwing in the soft coal, that issues in clouds of smoke from the towering chimneys seventy feet above. The lights in three rows of cabin windows glow; and the unceasing beat of the paddle-wheels mingles with the monotonous puff of the steam from the escape-pipes, and the occasional bursts of music from the open cabin doors. One who for the first time looks on one of these leviathans of the Mississippi, pursuing its stately course at night, does not wonder at the frightened negro, who, seeing for the first time a night-steamboat, rushed madly from the river's bank, crying that the angel Gabriel had come to blow the last trump.

When these boats have taken on their full load of cotton, they present a very different appearance. Then all the open space beneath the cabins is filled by a mass of cotton-bales. The hull is so sunken in the water that the lowest tier of cotton-bales is lapped by the little waves that ruffle the surface of the river. The stokers and furnaces are hid from view, and the cabins appear to be floating on one huge cotton bale. Generally a great wooden stern-wheel propels this strange craft, adding to the grotesqueness of the sight.

It may readily be understood, that vessels of this class, in which strength was subordinated to lightness, and economy to gingerbread decoration, seemed to be but poor materials for vessels-of-war. The tremendous recoil of a rifled cannon fired from one of those airy decks, meant to stand no ruder shock than the vibration caused by dancing pleasure-parties, would shake the whole frail structure to pieces. Yet the ingenuity born of necessity, and the energy awakened by the immediate prospect of war, led the Confederate engineers to convert some of these pleasure-palaces into the most terrible engines of destruction chronicled in the annals of war. The first step was to sweep off all the towering superstructure of decks, cabins, and saloons; tear away all the fanciful mouldings, the decorated staterooms, and carved and gilded stairways. This left a long, shallow hull, with a powerful engine in the centre, and great paddle-wheels towering on either side; the whole so light that the soldiers of Grant's army, when they first saw one, stoutly averred that "those boats could run on a heavy dew." The hull was then thinly plated with iron, and the prow lengthened, and made massive, until it formed the terrible "ram," fallen into disuse since the days of the Greek galleys, to be taken up again by naval architects in the nineteenth century. Then on the deck was built a pent-house of oak and iron, with sloping sides just high enough to cover the engine. The two towering smoke-stacks, the pride of the old river-steamers, were cut down to squat pipes protruding a foot or two above the strange structure. In the sides were embrasures, from which, when open, peered the iron muzzles of the dogs of war, ready to show their teeth and spit fire and iron at the enemy. This was the most powerful type of the river gunboat, and with them the Confederacy was fairly well provided; though it was not long before the war department of the United States was well supplied with similar ships. It was these iron-clad gunboats that used to rouse the anger of the doughty Admiral Farragut, who persisted in declaring them cowardly engines of destruction, and predicted that as they came into use, the race of brave fighting jack-tars would disappear. On one occasion the admiral was ploughing his way up the Mississippi above New Orleans, in one of Commodore Bailey's river iron-clads. The batteries of the enemy on either hand were pounding away at the ascending ships, hurling huge bolts of iron against their mailed sides, with a thunder that was deafening, and a shock that made the stricken ships reel. The admiral stood in the gun-room of one of the iron-clads, watching the men working the guns, in an atmosphere reeking with the smoke of the powder. A look of manifest disapproval was on his face. Suddenly an unusually well-directed shot struck a weak point in the armor, and, bursting through, killed two men near the admiral's position. He looked for a moment on the ghastly spectacle, then turning to an officer said, "You may stay here in your iron-clad room if you wish: as for me, I feel safer on deck." And on deck he went, and stayed there while the fleet passed through the hail of shot and shell.

The scarcity of iron in the Southern States prevented the naval authorities of the newly organized Confederacy from equipping a very large fleet of iron-clads. At the outbreak of the war, the Tredegar Iron Works at

Richmond was the only place in the South where iron plates of a size suitable for plating vessels could be rolled. The demand was of course far in excess of the facilities of the factory, and many were the make-shifts that ship-builders were forced to. Some vessels were plated only about the centre, so as to protect the boiler and engines. Others bore such a thin coat of iron that they were derisively called "tin-clads" by the sailors, who insisted that a Yankee can-opener was all that was necessary to rip the vessel up. Sometimes, when even a little iron was unattainable, bales of cotton were piled up around the sides, like breastworks, for the protection of men and engines. The vessel which captured the United States ship "Harriet Lane," at Galveston, was thus provided; and the defence proved very valuable. One great objection to the cotton-bale bulwarks was the very inflammable nature of the material, since a red-hot shot from the enemy, or a bit of blazing wadding from a gun, would set it smouldering with a dense black smoke that drove the men from their guns until the bales could be thrown overboard; thus extinguishing the fire, but exposing the men to the fire of the enemy.

One of the most striking features of the war of secession was the manner in which private citizens hastened to contribute towards the public defence. This was so no less in naval than in military circles. Perhaps the greatest gift ever made by a citizen to his Government was the gift by "Commodore" Vanderbilt to the United States of a magnificently equipped ship-of-war, which was named "The Vanderbilt" in honor of her donor, and did efficient service in maintaining the blockade on the Atlantic coast. Mr. James Gordon Bennett, the present owner of the "New-York Herald," put his yacht at the service of the Government, and was himself commissioned a lieutenant in the revenue service.

CHAPTER II.

FORT SUMTER BOMBARDED.—ATTEMPT OF THE "STAR OF THE WEST" TO RE-ENFORCE ANDERSON.—THE NAVAL EXPEDITION TO FORT SUMTER.—THE RESCUE OF THE FRIGATE "CONSTITUTION."—BURNING THE NORFOLK NAVY-YARD.

THE first purely warlike event of the civil war was the bombardment and capture of Fort Sumter in Charleston Harbor, by the troops of the State of South Carolina. At the time when it first became evident that civil war was inevitable, Fort Sumter was vacant. The only United States troops stationed at Charleston were two companies of artillery under Major Robert Anderson. The fortifications of Charleston Harbor consisted of Fort Moultrie on the main land (in which Anderson's command was stationed), Fort Pinckney, and Fort Sumter standing massive and alone in the centre of the harbor. Anderson, with his handful of troops in the most vulnerable of the three forts, saw day by day the secession sentiment growing stronger. Almost daily some of the privileges of the soldiery were cut off; such as the right of passing through the city, and the right to buy supplies in the public markets. Daily could be heard the drum and the tread of the newly organized bodies of State soldiers. Anderson saw that his position was a weak one, but could get no orders from headquarters. Finally he decided to assume the responsibility of evacuating Fort Moultrie and occupying Fort Sumter. To-day it hardly seems as though he could have thought of doing otherwise, but at that time it was a grave responsibility for a man to assume. The whole voice of the North was for compromise, and it was his part to commit the first overt act of war. But he was nobly upheld in his decision by his Northern brethren. Having decided, he lost no time in carrying his plan

FORT MOULTRIE.

into effect. His little corps of troops was drawn up at midnight on the parade, and for the first time informed of the contemplated movement. The guns of Fort Moultrie were hurriedly knocked from their trunnions, and spiked; the gun-carriages were piled in great heaps, and fired; and every thing that might in any way be used against the United States Government was destroyed. Then the work of evacuation was begun.

A small fleet of row-boats carried the troops to the entrance of the great, sullen fort, standing alone in the middle of the harbor, and made frequent trips bringing supplies and ammunition from the deserted fortress. All was done silently: the oars were muffled, and the commands of the officers were whispered, that no tidings should be told of the movement under way. Before sunrise all was completed; and when the rays of the rising sun fell upon the stars and stripes floating from the flagstaff of Sumter, the people of Charleston turned their eyes from the starry flag to the clouds of smoke arising from Fortress Moultrie, and comprehended that the war had begun. Newspaper correspondents and agents of the Federal Government, and the Southern leaders, rushed for the telegraph-wires; and the news soon sped over the country, that Sumter was occupied. The South Carolinians at once began to build earthworks on all points bearing on the fort, and were evidently preparing to drive Anderson and his troops out. Anderson promptly telegraphed to Washington for supplies and re-enforcements, and expressed his intention of staying as long as the walls stood. The Government was dilatory, but finally concluded to re-enforce the fort, and to that end secured the steamer "Star of the West," and began the work of provisioning her for the voyage. It was decided that she should carry no guns: that would look too much like war; and accordingly, on the 8th of January, this helpless vessel set out to the aid of the beleaguered garrison of Fort Sumter. The news was at once telegraphed to Charleston; and the gunners in the Confederate trenches shotted their guns, and awaited the appearance of the steamer. She hove into sight on the morning of the 12th, and when within range was notified, by a shot across her bows, that she was expected to stop. This signal being disregarded, the firing began in earnest; and the shot and shell fell thick about the ship, which kept pluckily on her course. But it was useless to persist. One shot struck the steamer near the bows, others whizzed through her rigging, and finally her captain saw a tug putting out from the land, towing a schooner crowded with armed men to cut off the "Star's" retreat. He gave the command "Hard a port." The ship's head swung round, and she steamed away, leaving the garrison to their fate. An old gunner who stood in a casemate of Fort Sumter, with the lanyard of a shotted gun in his hand, tells the story of how he begged Major Anderson to let him fire on the rebel batteries. "Not yet; be patient," was the response. When the shells began to fall thick about the steamer, he again asked permission to retaliate, but met the same response. Then when he saw the white splinters fly from the bow, where the enemies' shell had struck, he cried, "Now, surely, we can return *that!*" but still the answer was, "Be patient." When the "Star of the West," confessing defeat, turned and fled from the harbor, Anderson turned and walked away, curtly saying there was no need to fire then, but to save the load for the necessity that was coming.

MAJOR ROBERT ANDERSON.

The first naval operation of the war was the expedition fitted out to relieve Fort Sumter. In itself, this expedition was but an insignificant affair, ending in failure; but as the first warlike action on the part of the United States Government, it attracted the greatest attention throughout the nation. In preparing the vessels for sea, great care was taken to keep their destination secret, so that no warning should reach the Confederates,

FORT SUMTER UNDER FIRE.

who were lying in their batteries about Sumter, awaiting the first offensive action of the United States authorities to begin shelling the fortress. While the squadron was fitting out, it was generally supposed that it was intended to carry troops and munitions of war to Fort Pickens in Pensacola Harbor, which was invested by the Confederates. When the fleet finally sailed, each commander carried sealed orders, upon opening which he first found that the expedition was bound for Charleston Harbor. Notwithstanding all this secrecy, the destination of the fleet was telegraphed to the Confederates almost as soon as the last vessel dropped past Sandy Hook; and the fire from the circle of batteries about the doomed fort in Charleston Harbor began immediately. When the fleet arrived at its destination, the bombardment was well under way. To attempt to land troops or stores under the withering fire concentrated upon the fort, would have been madness. The only vessel of sufficient strength to engage the batteries, the "Pawnee," had been separated from the fleet by a gale a few nights before, and had not yet arrived. Sadly the sailors gave up the attempt, and, beating up and down outside the harbor bar, awaited the inevitable end of the unequal conflict. When, finally, after a heroic resistance of several days, Major Anderson and his little band, worn with constant vigilance and labor, destitute of provisions, and exposed to a constant hail of iron missiles from without and a raging fire within, agreed to capitulate, the United States steamship "Baltic," of the Fort Sumter expedition, took him on board and bore him safely to New York. The main purpose of the expedition had failed, it is true; but the Government had made its first decisive move, and public sympathy and confidence were excited.

The preparations for the coming struggle were now being pressed forward on every hand. An incident which occurred soon after the fall of Sumter awakened the greatest enthusiasm throughout the North. The United States frigate "Constitution" was lying at Annapolis, where she was being used by the authorities of the naval academy there for a schoolship. Although the State of Maryland had not seceded from the Union, yet secessionists were to be found in great numbers in all parts of the State. A number of them determined to seize the ship. Besides being a war-vessel of considerable strength, the "Constitution" — or "Old Ironsides," as she was affectionately called — was famous for her many exploits, and dear to the hearts of Americans for her long service under the stars and stripes. "If we can but capture the vessel, and turn her guns against the Union," thought the conspirators, "we will strike a heavy blow at the Northern sympathizers." And, indeed, it would have been a heavy blow to the nation had they captured the old frigate that did such service under Preble in the war with Tripoli; and that in the War of 1812 forced the British to strike their colors, and gave to the United States navy an equal place on the high seas with any nation of the world. The plans of the conspirators were well laid. The ship was manned by but twenty men, and lay above a bar, over which she could only be carried by the aid of a steam-tug. Fortunately the officers and crew were all loyal. For four days and four nights they watched the preparations being made on shore for their capture. Mysterious signals flashed from the surrounding hills. Armed bodies of men were seen drilling on the shore. All seemed to tend toward certain capture. Yet with no chance of escape the brave men kept vigilant guard, with guns shotted and always primed.

Near Annapolis was stationed the Eighth Massachusetts Infantry, with Gen. Butler in command. News was carried to the general of the perilous position of the "Constitution," and he at once determined to hasten to her relief. Just as the crew of the old frigate had abandoned all hope, the steamer "Maryland" entered the harbor, her guards and decks crowded with the men of the Eighth Massachusetts. Quickly the "Constitution" was prepared for sailing. Her anchors were slipped, all useless weight cast overboard, and, with the "Maryland" as tug, the stately frigate passed slowly over the bar, and out of the grasp of the conspirators.

The "Constitution" was not the only United States vessel that the Confederates were planning to seize. Soon after she escaped from their hands, an event occurred by which a vast quantity of naval stores, and the mutilated but still valuable hulls of some of the most powerful war-vessels in the United States navy, fell into their hands. The United States navy-yard at Norfolk was one of the most valuable of all the governmental possessions. In the great yard was government property amounting to more than twenty millions of dollars. Machine-shops, foundries, dwellings for officers, and a massive granite dry-dock made it one of the most complete navy-yards in the world. An enormous quantity of cannon, cannon-balls, powder, and small-arms packed the huge storehouses. In the magnificent harbor were lying some of the most formidable vessels of the United States navy, including the steam frigate "Merrimac," of which we shall hear much hereafter. Small wonder was it, that the people of Virginia, about to secede from the Union, looked with covetous eyes upon this vast stock of munitions of war lying apparently within their grasp. It did not take long for them to persuade themselves that they were right in seizing it; and, once decided, their movements were vigorous and open. Of their ability to capture the yard, and gain possession of all the property there, they felt no doubt. The first thing to be done was to entrap the ships so that they should be unable to get out of the harbor. Accordingly, on the 16th of April, three large stone-vessels were sunk directly in the channel, apparently barring the exit of the frigates most effectually. Indeed, so confident of success were the plotters, that in a despatch to Richmond, announcing the successful sinking of the stone-ships, they said, "Thus have we secured for Virginia three of the best ships of the navy." But later events showed, that, in boasting so proudly, the Virginians were committing the old error of counting chickens before they were hatched.

The condition of affairs within the navy-yard now seemed desperate. There appeared to be no chance of getting the vessels beyond the obstructions. The militia of Virginia was rapidly gathering in the town. Among the naval officers on the ships great dissension existed, as many were Southerners, about to resign their posts in the United States service to enter the service of their States. These men would, of course, give no active aid to any movement for the salvation of the United States property in the yard. Any assistance must come from the outside; the beleaguered could but passively await the course of events.

At seven o'clock on the night of April 21, the United States steamer "Pawnee," which had been lying under the guns of Fortress Monroe, hoisted anchor, and headed up the bay, on an errand of destruction. It was too late to save the navy-yard with its precious stores. The only thing to be done was to burn, break, and destroy every thing that might be of service to an enemy. The decks of the "Pawnee" were black with men, — soldiers to guard the gates, and complete the work of destruction within the yard; blue-jacketed tars to do what might be done to drag the entrapped vessels from the snare set them by the Virginians. It was a bright moonlight night. The massive hull of the ship-of-war, black in the cold, white rays of the moon, passed rapidly up the Elizabeth River. The sunken wrecks were reached, and successfully avoided; and about nine o'clock the "Pawnee" steamed into the anchorage of the navy-yard, to be greeted with cheers from the tars of the "Cumberland" and "Pennsylvania," who expected her arrival. The townspeople seeing the war-vessel, with ports thrown open, and black muzzles of the guns protruding, took to their houses, fearing she would open fire on the town. Quickly the "Pawnee" steamed to her moorings. The marines were hurriedly disembarked, and hastened to guard the entrances to the navy-yard. Howitzers were planted so as to rake every street leading to the yard. Thus secure against attack, the work of the night began. Nearly two thousand willing hands were set hard at work, cannon were dismounted and spiked, rifles and muskets dashed to pieces; great quantities of combustibles were piled up in the mammoth buildings, ready to be fired at a given signal. In the mean time, the bluejackets were not idle. It was quickly decided, that, of all the magnificent vessels anchored in the harbor, the "Cumberland" was the only one that could be towed past the obstructions in the river. All hands were set to work removing every thing of value from the doomed vessels to the "Cumberland." Gunpowder and combustibles were then arranged so as to completely destroy the vessels when ignited. When the moon went down at twelve o'clock, the preparations were complete. All the men were then taken on board the "Cumberland" and "Pawnee," save a few who were left to fire the trains. As the two vessels started from the moorings, the barracks were fired, the lurid light casting a fearful gleam upon the crowded yards and shrouds of the towering frigate. A little way out in the stream

DESTRUCTION OF NORFOLK NAVY-YARD

a rocket was sent up from the "Pawnee." This was the signal for the firing of the trains. The scene that followed is thus described by an eyewitness:—

"The rocket sped high in air, paused a second, and burst in showers of many colored lights; and, as it did so, the well-set trains at the ship-houses, and on the decks of the fated vessels left behind, went off as if lit simultaneously by the rocket. One of the ship-houses contained the old 'New York,' a ship thirty years on the stocks, and yet unfinished; the other was vacant. But both houses, and the old 'New York,' burned like tinder. The vessels fired were the 'Pennsylvania,' the 'Merrimac,' the 'Germantown,' the 'Plymouth,' the 'Raritan,' the 'Columbia,' and the 'Dolphin.' The old 'Delaware' and 'Columbus," worn-out and disabled seventy-fours, were scuttled, and sunk at the upper docks on Friday.

"I need not try to picture the scene of the grand conflagration that now burst like the day of judgment on the startled citizens of Norfolk, Portsmouth, and all the surrounding country. Any one who has seen a ship burn, and knows how like a fiery serpent the flame leaps from pitchy deck to smoking shrouds, and writhes to their very top around the masts that stand like martyrs doomed, can form some idea of the wonderful display that followed. It was not thirty minutes from the time the trains were fired, till the conflagration roared like a hurricane, and the flames from land and water swayed and met and mingled together, and darted high, and fell, and leaped up again, and by their very motion showed their sympathy with the crackling, crashing war of destruction beneath.

"But in all this magnificent scene the old ship 'Pennsylvania' was the centre-piece. She was a very giant in death, as she had been in life. She was a sea of flame; and when the iron had entered her soul, and her bowels were consuming, then did she spout forth from every porthole of every deck torrents and cataracts of fire, that to the mind of Milton would have represented her a frigate of hell pouring out unending broadsides of infernal fire. Several of her guns were left loaded, but not shotted; and as the fire reached them they sent out on the startled morning air minute-guns of fearful peal, that added greatly to the alarm that the light of the fire had spread through the country round about. The 'Pennsylvania' burned like a volcano for five hours and a half before her mainmast fell. I stood watching the proud but perishing old leviathan as this emblem of her majesty was about to come down. At precisely half-past nine o'clock the tall tree that stood in her centre tottered and fell, and crushed deep into her burning sides."

During this fearful scene the people of the little town, and the Virginia militia-men who had been summoned to take possession of the navy-yard, were no idle spectators. Hardly had the "Pawnee" steamed out into the stream, when the great gates were battered down, and crowds of men rushed in, eager to save whatever arms were uninjured. Throughout the fire they worked like beavers, and succeeded in saving a large quantity of munitions of war to be used by the Confederacy. The ships that had been fired all burned to the water's edge. One was raised, and re-appeared as the formidable "Merrimac" that at one time threatened the destruction of the whole Union navy.

A great amount of valuable property was saved for the Virginians by the coolness of a young boy, the son of one of the citizens of the town. This lad was within the gates of the navy-yard when the troops from the ships rushed in, and closed and barricaded them against the townspeople. He was frightened, and hid himself behind a quantity of boards and rubbish, and lay there a silent and immensely frightened spectator of the work of destruction. An officer passed near him directing the movements of two sailors, who were laying a train of gunpowder to an immense pile of explosives and combustibles in the huge granite dry-dock. The train passed over a broad board; and the boy, hardly knowing what he did, drew away this board, leaving a gap of eight inches in the train. When all the trains were fired, this was of course stopped at the gap; and the dry-dock was saved, and still remains in the Norfolk Navy-Yard.

CHAPTER III.

DIFFICULTIES OF THE CONFEDERATES IN GETTING A NAVY. — EXPLOIT OF THE "FRENCH LADY." — NAVAL SKIRMISHING ON THE POTOMAC. — THE CRUISE OF THE "SUMTER."

THE disparity of maritime importance between the North and the South, and the consequent difficulties to be overcome by the latter in getting a navy, have been already alluded to. As it has been stated, in river-steamers and ponderous rams the South was fairly well supplied; but what was really needed were ocean-going ships, to break the rigid blockade that was slowly starving the Confederacy into submission, — swift cruisers to prey on the commerce of the enemy, and powerful line-of-battle ships, which, by successfully coping with the vessels of the United States on the high seas, should secure for the Confederacy recognition, and possibly assistance, from the great powers of Europe. But how to get these without ship-yards, ship-builders, or seamen, was a task that baffled the ingenuity of the best minds in the South. Immediately upon the organization of the Confederate cabinet, an agent was sent to England to negotiate for vessels and guns. But, though this agent was a man of wonderful resources and great diplomacy, he found an almost insuperable obstacle in the universally recognized law of nations, to the effect that no neutral nation shall sell vessels or munitions of war to belligerents. It is true that this agent, Capt. Bulloch, did succeed in securing three ships, — the "Florida," the "Shenandoah," and the celebrated "Alabama;" but to do so cost an immense amount of diplomacy and the sacrificing of the strength of the vessels to the necessity which existed for making them appear to be merchantmen. To build an ironclad in a foreign port, was out of the question; and consequently ships so obtained were forced to fly from any well-equipped war-vessel, and only venture to attack unarmed merchantmen.

The United States vessels which were delivered into the hands of the Confederates by their officers were mainly small revenue cutters, of little use in naval warfare and soon given up or destroyed. Not a single ship of this class made any record of distinguished service for the Confederacy. Several merchant-vessels were captured by the Confederates, who concocted the most ingenious plans to secure success. One bright July morning the steamer "St. Nicholas" was lying at her dock in Baltimore, with steam up, and all prepared for her regular trip down the Chesapeake. Quite a large number of passengers had bought tickets, and lounged about the decks, waiting for the voyage to begin. Among the passengers were a number of mechanics, with tools in their hands, going down the bay in search of work. Shortly before the signal to cast off was given, a carriage was driven down the wharf, and a lady, heavily veiled, alighted, assisted by two gentlemen. The gentlemen stated that she was a French lady, and in ill-health. Accordingly she was at once assigned a stateroom, to which she retired. Soon after, the vessel cast off and headed down the bay. When fairly out of the harbor, the stateroom door opened, and instead of the frail, heavily veiled widow who went in, out strode a black-whiskered man, armed to the teeth. He had no trouble now in speaking English, and at once demanded the surrender of the ship. The honest mechanics dropped their tools, and, drawing concealed weapons, rallied around their leader. They had found the work they started out to seek. The ship was captured, and a new privateer was ready to prey on Northern merchant-ships. Once in the hands of the conspirators, the vessel was run into a little port where the passengers were landed, and a hundred and fifty more Confederates taken aboard. Under the command of Capt.

THE "FRENCH LADY."

Thomas (the "French lady"), the vessel proceeded to Fredericksburg, where she, and three brigs captured on the way, were delivered to the Confederate leaders. This adventure so favorably terminated, Thomas, with his officers, started back to Baltimore, to lay plans for the capture of some other unsuspecting craft. But fortune, which had thus far favored him, deserted him at last. On the vessel upon which the conspirators took passage were two police-officers of Baltimore. One of these officers recognized Thomas, and quietly laid plans for his capture. In the harbor at Baltimore stands Fort McHenry. Under its frowning casemates the ships of the United States could lie without fear of attack from the thousands of discontented men who made of Baltimore a secession city. The captain of the "Mary Washington" was ordered by Lieut. Carmichael, the officer of police, to bring the ship into the anchorage, under the guns of the fort. This soon came to the ears of Thomas, who with his men rallied on the deck, and, with revolvers drawn, seemed prepared to make a desperate resistance. They were soon convinced that the officers had ample power behind them, and therefore submitted. On arriving at the fort, a company of soldiers was sent aboard the boat, and the prisoners were marched ashore. But Thomas was not to be found. Search was made in all parts of the boat, without avail; and the officers had decided that he had jumped overboard, with the desperate intention of swimming ashore. Just as they were about to give up the search, a noise was heard that seemed to come from a bureau in the ladies' cabin. Search was made, and there, coiled up in a narrow bureau-drawer, lay the leader of the band. He had been there two hours, and was helpless from cramp and exhaustion. He was placed in a cell at Fort Lafayette; but later, having been given the privilege of walking about the fort, managed to escape by making floats of empty tomato-cans, and with their aid swimming almost two miles. He was afterwards recaptured, and remained a prisoner until released by reason of an exchange of prisoners between the North and South. Soon after his capture, the Federal authorities at Baltimore learned that plans had been made to capture other passenger steamers in the same way; but the ringleader being locked up, there was no difficulty in defeating the plans of the band.

During the first few weeks of the war, before active hostilities had fairly commenced, events of this nature were of almost daily occurrence. On the Potomac particularly, small cruisers were in continual danger of being captured, and put into commission under the Confederate flag. A trading schooner loaded with garden-produce, dropping lazily down the river to the bay, would suddenly be boarded by four or five armed men, her crew driven below, and the vessel run into some convenient port on the Virginia shore, to re-appear in a day or two with a small rifled cannon mounted on the fore-castle, and a crew thirsting to capture more vessels for the Confederacy. On one occasion a party of congressmen from Washington started down the Potomac for an excursion to Hampton Roads. Their vessel was a small tug, which carried a bow-gun carefully screened from observation by tarpaulin. A short distance down the river, a boat with a howitzer was seen putting out into the stream, and shaping its course directly across the bows of the tug. As the two boats drew nearer together, a demand came from the smaller that the tug should be surrendered "to the State of Virginia." Apparently yielding, the captain of the tug slowed up his vessel, and waited for his assailants to come alongside, which they did until suddenly confronted with the muzzle of a cannon, trained directly on their boat, and a loud voice demanding that they surrender at once, which they accordingly did, and were taken to Washington by their triumphant captors. Many such trivial events are chronicled by the newspapers of the time. The advantage gained by either side was small, and the only effect was to keep the war sentiment at fever-heat.

The first regularly commissioned man-of-war of the Confederate States was the "Sumter," an old passenger steamer remodelled so as to carry five guns. This vessel, though only registering five hundred tons, and smaller than many a steam-yacht of to-day, roamed over the high seas at will for more than a year, burning and destroying the merchant-vessels of the North, and avoiding easily any conflicts with the Northern men-of-war. Her exploits made the owners of American merchant-vessels tremble for their property; and the United States authorities made the most desperate attempts to capture her, but in vain. In his journal of Dec. 3, 1861, Capt.

Semmes of the "Sumter" writes with the greàtest satisfaction: "The enemy has done us the honor to send in pursuit of us the 'Powhattan,' the 'Niagara,' the 'Iroquois,' the 'Keystone State,' and the 'San Jacinto.'" Any one of these vessels could have blown the 'Sumter' out of water with one broadside, but the cunning and skill of her commander enabled her to escape them all.

It was on the 1st of June, 1861, that the "Sumter" cast loose from the levee at New Orleans, and started down the Mississippi on her way to the

BLOCKADING THE MOUTH OF THE MISSISSIPPI.

open sea. For two months workmen had been busy fitting her for the new part she was to play. The long rows of cabins on the upper deck were torn down; and a heavy eight-inch shell-gun, mounted on a pivot between the fore and mainmasts, and the grinning muzzles of four twenty-four-pounder howitzers peeping from the ports, told of her warlike character. The great levee of the Crescent City was crowded with people that day. Now and again the roll of the drum, or the stirring notes of "Dixie," would be heard, as some volunteer company marched down to the river to witness the departure of the entire Confederate navy. Slowly the vessel dropped down the river, and, rounding the English turn, boomed out with her great gun a parting salute to the city she was never more to see. Ten miles from the mouth of the river she stopped; for anchored off the bar below lay the powerful United States steamer "Brooklyn," with three other men-of-war, each more than a match for the infant navy of the Confederacy. Eleven days the "Sumter" lay tugging at her anchors in the muddy current of the great river, but at last the time of action arrived. The news came that the "Brooklyn" had started in chase of a vessel, and the mouth of the river was clear. Quickly the "Sumter" got under way, and with all steam up made for the channel over the bar. She was still six miles from the bar when the "Brooklyn" caught sight of her, and abandoning her first chase strove desperately to head her off. It was a time of intense excitement. Each vessel was about equally distant from the bar for which each was steaming at the highest possible speed. For the "Sumter," it was escape or die. It was too late to fly up the river to the sheltering guns of Fort St. Philip. Should the "Brooklyn" get within range, the "Sumter" was doomed. The "Brooklyn" was the faster vessel of the two, but had the wind in her teeth; while the "Sumter" had the advantage of wind and current. At length the pass was reached, and the "Sumter" dashed over the bar, and out on the smooth blue water of the Gulf of Mexico, well ahead of her powerful foe. The "Brooklyn" quickly rounded to, and a quick puff of smoke from amidships told the crew of the flying vessel that the terrible pivot-gun of their enemy had sent a warning message after them. But there was but a second of suspense, when a great jet of water springing from the surface of the gulf told that the bolt had fallen short. The "Brooklyn" then quickly crowded on all sail, and started in hot pursuit, but after four hours abandoned the chase, put up her helm, and started sullenly back for the river's mouth; while the tars of the "Sumter" crowded shrouds and bulwarks, and cheered heartily for the navy of the young Confederacy.

The "Sumter" was now fairly embarked on her career. The open sea was her territory, and all ships floating the stars and stripes at the masthead were to be her prey. She was not a strong vessel; and her orders were to avoid any battles with the powerful ships of the "Yankee" navy, but to seize and destroy all merchantmen that should come in her way. Her first purpose was to capture these vessels, and by selling them in neutral ports profit by the prize. But the neutral nations soon refused to admit all rebel prizes to their ports; and, as all the ports of the Confederacy were closed by the blockade, nothing was left but to burn the vessels when captured. Many a floating bonfire marked the way of the little "Sumter," and great was the consternation among the ship-owners of the North.

When four days out, the "Sumter" captured her first prize. She was a fine ship, the "Golden Rocket" of Maine, six hundred and ninety tons. With the United States flag fluttering at the peak, she came sailing proudly towards her unsuspected enemy, from whose peak the red flag of England was displayed as a snare. When the two vessels came within a mile of each other, the wondering crew of the merchantman saw the English flag come tumbling down, while a ball of bunting rose quickly to the peak of the mysterious stranger, and catching the breeze floated out, showing a strange flag,—the stars and bars of the Confederacy. At the same minute a puff of smoke from the "Long Tom" amidships was followed by a solid shot ricochetting along the water before the dismayed merchantman, and conveying a forcible, but not at all polite, invitation to stop. The situation dawned on the astonished skipper of the ship,—he was in the hands of "the Rebels;" and with a sigh he brought his vessel up into the wind, and awaited the outcome of the adventure. And bad enough the outcome was for him; for Capt. Semmes, unwilling to spare a crew to man the prize, determined to set her on fire. It was about sunset when the first boat put off from the "Sumter" to visit the captured ship. The two vessels were lying a hundred yards apart, rising and falling in unison on the slow rolling swells of the tropic seas. The day was bright and warm, and in the west the sun was slowly sinking to the meeting line of sky and ocean. All was quiet and peaceful, as only a summer afternoon in Southern seas can be. Yet in the midst of all that peace and quiet, a scene in the great drama of war was being enacted. Nature was peaceful, man violent.

For a time nothing was heard save the measured thump of the oars in the rowlocks, as the boats plied to and fro between the two ships, transporting the captured crew to the "Sumter." Finally the last trip was made, and the boat hoisted to the davits. Then all eyes were turned toward the "Golden Rocket." She lay almost motionless, a dark mass on the black ocean. The sun had long since sunk beneath the horizon; and the darkness of the night was only relieved by the brilliancy of the stars, which in those latitudes shine with wondrous brightness. Soon the watches on the "Sumter" caught a hasty breath. A faint gleam was seen about the companionway of the "Rocket." Another instant, and with a roar and crackle, a great mass of flame shot up from the hatch, as from the crater of a volcano. Instantly the well-tarred rigging caught, and the flame ran up the shrouds as a ladder of fire, and the whole ship was a towering mass of flame. The little band of men on the "Sumter" looked on the terrific scene with bated breath. Though they fully believed in the justice of their cause, they could not look on the destruction they had wrought without feelings of sadness. It was their first act of war. One of the officers of the "Sumter" writes: "Few, few on board can forget the spectacle, — a ship set fire to at sea. It would seem that man was almost warring with his Maker. Her helpless condition, the red flames licking the rigging as they climbed aloft, the sparks and pieces of burning rope taken off by the wind, and flying miles to leeward, the ghastly glare thrown upon the dark sea as far as the eye could reach, and then the deathlike stillness of the scene, — all these combined to place the "Golden Rocket" on the tablet of our memories forever." But it was not long before the crew of the "Sumter" could fire a vessel, and sail away indifferently, with hardly a glance at their terrible handiwork.

The "Sumter" continued on her cruise, with varying fortunes. Sometimes weeks would pass with no prizes to relieve the tedium of the long voyage. Occasionally she would run into a neutral port for coal or water, but most of the time was spent on the open sea. The crew were kept actively employed with drills and exercises; while the officers, yawning over their books or games, longed for the welcome cry from the masthead, "Sail ho!" In September the "Sumter" captured a brig, the "Joseph Park;"

and the boarding officer, on examining the log-book, found an entry made by her captain on the day of leaving Pernambuco: "We have a tight, fast vessel, and we don't care for Jeff Davis." The unlucky captain had holloaed long before he was out of the wood.

The "Joseph Park" was the last prize the tars of the "Sumter" had the pleasure of "looting" for many days. Up and down the tropic seas the cruiser travelled, loitering about the paths of ocean commerce to no avail. Often enough the long-drawn hail of the look-out in the cross-trees, "Sail ho-o-o-o!" would bring the jackies tumbling up from the forecastle, and set the officers peering anxiously through their telescopes. But the sails so sighted proved to be English, French, Spanish, any thing but American; and life aboard the "Sumter" became as dull as a fisher's where fish are not to be found. In September Capt. Semmes ran his vessel into a Martinique harbor, to make some needed repairs, and give the sailors a run ashore. Here they were blockaded for some time by the United States frigate "Iroquois," but finally escaped through the cunning of Semmes. Lying in the harbor near the "Sumter" were two Yankee schooners, whose captains arranged with the commander of the "Iroquois" to signal him if the "Sumter" should leave the harbor. If on passing the bar she headed south, a single red light should gleam at the masthead of the schooner; should her course lie northward, two lights would be displayed. Semmes, lying at anchor in the bay, and chafing over his captivity, determined to break away. He had noticed the frequent communications between the schooners and the man-of-war, and suspected that his course would be spied out. Nevertheless, he determined to dare all, and one black night slipped his cables, and with all lights out, and running-gear muffled, glided swiftly out of the harbor. In the distance he could see the lights of the "Iroquois," as she steamed slowly up and down in the offing, like a sentry on guard. Up in the cross-trees of the "Sumter" sat a sharp-eyed old quarter-master, with orders not to mind the "Iroquois," but to keep a close watch on the suspected schooners. Soon a light gleamed from the main-top of each. Semmes's suspicions grew. "They have signalled our course," said he: "we'll double." The ship's head was quickly brought about, and headed south; then all turned to watch the movements of the "Iroquois." She had headed northward, and was exerting every power to catch the flying vessel supposed to be just ahead. Satisfied with having so successfully humbugged the enemy, the "Sumter" proceeded leisurely on her course to the southward, leaving the "Iroquois" steaming furiously in the opposite direction. "I do think, however," writes Capt. Semmes in his log-book, "that a tough old quarter-master, and a grizzled boatswain's mate, who had clean shaven their heads in preparation for a desperate fight, were mightily disgusted."

The subsequent career of the "Sumter" was uneventful. She captured but few more vessels; and in January of the next year ran into the harbor at Gibraltar, where she was blockaded by a powerful United States frigate, and finally sold as being worn out. She had been in commission a little over a year, and in that time had captured eighteen vessels, burned seven, and released two on a heavy ransom to be paid to the Confederate Government at the end of the war. It is needless to say these ransoms were never paid. Capt. Semmes, with his crew, proceeded to England, and took command of a mysterious ship, "No. 290," just built at Liverpool, which soon appeared on the high seas as the dreaded "Alabama."

CHAPTER. IV.

THE POTOMAC FLOTILLA.—CAPTURE OF ALEXANDRIA.—ACTIONS AT MATTHIAS POINT.—BOMBARDMENT OF THE HATTERAS FORTS.

IN petty skirmishes and in general inactivity the forces of both contestants idled away the five months following the fall of Fort Sumter. The defeat of the Union armies at Bull Run had checked active operations along the Potomac. On either side of the river the hostile armies were drilling constantly to bring the raw recruits down to the efficiency of trained soldiers. Four hundred thousand men lay in hostile camps within sight of each other. From the national Capitol at Washington the stars and bars of the Confederate flag could be seen floating over the camp at Arlington. Occasionally the quiet would be broken by the crack of a rifle, as some straggler, on one side or the other, took a casual shot at the sentry pacing on the other side of the broad stream. Sometimes a battery would come driving down to the shore, select an advantageous spot, and begin an afternoon's target practice at the hostile camp; but the damage done was immaterial, and after wasting much powder and shot the recruits would limber up their guns and return to their camp. It would have been easy, at almost any time, for either army to have crossed the Potomac and invaded the territory of the enemy; but each hung back in apparent dread of taking the first decisive step.

Abraham Lincoln at this time illustrated the existing condition of affairs, by one of those stories which have made him celebrated as a *raconteur*. A number of politicians, calling at the White House, spoke of the apparent inactivity of the army authorities, and demanded that some decisive move should be made; some powerful preparations to beat back the enemy should he attempt to cross the Potomac. "Gentlemen," said Lincoln, with the twinkle in his eye that always foretold a story, "when I was a boy I saw an incident which I have always recollected, and which seems to me to resemble very much the attitude now assumed by the parties in this impending war. My father owned a dog, — a particularly vicious, aggressive, and pugnacious bull-terrier, — one of these fellows with heavy, short necks, and red, squinting eyes, that seem ever to be on the look-out for a fight. Next door to us lived a neighbor who likewise rejoiced in the possession of a canine of appearance and habits of mind similar to our pet. From the date of their first meeting these dogs had been deadly enemies, and had growled and yelped at each other through the picket-fence separating the two yards, until we were forced to keep at least one dog chained continually. The strained relations between the dogs became a matter of general interest, and speculations were rife among the neighbors as to the probable outcome of a hostile meeting. Those were the times when a lively dog-fight would draw the merchant from his counter, and the blacksmith from his anvil; and it is even on record that an honorable judge once hurriedly adjourned his court at the premonitory sounds of snarling in the court-house square. Well, the knowledge that two dogs, pining for a fight, were being forcibly restrained, was too much to be borne by the people of the village; and a

FLAG OF THE CONFEDERACY.

plot was concocted for bringing about a fight. One night two pickets were surreptitiously removed from the fence, leaving an opening of ample size to permit a dog to pass. In the morning our dog was sunning himself in the yard, when the neighbor's dog rushed to his side of the fence, and made remarks not to be borne by any self-respecting canine. Then began the usual performance of snarls and barks, and baring of white teeth, as the dogs made frantic efforts to get at each other. The neighbors assembled in a crowd, and the knowing ones predicted a lively time when those two dogs found the hole in the fence. Down the line of the fence the two curs walked, their eyes glaring, their jaws snapping, their tongues out, and dropping foam. The racket was tremendous. At each place where the pickets were a little spread, they redoubled their efforts to clinch. They approached the opening. The interest of the spectators redoubled. Now they reached the spot; sprung at each other; their jaws touched, — and each, dropping his tail, slunk away to his kennel. Gentlemen, the attitude of these armies reminds me of that dog-fight."

While the armies of the two contestants were thus idly resting upon their arms, the navy was obliged to discharge duties, which, while they brought some danger, did not gain glory for either officers or men. The joys of Washington society were not for the naval officers. The applicant for promotion, who, when asked by an examiner, "Where is the post of a colonel when his regiment is drawn up for battle?" responded promptly, "In Washington," had been serving in the army, and not with the naval corps. Besides the duties of the officers detailed upon the blockading service, there remained to the navy the arduous task of patrolling the Potomac River, and preventing as far as possible communication between the shores.

This work, as may be readily understood, demanded the most untiring vigilance and the most unflagging energy. The shores on each side of the Potomac are indented with bays and tributary streams in which a sloop or large row-boat can easily be concealed during the day. At night it was impossible to prevent boats laden with contraband goods, or conveying the bearers of secret despatches, slipping across the river from the northern side, and running into the concealment afforded by the irregularity of the Virginia shore-line. Even at this early period of the war, the vigorous blockade of the Confederate sea-ports had created a great lack of many necessaries in the Southern States. Particularly did the lack of quinine afflict the people of those malarial sections comprised within the limits of the South Atlantic and Gulf States. So great was the demand for this drug, that the enormous sums offered for it led many a speculative druggist north of Mason and Dixon's line to invest his all in quinine, and try to run it through the Potomac blockade. Of course, as the traffic was carried on in small boats, it was impossible to break it up altogether; though by the efforts of the navy it was almost destroyed.

Briefly stated, the duties of the Potomac flotilla may be said to have been to patrol the river from Washington to its mouth, to inspect both sides *daily* if possible, and to observe whether any preparations for batteries were being made at any point, and watch for any transports with troops or provisions, and convoy them to Washington. The flotilla consisted of small vessels, lightly armed; the "Pawnee," the heaviest of the fleet, being a sloop of less than thirteen hundred tons, with a battery of fifteen guns, none of long range. Clearly such an armada as this could be of but little avail against the earthworks which the Virginians were busily erecting on every commanding bluff.

Toward the later part of May, 1861, the Federal Government determined to send troops across the river and occupy the city of Alexandria. The "Pawnee" had for some days been lying off the town, completely covering it with her batteries. She had held this position without making any offensive movement; as her commander understood, that, even should he compel the town to surrender, he had not the men necessary for holding the position. On the morning of the 24th, Commander Rowan saw two steamers coming down the river, laden with Federal troops. He at once sent a boat ashore, and demanded the surrender of the city, which was immediately evacuated by the Virginian troops. When the army of occupation landed, it proved to be Ellsworth's famous Zouave Regiment, made up largely of the firemen and "Bowery boys" of New York City. Ellsworth, while marching through the streets at the head of his command, saw a Confederate flag floating from a mast on top of a dwelling. With two of his men he proceeded to enter the house, go on the roof, and tear down the flag. As he came down the stairs, a man carrying a gun stepped from a doorway, and demanded what he did there. "This is my trophy," cried Ellsworth, flourishing the bit of striped bunting. "And you are mine," responded the man, quickly bringing his gun up, and discharging it full into Ellsworth's breast. The two Zouaves, maddened at the death of their commander, shot the slayer through the brain, and plunged their bayonets into his body before he fell. Ellsworth's death created the greatest excitement in the North, as it was almost the first blood shed in the war. While the capture of Alexandria was in itself no great achievement, it was of importance as the first move of the Northern armies into Virginia.

Had the efforts of the navy towards keeping the Potomac clear of hostile batteries been supplemented by a co-operating land force, an immense advantage would have been gained at the very outset. As it was, all that could be done was to temporarily check the exertions of the enemy. A battery silenced by the guns from the ships in the daytime could be, and usually was, repaired during the night, and remained a constant menace to the transports going to or from Washington. Under such circumstances, the work of the Potomac flotilla could only be fatiguing and discouraging. Much of it had to be performed in row-boats; and the crews of the various vessels were kept rowing up and down the banks of the river, making midnight excursions up creeks to examine suspected localities, and lying in wait for smugglers, and the mail-carriers and spies of the enemy. They were in continual danger of being opened upon by masked batteries and concealed sharp-shooters. The "prize money," the hope of which cheers up the man-o'-wars-man in his dreariest hours, amounted to nothing; for their prizes were small row-boats and worthless river-craft. The few engagements with the enemies' batteries brought little glory or success. In one battle on the 29th of May, 1861, a flotilla, consisting of the "Thomas Freeborn" (a paddle-wheel steamer, carrying three guns), the "Anacostia," and the "Resolute" (a little craft of ninety tons and two guns), engaged the batteries at Aquia Creek, and pounded away with their pygmy guns for two hours, without doing any visible damage. Two days later the bombardment was renewed, and two of the vessels were slightly damaged. A more serious event occurred at Matthias Point in the latter part of June. Matthias Point was one of the chief lurking-places of the Confederate guerillas, who, concealed in the dense undergrowth along the banks of the Potomac, could pour a destructive fire into any vessels that passed. Commander J. H. Ward of the "Freeborn" planned to break up this ambush, sending a landing party to cut away the trees and undergrowth. The landing party, commanded by Lieut. Chaplin, was to be covered by the guns of the "Freeborn" and "Reliance." It was late in the afternoon when they pushed off for the shore. All seemed quiet; and the bursting of the shells, which were occasionally dropped into the woods, seemed to have driven the enemy away. Hardly, however, had the sailors begun the work of hewing down the undergrowth, when from all quarters a hot fire was begun, driving them to their boats in a rout. The decks of the two vessels were swept by the storm of lead. Commander Ward, while sighting the bow-gun of the "Freeborn," was struck in the abdomen by a bullet, and died in a few minutes. On the shore the sailors were hurrying into the boats and pushing off to avoid capture. Lieut. Chaplin acted with great bravery, and succeeded in getting all his men away, with their muskets. The last man left on the shore was unable to swim; and Chaplin, taking him on his shoulders, bore him safely to the boat. Though the fire of the enemy was concentrated on the two, neither was hurt, although a minie-ball passed through the lieutenant's cap.

Two months later this same locality was the scene of another bloody disaster to the Union arms. On the 16th of August the "Resolute" and the "Reliance" were ordered to make a reconnoisance of the neighborhood of Matthias Point. After steaming about the shore for some time, and noticing nothing of a suspicious character, a boat was seen on the Virginia shore, and an officer and five men despatched to capture her. They had just reached her, and were in the act of making fast, when a volley of musketry was fired from the bushes not more than five yards away, and three of the crew were instantly killed, and one wounded. The watchers on the war-vessels, lying in the river, sprang to their guns, and threw several rounds of shell into the cover that sheltered the enemy, soon driving them away. The two uninjured men in the boat succeeded in getting her away with her load of dead and dying.

It is easy to understand how exasperating, how infuriating, such service as this must have been to the officers and men of the navy. For a man to risk his life in the heat and excitement of a battle, is as nothing to the feeling that one may be at any time caught in a death-trap, and slaughtered in cold blood.

A more successful expedition was organized in October, by Lieut. Harrill of the steamer "Union." He had been informed that a large schooner was lying in Quantico Creek, and that the Confederates were massing a number of troops there for the purpose of crossing the river. He at once determined to destroy the schooner. Accordingly he manned three boats at half-past two in the morning, and in the darkness proceeded, with muffled oars, toward the mouth of the creek. Here some difficulty was experienced, as the entrance is narrow and obstructed by sandbars; but working energetically, and in perfect silence, the sailors overcame all obstacles. Once in the creek, they pulled rapidly along within pistol-shot of the shore, until the tall masts of the schooner could be descried in the darkness. One sentry was on guard, who fled wildly as he saw the mysterious boat emerge from the darkness of the night. The grappling-irons were thrown aboard, and the jackies swarmed nimbly up the sides, and began the work of destruction. A huge pile of combustibles was made in the cabin, and hastily set on fire. The flames spread rapidly; and, though they insured the destruction of the schooner, they also lighted up the creek, showing the boats with the sailors bending to their oars to escape the storm of bullets that they knew must follow. The glare of the burning schooner, the reflection of the flames on the water, the flash of the rifles from the shores made a wild picture. Occasionally a flash from the river was followed by a deep boom, as a heavy shot left the muzzle of a cannon on the steamers. But through it all, the men escaped; and the projected invasion of the Confederates was abandoned, owing to the loss of their schooner.

All through the war this untiring patrol of the Potomac was continued. Among miasmatic vapors and clouds of noxious insects on mud-flats, in narrow channels whose densely wooded banks might conceal legions of

NAVAL PATROL ON THE POTOMAC.

hostile sharp-shooters, the river navy kept up its work. Earning but little glory, though in the midst of constant peril, the officers and men kept up their work, and contributed not a little to the final outcome of the great conflict.

All this time the officers of the naval vessels, riding at anchor in

Hampton Roads, were chafing under the enforced idleness. Even the occasional artillery duels with which their army brethren whiled away the time were denied to the wistful blue-jackets. Beyond an occasional chase, generally useless, after a fleet blockade-runner, the sailors had absolutely no employment. At last, however, the opportunity came. The first great naval expedition of the war was set under way.

From Cape Henry, at the mouth of the James River, the coast of Virginia and North Carolina sweeps grandly out to the eastward, like a mammoth bow, with its lower end at Beaufort, two hundred miles south. Along this coast-line the great surges of mighty ocean, rolling with unbroken course from the far-off shore of Europe, trip and fall with unceasing roar upon an almost uninterrupted beach of snowy sand, a hundred and more miles long. Near the southern end of this expanse of sand stands a lighthouse, towering solitary above the surrounding plain of sea and sand. No inviting beacon giving notice to the weary mariner of safe haven is this steady light that pierces the darkness night after night. It tells of treacherous shoals and roaring breakers; of the loss of many a good ship, whose ribs, half buried in the drifting sand, lie rotting in the salt air; of skies ever treacherous, and waters ever turbulent. It is the light of Hatteras.

Some twenty miles below Cape Hatteras light occurs the first great opening in the stretch of sand that extends south from Cape Henry. Once he has passed through this opening; the mariner finds himself in the most peaceful waters. The great surges of the Atlantic spend themselves on the sandy fringe outside, while within are the quiet waters of Pamlico and Albemarle Sounds, dotted with fertile islands, and bordering a coast rich in harbors. The wary blockade-runner, eluding the watchfulness of the United States blockaders cruising outside, had but to pass the portals of Hatteras Inlet, to unload at his leisure his precious cargo, and load up with the cotton which grew in great abundance on the islands and fertile shores of the sound.

Recognizing the importance of this harbor, the Confederates had early in the war fortified the point north of Hatteras Inlet. Shortly after the fall of Fort Sumter, a Yankee skipper, Daniel Campbell, incautiously running his schooner the "Lydia Francis" too near the stormy cape, was wrecked, and sought shelter among the people at the inlet. When, some days after, he proposed to leave, he was astounded to find that he had been delivered from the sea only to fall a prey to the fortunes of war. He was kept a prisoner for three months; and on his release, going directly to Fortress Monroe, he proved that he had kept his eyes open to some purpose. He reported to flag-officer Stringham that the Confederates had two batteries, — one of ten, the other of five guns, — known as Fort Hatteras and Fort Clark. With these two forts the Confederates claimed that they could control the entrance to Albemarle Sound.

As soon as this information was received, an expedition for the destruction of these forts was organized. It was necessarily chiefly naval, although a land force under Gen. Butler went with the fleet. On Aug. 25, 1861, Hampton Roads presented a scene of the greatest activity. The fleet seemed to have awakened from a long sleep. Every vessel was being hastily prepared for sailing. Two transports, the "George Peabody" and the "Adelaide," were crowded with the soldiers of Gen. Butler's command. From the mainmast of the flag-ship "Minnesota" waved the signal-flags, changing constantly as different orders were sent to the commanders of the other war-ships. At two o'clock three balls of bunting were run up to the truck, and catching the breeze were blown out into flags, giving the order, "Get under way at once." From the surrounding men-of-war came the shrill pipe of the boatswains' whistle, and the steady tramp of the men at the capstan bars as they dragged the anchors to the cat-heads. The nimble blue-jackets, climbing about the shrouds and yards, soon had the snowy clouds of canvas set. The wind was fresh; and with bands playing, and cheers of blue-jackets and soldiers, the stately squadron sailed down the bay.

But none on board, save the superior officers, knew whither the fleet was bound. Hardly were they fairly on the Atlantic, when the course was shaped to the southward, and that much was settled. But whether New Orleans, Charleston, or Beaufort was the point to be attacked, the sailors did not know.

THE FLEET OFF HATTERAS.

The squadron which sailed from Hampton Roads consisted of the war-vessels "Minnesota," "Wabash," "Pawnee," "Monticello," and "Harriet Lane;" the transports "George Peabody" and "Adelaide;" and the tug "Fanny." Soon after rounding Cape Henry, the vessels became separated; and when the other vessels reached Hatteras, on the 27th, the "Minnesota" and "Wabash" were nowhere to be seen. As these were the most powerful frigates of the fleet, great fears were felt for the success of the expedition; but at last they appeared on the horizon. A place for landing was selected, and the vessels withdrew into the offing to spend the night. It was determined to begin the attack early the next day.

The morning dawned clear, with a calm sea. At four o'clock the men were summoned to breakfast. At seven the operation of landing the troops was begun. All the surf-boats, barges, and life-boats in the fleet were put to the work. The great war-vessels moved into position, and prepared to cover with a terrific fire the landing of the troops. The first shot was fired by the "Wabash," and the cannonading was at once taken up by the rest of the fleet. The vessels were placed so that a whole broadside could be discharged at once. Thousands of pounds of iron balls were thrown into the forts. Under cover of the cannonading, the disembarkation of the troops began.

But the opposition of the enemy was not the only difficulty to be met. During the time consumed in getting ready to land, heavy banks of clouds had been crawling up from the horizon, and the soft wind of morning had grown into a steady blow. Cape Hatteras was true to its reputation. On the shelving beach, where the troops must land, the great rollers were breaking in torrents of foam. The first life-boats that attempted the landing were swamped, and the soldiers reached the land wet and chilled through. The surf-boats were stove in. The barges, which had been relied upon to land men in large numbers, proved unmanageable, and were towed away by the "Harriet Lane." When the attempt to land the troops was given up, it was found that but three hundred and twenty men had been landed. This was too small a party to storm the forts, and the issue of the battle depended upon the great guns of the navy.

By this time the gunners on the ships had calculated the exact range, and were firing with fearful effect. Broadside followed broadside, with

ATTACK ON THE HATTERAS FORTS.

the regularity of machinery. It was war without its horrors for the blue-jackets, since bad marksmanship or poor powder prevented the Confederate gunners doing any damage. On the gun-deck of the superb frigate

"Minnesota," the jackies were working their guns as coolly as though they were on drill. The operations of loading and firing were gone through with like clock-work. The officers could watch the course of the shells until they struck, and instruct the men, without undergoing any danger.

But in the forts the scene was one of terror. As soon as the gunners of the fleet had secured the range, the shells began crashing into the fort, bewildering the untried soldiers, and driving them from their guns. A shell falling in the fort, and bursting, would sweep clean a space thirty feet square. It was madness to try to work the guns. All sought refuge in the bomb proofs, and an occasional shot was all that showed the presence of any defenders in the forts. Soon the Confederates decided to abandon Fort Clark, the smaller of the two, and mass their forces in Fort Hatteras. As a ruse, to check the bombardment of the ships, the flags on both forts were hauled down. This was, of course, taken as a token of surrender; and as the cannonading stopped, and the clouds of gray gunpowder-smoke lifted, the shrouds of the bombarding squadron were filled with men, and cheer upon cheer rang out in honor of the victory. Soon the troops occupied the deserted battery, and the "Monticello" was ordered into the inlet to take possession of Fort Hatteras. She had proceeded only a little way, however, when suddenly a heavy fire was opened upon her from the fort, and at the same time a large body of re-enforcements was seen approaching from the south. The gunners came down from the shrouds, stopped cheering, and began their work again. For a time the "Monticello" was in a dangerous position. In a narrow and unknown channel, she was forced to retreat slowly, under heavy fire from the fort, being hit eight times. The heavy fire of the other vessels, however, soon drove the Confederate gunners from their guns. The sailors worked untiringly, and seemed enraged by the deceit practised by the enemy. One man, while sponging out a gun, preparatory to reloading it, dropped his sponge overboard. Quick as thought he vaulted the gunwale, and re-appeared on the surface of the water swimming for the sponge. Recovering it, he in a few moments crawled dripping through a porthole, to report respectfully to the captain of the gun: "Just come aboard, sir."

The fort abandoned by the Confederates had been occupied by the troops that had been landed; and, under cover of the furious bombardment, the work of landing was vigorously prosecuted. Night came, and with it a gale so heavy that the vessels had to desert their stations, and withdraw into the offing. When the morning broke, however, the sea had calmed sufficiently to allow the gunners to again set about their terrible work.

The second day's firing was even more accurate than that of the first; and the gray-coats were soon compelled to retire to the bomb-proofs, and abandon all attempt to return the fire of the ships. Soon three shells in rapid succession burst close to the magazine of the fort, telling plainly to the affrighted defenders that nothing was left for them but surrender. A white flag was raised, and Commodore Barron went off to the fleet to formally surrender the forts and the eight hundred men of his command. When the terms were concluded, the defeated soldier turned to flag-officer Stringham, and asked if the loss of life on the ships had been very large. "Not a man has been injured," was the response. "Wonderful!" exclaimed the questioner. "No one could have imagined that this position could have been captured without sacrificing thousands of men." But so it was. Without the loss of a man, had fallen a most important post, together with cannon, provisions, and nearly seven hundred men.

CHAPTER V.

THE "TRENT" AFFAIR. — OPERATIONS IN ALBEMARLE AND PAMLICO SOUNDS. — DESTRUCTION OF THE CONFEDERATE FLEET.

EARLY in the war an event occurred which for a time seemed likely to bring England to the aid of the Confederates. The Confederate Government had appointed as diplomatic commissioners to England two gentlemen, Messrs. Mason and Slidell. They had escaped from Mobile on a fleet blockade-runner, and reached Havana, where they remained a week waiting for the regular English packet to convey them to Liverpool. While in Havana they were lavishly entertained by the colony of Confederate sympathizers there; and feeling perfectly safe, now that they were outside the jurisdiction of the United States, they made no attempt to conceal their official character, and boasted of the errand upon which they were sent.

The United States frigate "San Jacinto," which was one of the many vessels kept rushing about the high seas in search of the privateer "Sumter," happened to be in the harbor of Havana at this time. She was commanded by Capt. Wilkes, an officer who had made an exhaustive study of international law, particularly as bearing upon the right of a war-vessel to search a vessel belonging to a neutral nation. Capt. Wilkes, knowing that by capturing the Confederate commissioners, he could win for himself the applause of the entire North, determined to make the attempt. By a study of his books bearing on international law, he managed to convince himself that he was justified in stopping the British steamer, and taking from it by force the bodies of Messrs. Mason and Slidell. Accordingly he set sail from the harbor of Havana, and cruised up and down at a distance of more than a marine league from the coast, awaiting the appearance of the vessel. Five days after the "San Jacinto's" departure, the commissioners set sail in the British mail-steamer "Trent." She was intercepted in the Bahama Channel by the "San Jacinto." When the man-of-war fired a blank cartridge as a signal to heave to, the commander of the "Trent" ran the British flag to the peak, and continued, feeling secure under the emblem of neutrality. Then came a more peremptory summons in the shape of a solid shot across the bows; and, as the incredulous captain of the "Trent" still continued his course, a six-inch shell was dropped within about one hundred feet of his vessel. Then he stopped. A boat put off from the "San Jacinto," and made for the "Trent." Up the side of the merchant-vessel clambered a spruce lieutenant, and demanded the immediate surrender of the two commissioners. The captain protested, pointed to the flag with the cross of St. George waving above his head, and invoked the power of her Britannic majesty, — all to no avail. The two commissioners had retired to their cabins, and refused to come out without being compelled by actual force. The boat was sent back to the "San Jacinto," and soon returned with a file of marines, who were drawn up with their muskets on the deck of the "Trent." Every British ship which carries mails carries a regularly commissioned officer of the navy, who is responsible for them. This officer on the "Trent" was somewhat of a martinet, and his protests at this violation of the rights of a neutral vessel were very vigorous. When the first gun was fired, he rushed below, and soon re-appeared in all the resplendent glory of gold lace and brass buttons which go to make up a naval uniform. He danced about the deck in an ecstasy of rage, and made the most fearful threats of the wrath of the British people. The passengers too became excited, and protested loudly. Every thing possible was done by the people of the "Trent" to put themselves on record as formally protesting. Nevertheless, the commissioners were taken away, carried to New York, and from there sent into confinement at Fort Warren.

When the news of this great achievement became known, Wilkes was made the lion of the hour. Unthinking people met and passed resolutions of commendation. He was tendered banquets by cities. He was elected a member of learned societies in all parts of the country, and was generally eulogized. Even the Secretary of the Navy, who should have recognized the grave troubles likely to grow out of this violation of the principles of neutrality, wrote a letter to Capt. Wilkes, warmly indorsing his course, and only regretting that he had not captured the steamer as well as the two commissioners.

But fortunately we had wiser heads in the other executive departments of the government. President Lincoln and Secretary Seward quickly disavowed the responsibility for Wilkes's action. Letters were written to the United States minister in England, Charles Francis Adams, alluding to the proceeding as one for which Capt. Wilkes as an individual was alone responsible. And well it was that this attitude was taken: for hardly had the news reached England, when with one voice the people cried for war. Sympathizing with the South as they undoubtedly did, it needed but this insult to the British flag to rouse the war spirit of the nation. Transports loaded with troops were immediately ordered to Canada; the reserves were called out; the ordnance factories were set running day and night; while the press of the nation, and the British minister at Washington, demanded the immediate release of the captives, and a full apology from the United States.

The matter was conducted on this side with the utmost diplomacy. We were undoubtedly in the wrong, and the only thing was to come out with as little sacrifice of national dignity as possible. The long time necessary for letters to pass between this country and England was an important factor in calming the people. Minister Adams said, that, had the Atlantic cable then been in operation, nothing could have prevented a war. In the end the demands of Great Britain were acceded to, and the commissioners proceeded on their way. The last note of the diplomatic correspondence was a courteous letter from President Lincoln to the British minister, offering to allow the British troops *en route* for Canada to land at Portland, Me., and thus avoid the long winter's march through New Brunswick. The peaceful settlement of the affair chagrined the Confederates not a little, as they had hoped to gain Great Britain as a powerful ally in their fight against the United States.

Soon after the capture of the forts at Hatteras Inlet, the authorities of the Union again turned their attention in that direction, with the result of sending the Burnside expedition to Albemarle Sound.

The coast of North Carolina is honeycombed with rivers, inlets, and lagoons, which open into the two broad sounds known as Pamlico and Albemarle, and which are protected from the turbulence of the Atlantic by the long ridge of sand which terminates at Cape Hatteras. While the capture of the Hatteras forts had given the Union authorities control of Hatteras Inlet, the chief entrance to the sounds, yet the long, narrow island was broken by other lesser inlets of a size sufficient to permit the passage of light-draught steamers. The Confederates had quite a fleet of swift, light vessels of insignificant armament, often only a single gun, with which they occasionally made a descent upon some coaster or merchantman, running close inshore, and dragged her in as a prize. With these swift steamers, too, they effectually controlled all navigation of the sounds. But the greatest advantage that they derived from their control of the sounds was the vast facilities given them for constructing, at their leisure, powerful iron-clads in some of the North Carolina ship-yards; then sending them to reduce the Hatteras forts, and so out into the Atlantic to fight for the destruction of the blockade. All these conditions were clear to the authorities of the Union; and therefore, in the early part of January, 1862, a joint military and naval expedition was fitted out for operation against the Confederate works and steamers in these inland waters. It was in the early days of the war; and the flotilla was one of those heterogeneous collections of remodelled excursion-steamers, tugs, ferry-boats, and even canal-boats, which at that time was dignified with the title of "the fleet." In fitting out this expedition two very conflicting requirements were fol-

lowed. In the most favorable circumstances, the channel at Hatteras Inlet is seldom over seven and a half feet: consequently the vessels must be of light draught. But the Confederate steamers in the sounds carried heavy rifled cannon, and the armament of the forts on Roanoke Island was of the heaviest: therefore, the vessels must carry heavy guns to be able to cope with the enemy. This attempt to put a heavy armament on the gun-deck made the vessels roll so heavily as to be almost unseaworthy.

In addition to the armed vessels belonging to the navy, a number of transports accompanied the expedition, bearing the army corps under the command of Gen. Burnside; and the whole number of craft finally assembled for the subjugation of the North Carolina sounds was one hundred and twenty. This heterogeneous assemblage of vessels was sent on a voyage in the dead of winter, down a dangerous coast, to one of the stormiest points known to the mariner. Hatteras was true to its reputation; and, when the squadron reached the inlet, a furious north-easter was blowing, sending the gray clouds scudding across the sky, and making the heavy rollers break on the beach and the bar in a way that foretold certain destruction, should any hardy pilot attempt to run his ship into the narrow and crooked inlet. Outside there was no safe anchorage, and the situation of the entire squadron was most precarious. Several serious mishaps occurred before the vessels got into the small and altogether insufficient harbor between the seaward bar and the "bulkhead" or inner bar. The first vessel to come to grief was one of the canal-boats laden with hay, oats, and other stores. She was without any motive power, being towed by a steam-tug, and, getting into the trough of the sea, rolled and sheered so that she could not be towed. The heavy rolling started her seams, and it was soon evident that she was sinking. With the greatest caution a boat was lowered from one of the steamers, and put off to rescue the crew of the foundering craft. Laboriously the sailors worked their way through the tossing sea to the lee side of the "Grape-shot," and after much difficulty succeeded in taking off all on board, and the return trip was commenced. All went well until the boat came under the lee of the steamer, and the men were about to clamber up the sides. Suddenly an immense sea lifted the vessel high in the air; and in an instant the boat was swamped, and the men were struggling in the icy water. All were ultimately saved, but it was with the greatest difficulty. The "Grape-shot," left to her fate, went ashore some fourteen miles above Hatteras. Her cargo served some practical use, after all; for some horses from the wreck of the "Pocahontas" managed to reach the shore, and kept themselves alive by munching the water-soaked hay and oats.

The "Pocahontas" was one of the steamers chartered by the war department as a horse transport. Her actions during this gale furnish a fair illustration of the manner in which the Government was often deluded into purchasing almost valueless ships. She started with the Burnside expedition from Hampton Roads, freighted with one hundred and thirteen horses. As soon as the gale off Hatteras came on, she began to show signs of unseaworthiness. First the boilers gave way, loosened from their places by the heavy rolling of the ship. All progress had to be stopped until they were patched up. Then down fell the grates, extinguishing the fires. Then the steering-gear was broken; and, getting into the trough of the sea, she rolled until her smoke-stack broke its moorings and fell over. Finally she sprung a leak and was run ashore. The crew were all saved, but for a long time their chances for life seemed small indeed. Ninety of the horses were lost, some having been thrown overboard ten miles from the land. Others were left tied in their stalls, to perish when the ship went to pieces in the breakers. Those that were thrown overboard near the beach swam ashore through breakers in which no boat nor man could live, and, finding the waste and wreckage from the cargo of the "Grape-shot," lived for days on the hay and oats, soaked with sea-water though they were.

For two days this gale continued. The out-look for the fleet seemed hopeless. The inner bar of the harbor was absolutely impassable. Between the outer bar and the inner were packed seventy vessels. This space, though called a harbor, was almost unsheltered. Crowded with vessels as it was, it made an anchorage only less dangerous than that outside. Although the vessels were anchored, bow and stern, the violence of the sea was such that they frequently crashed into each other, breaking bulwarks, spars, and wheel-houses, and tearing away standing-rigging. A schooner breaking from its anchorage went tossing and twirling through the fleet, crashing into vessel after vessel, until finally, getting foul of a small steamer, dragged it from its moorings; and the two began a waltz in the crowded harbor, to the great detriment of the surrounding craft. At last the two runaways went aground on a shoal, and pounded away there until every seam was open, and the holds filled with water.

A strange mishap was that which befell the gunboat "Zouave." She was riding safely at anchor, remote from other ships, taking the seas nobly, and apparently in no possible danger. Her crew occupied themselves in going to the assistance of those in the distressed vessels, feeling that their own was perfectly safe. But during the night, the tide being out, the vessel was driven against one of the flukes of her own anchor; and as each wave lifted her up and dropped her heavily on the sharp iron, a hole was stove in her bottom, sinking her so quickly that the crew took to the boats, saving nothing.

But the most serious disaster was the total wreck of the "City of New York," a large transport, with a cargo of ordnance stores valued at two hundred thousand dollars. Unable to enter the inlet, she tried to ride out the gale outside. The tremendous sea, and the wind blowing furiously on shore, caused her to drag her anchors; and those on board saw certain death staring them in the face, as hour by hour the ship drifted nearer and nearer to the tumbling mass of mighty breakers, that with an unceasing roar, and white foam gleaming like the teeth of an enraged lion, broke heavily on the sand. She struck on Monday afternoon, and soon swung around, broadside to the sea, so as to be helpless and at the mercy of the breakers. Every wave broke over her decks. The condition of her crew was frightful. In the dead of winter, the wind keen as a razor, and the waves of icy coldness, the body soon became benumbed; and it was with the greatest effort that the men could cling to the rigging. So great was the fury of the wind and waves, that no assistance could be given her. For a boat to venture into that seething caldron of breakers would have been throwing away lives. So the crew of the doomed ship were left to save themselves as best they might. The night passed away, and Tuesday morning saw the gale still blowing with unabated force. Hoping to lessen the strain on the hull, they cut away the foremast. In falling, it tore away the pipes, and the vessel became a perfect wreck. Numbed with cold, and faint for lack of food, the crew lashed themselves to the bulwarks and rigging; and so, drenched by the icy spray, and chilled through by the wind, they spent another fearful night. The next day the fury of the storm seemed to have somewhat abated. The sea was still running high, and breaking over the almost unrecognizable hulk stranded on the beach. With the aid of a glass, sailors on the other ships could see the inanimate forms of the crew lashed to the rigging. It was determined to make a vigorous attempt to save them. The first boat sent out on the errand of mercy was watched eagerly from all the vessels. Now it would be seen raised high on the top of some tremendous wave, then, plunging into the trough, it would be lost from the view of the anxious watchers. All went well until the boat reached the outermost line of the breakers, when suddenly a towering wave, rushing resistlessly along, broke directly over the stern, swamping the boat, and drowning seven of the crew. Again the last hope seemed lost to the exhausted men on the wreck. But later in the day, the sea having gone down somewhat, a steam-tug succeeded in reaching the wreck and rescuing the crew. The second engineer was the last man to leave the ship. He remained lashed to the mast until all were taken on the tug. Then, climbing to the top-mast, he cut down the flag that had waved during those two wild days and nights, and bore it safely away.

After this gale died away, the work of getting the squadron over the inner bar was begun. It was a tremendous task. Many of the ships drew too much water for the shallow channel, and it was necessary to remove large parts of their cargoes. The bar, which is known as Buckhead Shoal, was an expanse of quicksand a mile wide, with a tortuous channel ever changing with the shifting sands. Many of the ships stranded, and the tugs were constantly busy in towing them off. Scarcely would one be safely afloat, than another would "bring up all standing" on some new shoal. Two weeks elapsed before all the vessels were safe within the landlocked sound. They were none too soon; for hardly had the last vessel crossed the bar, than the black gathering clouds, the murky, tossing sea, and the foaming billows breaking on the bar, foretold another of the storms for which Cape Hatteras is famed. Through the storm a queer-looking craft was seen approaching the fleet. It was found to be a boat-load of escaping slaves, who had put to sea at random, feeling sure of finding "de Yankees" somewhere. From these men much valuable information was obtained.

Up to this time no one in the fleet, excepting the superior officers, was informed as to the exact destination of the expedition. Now as the signal to get under way blew out from the foremast of the flag-ship, and as the prow of the leading vessel was turned to the northward, all knew, and all cried, "Roanoke Island." This island was heavily fortified by the Confederates, and from its position was a point of considerable strategic importance. It guards the entrance to Pamlico Sound from Albemarle Sound, and into Pamlico Sound open great bays and rivers that penetrate far into the interior of Virginia and North Carolina. On this island the Confederates had erected three forts of formidable strength. These forts commanded the channel through which the vessels would have to pass; and to make the task doubly dangerous, the channel was obstructed with sharpened piles and sunken hulks, so as to be apparently impassable. Beyond the obstructions was the Confederate fleet, which, though insignificant compared with the attacking squadron, was formidable in connection with the forts. It was the task of the invaders to capture these forts, and destroy the fleet.

It was on Feb. 5 that the squadron prepared to leave its moorings at Hatteras Inlet. It was an imposing spectacle. The flag-ship "Philadelphia" led the naval squadron, which advanced with the precision of a body of troops. Behind, with less regularity, came the army transports. About one hundred vessels were in the three columns that moved over the placid waters of the sound toward the forts. It was five in the afternoon of a short February day that the fleet came in sight of the forts. Signals were

CONTRABANDS ESCAPING TO FLEET.

made for the squadron to form in a circle about the flag-ship. The early darkness of winter had fallen upon the scene. The waters of the sound were smooth as a mill-pond. From the white cottages on the shore gleamed lights, and brilliant signal-lanterns hung in the rigging of the ships. Through the fleet pulled swift gigs bearing the commanders of the different vessels.

The morning dawned dark and rainy. At first it was thought that the fog and mist would prevent the bombardment, but all doubt was put at an end by the signal, "Prepare for action," from the flag-ship. The drums beat to quarters, and soon the guns were manned by sailors stripped to the waist. The magazines were opened; and the surgeons cleared away the cock-pits, and spread out their glistening instruments ready for their work.

The fleet got under way, and stood up the channel almost to the point where the obstructions were planted. Beyond these were the gunboats of the enemy. The cannonade was begun without loss of time. A portion of the fleet began a vigorous fire upon the Confederate gunboats, while the others attacked the forts. The gunboats were soon driven away, and then the forts received the entire fire. The water was calm, and the aim of the gunners was admirable. The forts could hardly respond to the fire, since the great shells, plunging by hundreds into the trenches, drove the men from their guns into the bomb-proof casemates. The officers of the ships could watch with their glasses the effect of every shell, and by their directions the aim of the gunners was made nearly perfect.

While the bombarding was going on, Gen. Burnside set about landing his troops near the southern end of the island. The first boat was fired upon by soldiers concealed in the woods. The "Delaware" instantly pitched a few shells into the woods from which the firing proceeded, and in a few minutes the enemy could be seen running out like rats from a burning granary. The landing then went on unimpeded. The boats were unable to get up to the bank, owing to shoal water; and the soldiers were obliged to wade ashore in the icy water, waist-deep, and sinking a foot more in the soft mud of the bottom.

The bombardment was continued for some hours after nightfall. A night bombardment is a stirring scene. The passionate and spiteful glare of the cannon-flashes; the unceasing roar of the explosions; the demoniac shriek of the shells in the air, followed by their explosion with a lightning flash, and crash like thunder; the volumes of gray smoke rising upon the dark air, — make up a wonderful and memorable sight.

In the morning the bombardment was recommenced, and the work of landing troops went on. Eight gunboats were sent to tear away the obstructions in the channel; and there beneath the guns of the enemy's fleet, and the frowning cannon of the forts, the sailors worked with axe and ketch until the barricade was broken, and the eight ships passed to the sound above the forts. In the mean time, the troops on the island began the march against the forts. There were few paths, and they groped their way through woods and undergrowth, wading through morasses, and tearing their way through tangled thickets to get at the enemy's front. The advance was slow, but steady, until the open field before the forts was reached; then a change was ordered, led by the famous Hawkins Zouaves, who rushed madly upon the fort, shouting their war cry of *Zou, zou, zou!* Like a resistless flood the attackers poured over the earthworks, and the frightened defenders fled. Before five o'clock the entire island was in the hands of the troops, and the fleet had passed the barricade. During the bombardment the vessels sustained severe injuries. An act of heroism which made the hero celebrated was that of John Davis, gunner's mate on board the "Valley City." A shell entered the magazine of that ship, and exploded, setting the wood-work on fire. An open barrel of gunpowder stood in the midst of the flames, with sparks dropping about it. At any moment an explosion might occur which would shatter the vessel to fragments. Men shrank back, expecting every moment to be their last. With wonderful presence of mind Davis threw himself across the open end of the barrel, and with his body covered the dangerous explosive until the fire was put out.

As soon as the stars and stripes were hoisted on the flagstaffs of the forts, the Confederate fleet, which had been maintaining a desultory fire, fled up the sound, after setting fire to one schooner which had hopelessly crippled in the battle. She blazed away far on into the night, and finally, when the flames reached her magazine, blew up with a tremendous report, seeming like a final involuntary salute paid by the defeated enemy to the prowess of the Union arms. When quiet finally settled down upon the scene, and Gen. Burnside and Commander Goldsborough counted up their gains, they found that six forts, twenty-five hundred prisoners, and forty-two great guns had fallen into the hands of the victors. The Union loss was forty killed and two hundred wounded.

The next day was Sunday. It was considered highly important that the success of the day before should be vigorously followed up; and an expedition of fourteen vessels, under Capt. Rowan, was ordered to follow the retreating Confederate fleet and destroy it. The flying squadron was chased as far as Elizabeth City on the Pasquotauk River. Here night overtook the pursuers; and they came to anchor at the mouth of the stream, effectually cutting off all hope of retreat. The Confederates in the vessels lying off the town passed an anxious night. Outnumbered two to one by the pursuing vessels, they saw no hope of a successful resistance. With a courage which in view of the facts seems to be almost foolhardy, they determined to stick to their ships, and fight to the death. The feelings of the inhabitants of the town were hardly less gloomy. So thoroughly impregnable had they considered the forts at Roanoke Island, that they had made absolutely no preparations for defence; and now they found their homes upon the eve of capture. The victorious army had not yet had an opportunity to show the merciful way in which the inhabitants of captured cities were treated throughout the war; and the good people of Elizabeth City may be excused for fearing, that, with the destruction of their fleet, they were to be delivered into the merciless hands of a lawless enemy.

Morning dawned bright and clear. With the greatest deliberation the preparations for action were made on the attacking vessels. It was discovered, that, owing to the continuous firing during the Roanoke Island engagement, but twenty rounds of ammunition per gun were left to each vessel. It was accordingly ordered that no long-distance firing should be done; but each vessel should dash at the enemy, run him down if possible, and then board and fight it out, hand to hand. Early in the morning the fleet started up the river. The enemy's fleet was soon sighted, lying behind the guns of a small battery on Cobb's Point. When within long range, battery and vessels opened a tremendous fire with eighty-pound rifles. The approach of the squadron continued until when within three-quarters of a mile the signal was flung out from the mast of the flag-ship, "Dash at the enemy." Then full speed was put on, and firing commenced from bow-guns. The Confederates became totally demoralized. The battery was abandoned when the first vessel poured her broadside into it as she passed. Before the enemy's fleet was reached, many of his vessels were fired and abandoned. The United States steamship "Perry" struck the "Sea-Bird" amidships, sinking her so quickly that the crew had scarce time to escape. The crew of the "Delaware" boarded the "Fanny," sabering and shooting her defenders until they fled over the side into the water. The victory was complete and overwhelming. Three or four of the victorious vessels at once proceeded to the town, where they found the enemy in full retreat and compelling the inhabitants to set fire to their houses. This was quickly stopped, and the invaders became the protectors of the conquered people.

The power of the Confederates in this part of the country being so effectually destroyed, the navy was divided into small detachments and sent cruising up the lagoons and rivers opening into the North Carolina sounds, merely to show the people the power of the United States Government, and to urge them to cease their resistance to its authority. Three vessels were sent to Edenton. As they came abreast of the village, a company of mounted artillery precipitately fled. A detachment of marines sent ashore found a number of cannon which they destroyed, and a nearly completed schooner to which they set fire. Other small places were visited, generally without any opposition being encountered.

A somewhat larger force was sent to a small town named Winton, as it had been rumored that a force of Union men were there disputing the authority of the Confederate Government, and the navy wished to go to their assistance. The "Delaware" and "Hudson," in advance of the squadron, came within sight of the landing and warehouses of Winton about four in the afternoon. The town itself was hidden from the view of the vessels by a high bluff. It was a clear, quiet afternoon, and all seemed peaceful. The long wharf, running out into the stream, was deserted by all save a negro woman, who, roused from her occupation of fishing, gazed inquisitively at the strange vessels. The place looked like a commercial port going to seed on account of the blockade. The two vessels proceeded on their way unmolested, ranging past the wharf, and apprehending no danger. Suddenly from the woods on the bluff a terrific fire was poured upon the vessels. The negress, having served her end as a decoy, fled hastily to shelter. The bluffs seemed to be held by two batteries of light artillery and a considerable force of armed men. Fortunately the aim of the artillery men was bad, and the vessels sustained no severe damage. Still, they were in a precarious position. The "Delaware" was too near to bring her battery to bear, and was obliged to turn slowly in the narrow channel. The "Perry," more fortunately situated, opened at once on the enemy with shrapnel. But the contest was unequal, and the two vessels were forced to retreat down the river about seven miles, there to await the remainder of the squadron.

Two days after, the flotilla began the advance up the river, shelling the town as they ascended. Once opposite the town, the troops were landed, and the Hawkins Zouaves soon had possession of the bluff and town. Knapsacks, ammunition, and muskets in considerable quantity fell into the hands of the victors; and, after burning the barracks of the enemy, the squadron returned to the base of operations at Roanoke Island.

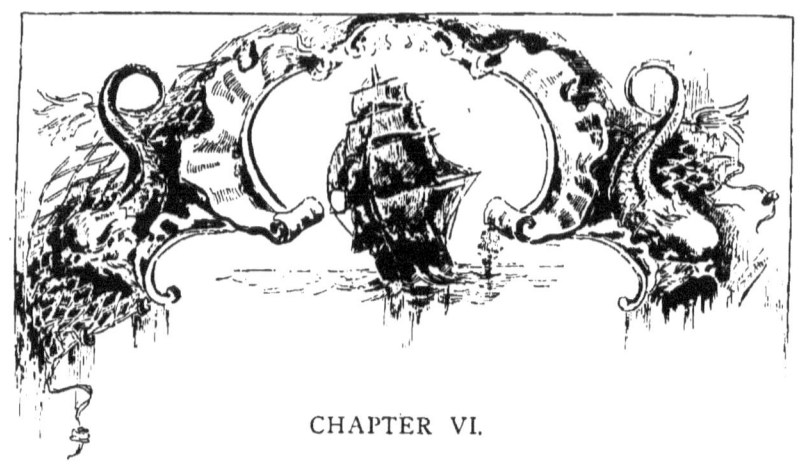

CHAPTER VI.

REDUCTION OF NEWBERN.—EXPLOITS OF LIEUT. CUSHING.—DESTRUCTION OF THE RAM "ALBEMARLE."

AFTER the destruction of the Confederate flotilla at Elizabeth City, and the affair at Winton, the Union fleet remained quietly at anchor off Roanoke Island, or made short excursions up the little rivers emptying into the sounds. Over a month passed in comparative inaction, as the ships were awaiting supplies and particularly ammunition. When finally the transports from New York arrived, and the magazines of the war-vessels were filled with shot and shell and gunpowder, they again turned their attention to the enemy. The victories already won had almost driven the Confederates from that part of North Carolina which borders on the sounds. Roanoke Island, Elizabeth City, Edenton, and Plymouth had one after the other yielded to the persuasive eloquence of the ship's cannon, and there was left to the Confederates only one fort, — Newbern, on the River Neuse. As a city Newbern is insignificant ; but as a military post it was of a good deal of importance, and the Confederates had made active preparations for its defence.

It was on the 12th of March, 1862, that Commander Rowan started from Hatteras Inlet with a flotilla of thirteen vessels, and army transports bearing three thousand men. The long column steamed down the placid waters of Pamlico Sound, and, turning into the Neuse River, anchored about fifteen miles below the city. Although the night before the battle, and within sight of the white steeples of the menaced city, all was quiet and peaceful. The banks of the broad stream were densely wooded, and from them could be heard at times the cry of the whip-poor-will, or the hoot of the night-owl. The vessels were anchored far out in the middle of the stream, so as to avoid the deadly bullets of any lurking sharp-shooters. The look-outs kept a close watch for floating torpedoes; while the sailors off duty spun their yarns in the forecastle, and bet pipes and tobacco on the result of the coming battle. The jolly tars of the Burnside expedition had hardly yet learned that war was a serious matter. They had met with but little serious resistance, had captured powerful forts without losing a man, had chased and destroyed the Confederate fleet without any serious damage to their own, and felt, accordingly, that war was a game in which it was their part always to win, and the part of the enemy to run away. Certainly the fight at Newbern did nothing to dispel this idea.

When morning broke, the shrill piping of the boatswain's whistle brought the crew to their places on deck. Breakfast was served, and leisurely eaten; for it is one of the established theories of the navy, that sailors can't fight on empty stomachs. Breakfast over, the work of landing the troops was begun. The point chosen was a broad beach fringed with woods near the anchorage of the vessels. Before landing the troops, the ships threw a few shells into the woods, to make certain that they concealed no ambuscade, as in the disastrous affair at Matthias Point. After two dozen shells had burst, mowing down trees, and driving out frightened animals in plenty, but no sharp-shooters, the long-boats put off from the transports bearing the soldiers for the land attack. As soon as six or seven hundred were landed, they formed in column, and moved rapidly up the beach. The others followed as rapidly as they could be put on shore. The gunboats steamed slowly up the river, keeping abreast of the troops, and throwing shells into the woods ahead of the attacking column. Had any Confederates prepared to resist the march, they must have been driven out of the forest before the Federals came within musket-range. Not an atom of resistance was made. The plans of the invaders seemed irresistible. About half-past four in the afternoon, a puff of smoke rose from the river-bank far ahead of the leading vessel, and in a few seconds a heavy shell plunged into the water a hundred yards ahead of the flotilla. The enemy was getting awake to the situation. The gunboats soon returned the fire, and the cannonading was continued at long range, without damage to either side, until sundown, when the troops went into camp, and the vessels chose an anchorage near by.

At daylight the next morning, the advance was resumed. The day was so foggy that the usual signals between the vessels could not be seen, and orders from the flag-ship had to be carried by boat. The fleet proceeded up the river; and, when the fog lifted, the ramparts of Fort Dixie — the one that had fired on them the night before — were visible. A vigorous bombardment was at once begun; but the fort failed to reply, and a storming-party sent ashore found it empty. Hoisting the stars and stripes above the deserted bastions, the ships went on. Soon they reached Fort Ellis. Here the firing was sharp on both sides. The fort was a powerful earthwork, well armed with rifles ranging from thirty-two to eighty pounders. The Confederates did but little damage with their guns; their aim being bad for want of practice, and their powder of poor quality. Still, they fought on with great courage until a shell from the "Delaware" burst in the magazine, firing the powder there, and hurling the fort, with large numbers of its brave defenders, high in the air. This ended the fight with Fort Ellis, and the fleet continued its way up the river.

Shortly after passing Fort Ellis, two rows of obstructions were met in the channel. The lower barrier was composed of a series of piles driven into the river-bottom, and cut off below the water; back of these came a row of pointed and iron tipped piles pointing down stream at such an angle as to be likely to pierce the hull of any vessel that should run upon them. Entwined about these piles was a cable connecting with thirty powerful torpedoes. That any vessel could pierce such a barrier seems almost incredible; yet all the vessels of the flotilla passed, and but two were seriously injured. One of the sharp iron piles drove through the bottom of the "Barney," sending the crew to the pumps, and the carpenter down into the hold with his felt-covered plugs. But her damages were quickly repaired, and she went on with the rest of the fleet. Right under the guns of Fort Thompson the second line of obstructions was encountered. It consisted of a line of sunken vessels closely massed, and a *cheval-de-frise* of stakes and logs, that blocked the entire river, save a small passage close in shore under the guns of the battery. Here was more hard work for the sailors; but they managed to creep through, and ranging up in line, broadside to Fort Thompson, they opened a vigorous cannonade upon that work. The condition of the garrison of the fort was desperate. The troops that had marched up the beach abreast of the vessels began a vigorous attack on the landward face of the fort, while the vessels in the river kept up a vigorous fire on the water-front.

FLAG OF SOUTH CAROLINA.

Soon the gunners of the fort were called away from the river-front to meet the hot assault of the soldiers on the land; and, as the conflict grew close, the ships ceased firing, lest their shell should mow down foe and friend alike. Leaving the enemy to the attention of the soldiery, the ships proceeded up the river past two deserted forts that gave no answer to vigorous shelling. Just as the last vessel was passing Fort Thompson, the attacking troops, with a cheer, rushed upon the ramparts; and in a minute the stars and stripes were fluttering from the flagstaff. This was the last resistance encountered, and at two P.M. the victors were in full possession of the city. The war-ships sped up the river after three Confederate steamers that were endeavoring to escape, and soon captured them. One was run ashore and burned, while the other two were added to the conquering fleet. As a last resort, the flying enemy sent down a huge fire-raft, in the hope of burning some of the Union vessels; but this was stopped by the piers of a railroad bridge, and, burning that, effectually cut off Newbern's communication with the world. During the entire two days' engagement, the navy did not lose a man on the ships. Two of a small landing-party were killed, and eleven wounded; while of the soldiers there were killed eighty-eight, and wounded three hundred and fifty-two. This victory gave to the United States the entire control of the North Carolina sounds and tributary navigable waters.

For years after this, the sounds were occupied by a small squadron of the United States navy, mainly blockading cruisers. It was during these three years of occupation that Lieut. W. B. Cushing performed those wonderfully daring deeds that made him a name and fame apart from all other war-records. These feats so particularly belong to Cushing's record, rather than to the history of any years of the war, that they may well be considered together here. The wonderful exhibitions of daring by which this young officer earned his promotion to the rank of a commander, while still hardly more than a boy, were the ascent of New River Inlet in the steamer "Ellis," for the purpose of destroying the enemy's salt-works, and a blockade-runner at New Topsail Inlet; and. finally, the great achievement of his life, the destruction of the ram "Albemarle" in the Roanoke River.

Lieut. Cushing entered the navy during the first year of the civil war, being himself at that time but nineteen years old. A comrade who served with him at the time of the destruction of the "Albemarle" describes him as about six feet high, very slender, with a smooth face, and dark wavy hair. Immediately upon his joining the navy, he was assigned to duty with the blockading squadron on the Atlantic coast. He distinguished himself during the first year of the war, at a time when the opportunities of the service were not very brilliant, by unfailing vigilance, and soon won for himself the honor of a command. In November, 1862, he was put in command of the steamer "Ellis," and ordered to preserve the blockade of New River Inlet on the North Carolina coast, not far from the favorite port of the blockade-runners, Wilmington. The duties of a blockading man-of-war are monotonous, at best. Lying at anchor off the mouth of the blockaded harbor, or steaming slowly up and down for days together, the crew grow discontented; and the officers are at their wits' end to devise constant occupation to dispel the turbulence which idleness always arouses among sailors. Inaction is the great enemy of discipline on board ship, and it is for this reason that the metal and trimmings aboard a man-of-war are so continually being polished. A big brass pivot-gun amidships will keep three or four jackies polishing an hour or two every day; and petty officers have been known to go around secretly, and deface some of the snowy wood-work or gleaming brass, when it seemed that surfaces to be polished were becoming exhausted. It is no unusual thing to set a gang of sailors to work rubbing away with polish on the flukes of the great anchors, merely to give them work. But while this sort of occupation may drive dull care away from the heart of Jack, his officers are not so easily entertained; and the dull routine of blockading duty at an unfrequented port is most wearisome to adventurous spirits. Particularly was this the case with Lieut. Cushing, and he was constantly upon the look-out for some perilous adventure. One day late in November, information was brought to him that the enemy had established large salt-works at Jacksonville, thirty-five miles up the river. Even thus early in the war, the vigorous blockade was beginning to tell upon the supplies of the Confederates; and one of the articles of which the Southern armies were in the greatest need was salt. The distress caused by the lack of it was great. Many of the soldiers were in the habit of sprinkling gunpowder upon their food to give it a flavor approaching that of salt. In olden days, particularly in the British navy about the end of the eighteenth century, it was the custom for the captains to issue to their crews, before going into battle, large cups of grog with gunpowder stirred in. It was believed that this mixture made the men fight more desperately. But this theory of the doughty sea-dogs of past generations no longer finds any support, and doubtless the soldiers of the Confederacy felt they could fight better upon salt than on their enforced seasoning of gunpowder. At Manassas Junction, when the Confederate army by a rapid movement captured a large provision train, the rush of the soldiers for two or three cars laden with salt was so great that a strong guard had to be stationed to beat back pilferers, and secure a proper division of the much-prized seasoning.

The officers of the Union navy were well informed of this scarcity of salt throughout the South, and accordingly made it a point to destroy all salt-works along the coast. The officers of the Gulf squadron were constantly employed in raiding establishments of this character, of which there were numbers along the coast of Louisiana, Alabama, and Mississippi. Cushing, on hearing of the existence of salt-works in the district over which he stood guard, determined to destroy them. But to do this was a matter of no small peril. Jacksonville was thirty-five miles up a small stream, in the heart of a country teeming with Confederate troops and their guerilla sympathizers. The densely wooded shores could conceal sharp-shooters, who could easily pick off every man stationed on the steamer's deck. At any point of the entire distance a masked battery might be stationed, that could blow the invading craft out of water, and leave none of her crew uncaptured to tell the tale. Nevertheless, the intrepid young commander determined to make the attempt. His vessel was a small steamer, mounting one heavy gun amidships and two smaller cannon on each side. Without any mishap the "Ellis" and her crew reached the town about noon. On the way up the river a dense column of black smoke appeared ahead, rising above the forest. All thought that the Confederates, hearing of their approach, had evacuated the town, firing it as they retreated. All possible steam was put on, and the little gunboat dashed up the river in the hope of saving some of the property of the inhabitants. But, on rounding an abrupt curve in the river, the mystery was solved by the appearance of a fine schooner, loaded with cotton and turpentine, and drifting helplessly, a mass of crackling flames, down the stream. She was clearly a blockade-runner, freighted with the chief products of the country, and had been waiting a chance to slip out past the blockader, and run for some friendly port. Cushing's bold move up the river had entrapped her neatly, and her owners had fired her and fled. The fire was a magnificent sight. The inflammable cargo, the tarry ropes and cordage, fed the flames, which leaped from hull to main-truck. The cotton burned sullenly, giving forth immense clouds of dense, black smoke. To save her was hopeless, and the "Ellis" kept out of the way of the flying fire-brands and continued on. The expected salt-works were not found, however; and the only trophies to be obtained at the town were about twenty-five stand of arms and two schooners, evidently blockade-runners. The post-office was also visited, and a large mail captured and removed, in the hope of finding therein some valuable information regarding the movements of the enemy. The town itself was one of the sleepy little Southern villages, with wide streets, grass-grown and lined with live-oaks. Children, and boys too young to have been drafted into the Southern army, followed the sailors and marines curiously as they strolled up and down the silent streets. The war had robbed the little city of its men; the blockade had robbed it of its little coasting-trade. Such an air of quiet and desolation hung about the place, that the inhabitants probably welcomed the advent of even the hostile sailors as being something to break the monotony. After a stoppage of an hour and a half, the "Ellis" started down the river. The quiet of the upward voyage had dispelled any thoughts of danger, but about five o'clock suspicions were re-awakened by the sight of a small encampment on the bank. A few shells thrown over the tents quickly sent the campers scurrying into the woods; and, as the camps seemed to have no artillery, the "Ellis" continued without further hostilities. A short distance down the stream the Confederates opened upon them with two guns mounted on a lofty bluff. Cushing, ever ready for a skirmish, stopped his engine, and cleared away the big pivot-gun for action. The battle-flag was hoisted at the fore, and the crew, with three cheers, set about the work. About an hour of artillery practice followed, when, the enemy being driven from his guns, the "Ellis" proceeded on her way. It was now growing dark, and the tide was rapidly falling. The two pilots on the steamer agreed that daylight and high tide were necessary to get the vessel safely out of the river. With great reluctance Cushing ordered the anchor to be let fall, and proceeded to make preparations for the night. On both banks of the river could be seen the flash of lanterns, proving that the Confederates were aware of the steamer's presence, and were contemplating an attack. To resist such an attack if made in force during the night, seemed almost hopeless; yet the sailors went cheerfully about the work of preparation, getting out cutlasses and revolvers, and putting up the boarding-nettings over the sides. In watchful anxiety the hours wore away. No sound escaped the vigilant ear of the men on duty. But the enemy evidently had abandoned the attack, and when morning broke none were to be seen. With light hearts, and feeling that the worst was past, the little party continued their way, only to find that the worst was yet to come. Soon after daylight, the pilot, mistaking the channel, ran the ship so solidly aground that there was clearly no hope of extricating her. All this time she had been towing one of the captured schooners; and Cushing, with quick decisiveness, ordered that every thing should be removed from the "Ellis" to the schooner. This was quickly done, leaving nothing but the great pivot-gun aboard.

But even when so greatly lightened, the ship would not float, and Cushing saw that all was lost. As a final expedient he sent a boat's crew back after the cannon that the enemy had abandoned the day before, intending to construct a land-battery with them, and so keep his ship. But the Confederates had already removed the guns, so this forlorn hope failed. Orders were then given for the crew to take the schooner, and drop down the river for a mile or two. The young captain expressed his intention of remaining aboard his craft, and asked for six volunteers to help him fight the pivot-gun. They were quickly found; and, while the remainder of the crew dropped down the river in the schooner, the devoted little band calmly awaited the beginning of the attack. They did not have long to wait. Soon a cannon boomed from the bank, and a heavy shell whizzed over their heads. Then another, from another direction, and a third, and a fourth, each from a distinct battery. They were hopeless odds, yet Cushing and his command fought on until the gunners, getting the range, dropped shot after shot into the doomed vessel. Then fire broke out in three or four places. This was too much; and the seven daring men took to a small boat, and rowed to the schooner. First, however, they loaded the long gun, and turned it on the enemy, in order, as Cushing said, "that she might fight for herself when we could do so no longer." Once in the schooner, they sailed rapidly down the river; and just as they reached the sound a deep boom announced that the fire had reached the magazine, and the "Ellis" was blown into a million pieces. Daring as this adventure was, Cushing was much distressed at its termination; and in his official report he asks for a general court of inquiry, to determine whether he had properly upheld the honor of the nation's flag.

Another daring expedition was undertaken by Cushing when in command of the "Monticello." This was in February, 1864. He was cruising off Cape Fear River. At Smithville, a small town some distance up the river, was a Confederate army-post. Cushing's plan was to proceed up the river in row-boats, burn any vessels that might be at the dock, capture the commanding officers, and escape before the enemy could recover from the surprise. It was a rash and rather useless expedition, but Cushing successfully carried it out. With two boats and twenty men, he went quietly past the guns of the fort, concealed by the blackness of a cloudy night, ascended the river to the town, and landed directly in front of the hotel. A high bank concealed the party from view, and lying in ambush here they managed to capture some negroes, from whom the desired information was obtained. Then with two officers and a seaman, Cushing walked from the deck to Gen. Herbert's headquarters in so open a manner as to disarm suspicion. Entering the house they met an engineer officer, who tried to raise an alarm, but was quickly captured and gagged. The adjutant-general, never dreaming that any enemy could be so near him, supposed it was a mutiny, and fled hastily, half dressed, to the woods, not even calling out the garrison. Cushing then with his speechless prisoner walked calmly back before the long barracks that sheltered a thousand hostile soldiers, and within a few yards of the sentry on the wharf. Only when the affrighted adjutant-general returned from his hasty trip to the woods did the Confederates know that an enemy had been in their midst. Then there was great excitement, arresting of sentries, calling out of guards, and signalling to the fort that hostile boats were in the harbor. But all too late. Cushing's coolness, courage, dash, and invincible luck had carried him scot free through another dare-devil adventure.

From the "Monticello" Cushing made yet another dangerous excursion into the enemy's country. On this occasion he had a more adequate purpose for his perilous errand. It was believed that the Confederate ram "Raleigh" was in the Cape Fear River above the town of Smithville, the scene of the last adventure. Cushing obtained permission from his superior officer to ascend the river, and try to blow up the ram with a torpedo. On the night of the 23d of June he started, taking with him Jones and Howarth, the officers who had been with him in the previous trip, and fifteen men. The night was pitchy dark, and all went well as they passed the fort and the little town of Smithville. Fifteen miles from the river's mouth, they saw the moon suddenly break through the clouds; and the surface of the river suddenly became bright, revealing to the sentries on shore the Yankee boat fifteen miles within Confederate territory. Quickly the boats turned about, and headed down the river; but this was a mere feint, as Cushing doubled as soon as he reached the shadow of the opposite bank, and continued his course into the hostile territory. Toward morning, when within about seven miles of Wilmington, a very stronghold of the Confederates, he landed, and hid his boat in a neighboring swamp. The men lay in hiding all day; and, just as they were about to start out again, they captured two boats with a Wilmington fishing-party. During the second night Cushing crept cautiously up to within three miles of Wilmington, closely examining the defences of the town and the obstructions in the river. At daybreak he rowed up one of the creeks until he found the road between Fort Fisher and Wilmington. Here he crouched by a hedge until a mounted mail-carrier came by from the fort. The soldier was captured and dismounted, vastly astonished at the sight of a blue-jacket in that region. Presently, along came the carrier from the town, on the way to the fort. He too was astonished at the sight, but flung back a scornful answer to the demand that he surrender, and galloped hastily away. In an instant Cushing was on the back of the captured horse, and after him; but the fugitive was too well mounted, and escaped. Matters were now becoming very serious. The runaway would doubtless give the alarm everywhere. Immediate flight was imperative. The men had been away from the boat for some hours, and were famished. Food must be had. But how to get it? Cushing's solution of the problem was characteristic. Having captured some other prisoners, he learned that a store was to be found about two miles off. A prisoner about Howarth's size was ordered to strip, and Howarth put on his clothing. The change from the trim blue uniform of a Yankee naval officer to the slouchy jeans jumper and overalls of a North Carolina "cracker" was somewhat amusing, but the disguise was complete. Mounting the captured horse, Howarth rode off in the character of a "poor-white" farmer come in to do his marketing. He chatted freely with the people he met along the road, and securing his provision, returned to the boat without arousing the least suspicion. Snugly ensconced in the thick bushes, the party then proceeded to sup, and after the meal amused themselves in cutting telegraph-wires, and at dark returned to the boat. This was the third night in the river, and Cushing prepared to return. Embarking with his prisoners, he pulled up to the "Raleigh," and found that she would not need his attentions, as she was already a total wreck. Then he began the descent of the river. When a little way down the prisoners were set adrift, with neither sails nor oars in order that they might not report the occurrence too soon. The blue-jackets continued their pull down the river. Just as they reached the mouth the moon shone out, and a quick hail came from a guard-boat. Cushing made no answer, but in a low voice urged his men on, intending to attack the enemy. But in an instant more three boats came out of the shadow, and at the same instant five appeared on the other side. One opening seemed left for the beleaguered boat to dash through. At it they went, but a schooner filled with troops suddenly appeared blockading this last exit. It looked as though all was up, and those in the boat saw before them the cheerful prospect of execution as spies. But Cushing's pluck and self-possession, which had never yet failed, still stood by him. He resorted to strategy, and, like the hunted fox, threw his pursuers off the track by doubling. He made a dash so rapid and determined towards the western bar, that all the boats of the enemy rushed to block that point. For an instant his own was in the shadow of a cloud. In that instant he had turned, and headed at full speed for New Inlet. His men were as cool as he. With a few vigorous pulls the boat shot out into the breakers where the enemy dared not follow it, and soon after the cutter was hoisted to the davits of the "Monticello," uninjured, after a stay of three nights in the heart of the enemy's country.

It was near the end of the great war that Cushing performed the greatest feat of daring of his adventurous career; and, as on the previous occasions, the scene of the exploit was in the waters tributary to the North Carolina sounds. Early in the spring of 1863 it became evident to the officers of the Union squadron in the sounds, that the Confederates were making arrangements to drive the Yankee ships from those waters, and to re-open the coasting-trade to the people of North Carolina. The chief source of alarm to the fleet was a heavy iron-clad which was reported to be building on the Roanoke River above Plymouth. Full descriptions of this vessel were in the hands of the Union officers; and they saw clearly that, should she be completed, no vessel of the sound squadron, nor perhaps the entire navy, would be able to do battle against her successfully. The river was too shallow for the war-vessels to go up to the point where the ram was being built, and the channel at Hatteras Inlet was not deep enough for iron-clads to be brought in to compete with the enemy when finished. The naval authorities repeatedly urged the army to send an expedition to burn the boat; but Major-Gen. Foster, in command of the department of North Carolina, declared it was of no importance, as the Confederates would never put it to any use. Time showed a very different state of affairs. In April, 1864, the ram was completed, and named the "Albemarle." Her first work was to co-operate with ten thousand Confederate troops in the re-capture of Plymouth, which was accomplished with very little difficulty. Lieut. Flusser was at Plymouth with four small gunboats, and remained bravely at his post as he saw the powerful ram bearing down upon him. It was half-past three in the morning, and the chill, gray dawn was just breaking over the earth. Above the river hung a mist, through which the great body of the ram could be seen coming doggedly down to the conflict. The "Miami" and "Southfield" were lashed together; and, at the order of Commander Flusser, they started to meet the iron-clad, firing quickly and with good aim. The "Albemarle" came on silently, disdaining to fire a gun. With a crash she struck the "Miami" a glancing blow on the port-bow, gouging off two great planks. Sliding past the wounded craft, she plunged into the "Southfield," crushing completely through her side, so that she began to settle at once. The lashings between the gunboats parted, and the "Southfield" sank rapidly, carrying part of her crew with her. As the "Albemarle" crashed into the two vessels, she fired her bow-gun several times, killing and wounding many of the Union sailors, and killing Lieut. Flusser. When she turned and made a second dash for the "Miami," the latter fled down the stream, knowing that to dare the power of the enemy was mere madness. The "Albemarle" steamed back to Plymouth, and by her aid the town was easily re-captured by the Confederates.

The squadron in the sounds was now in a state of the greatest anxiety. At any moment the impregnable monster might descend the river and destroy the frail wooden gunboats at her leisure. Preparations were made for a desperate battle when the time should come. Captains were instructed to bring their ships to close quarters with the enemy and to endeavor to throw powder or shells down her smoke-stack. Every possible means by which a wooden steamer might cope with an iron-clad was provided.

On the 5th of May the ram put in an appearance, steaming down the river. Deliberately she approached within easy range, then let fly a shot at the "Mattabesett" which knocked her launch to pieces and wounded several men. The "Mattabesett" ran up to within one hundred and fifty yards of the "Albemarle," and gave her a broadside of solid shot from nine-inch Dahlgrens and one hundred-pounder rifles. When these shot struck a sloping place on the ram's armor, they glanced off. Those that struck full on the plating simply crumbled to pieces, leaving no dent to tell of the blow. One beautifully aimed shot struck the muzzle of one of the cannon on the ram and broke it. The gun was used throughout the fight, however, as the "Albemarle" carried but two and could not spare one of them. The "Sassacus" followed in line of battle. She delivered her broadside in passing. The ram rushed madly at her, but was evaded by good steering. Then the "Sassacus" in turn rushed at the ram at full speed, thinking to run her down. She struck amidships at right angles, and with the crash of the collision came a hundred-pound shot from the ram, that passed through the wooden ship from end to end. Still the engines of the "Sassacus" were kept going, in the hope of pushing the "Albemarle" beneath the water. The iron-clad careened slowly, the water washed over her after-deck; the crew of the "Sassacus," far out on the bow, tried vainly to drop shells and packages of powder down the ram's smoking chimneys. It was a moment of intense excitement. But the ram was too much for her assailant. Recovering from the shock of the collision, she slowly swung around until her bow-gun could be brought to bear on her tormentor, when she let fly a ponderous bolt. It crashed through the side of the steamer and plunged into her boiler. In an instant hot, scalding steam filled the engine-room and spread over the whole ship. Cries of agony arose on every side. Twenty-one of the crew were terribly scalded. Nothing remained but retreat; and the "Sassacus" steamed away from her enemy, after making one of the bravest fights in naval history. In the mean time the other gunboats were pounding away at the ram. The "Miami" was trying in vain to get an opportunity to discharge a large torpedo. Two other vessels were spreading nets about the great ship, trying to foul the propeller. The action continued until dark, when the ram withdrew, uninjured and without losing a man. She had fought alone for three hours against six ships, and had seriously damaged every one of her adversaries. It must also be remembered that she carried but two guns.

The "Albemarle" lay for a long time idle at her moorings in Roanoke

River, feeling sure that at her own pleasure she could go into the sounds, and complete the destruction of the fleet. Lieut. Cushing, then twenty-one years old, begged permission to attempt to destroy her. The authority was gladly granted by the navy department, and Cushing began making his plans for the adventure. His first plan was to take a squad of men, with two steam-launches, up the Roanoke, and blow the ram up by means of a torpedo. The launches were sent from New York, but one was swamped while crossing Delaware Bay.

Cushing, however, was not the man to be balked by an accident: so, cutting down his force one-half, he prepared for the start. Thirteen officers and men made up the little party which seemed bound to certain death. The spirit which animated the blue-jackets during the war may be imagined from the fact that many sailors tried to purchase the privilege of going on this perilous expedition, by offering their month's pay to those who had been selected. To understand what a forlorn hope the little boat-load of men were cherishing, we must understand what were the defences of the "Albemarle." She lay at a broad wharf, on which was encamped a large guard of soldiers as well as her crew. Above and below her, great fires were kept burning on the shores, to prevent any boat approaching unseen. She was surrounded by a boom, or "water-fence," of floating logs, about thirty feet from her hull, to keep off any torpedo-boats. From the mouth of the Roanoke to her moorings was about eight miles; the shores being lined on either side by pickets, and a large picket-station being established in mid-stream about one mile below Plymouth.

To attempt to penetrate this network of defences seemed to be fool-hardy. Yet Cushing's record for dash and courage, and his enthusiasm, inspired his comrades with confidence; and they set out feeling certain of success. On the night of the 27th of October, the daring band, in their pygmy steamer, steamed rapidly up the river. No word was spoken aboard. The machinery was oiled until it ran noiselessly; and not a light shone from the little craft, save when the furnace-door was hastily opened to fire up. The Confederate sentries on the bank saw nothing of the party; and, even when they passed the picket schooners near the wreck of the "Southfield," they were unchallenged, although they could see the schooners, and hear the voices of the men, not more than twenty yards away. Not until they came into the fitful glare of the firelight were they seen, and then quick hails came from the sentries on the wharf and the "Albemarle's" decks. But the light on the shore aided the adventurers by showing them the position of the ram. They dashed up alongside, amid a shower of bullets that seemed to fill the air. On the decks of the ram all was confusion, the alarm rattles were sprung, the bell rung violently. The launch running alongside came into contact with the row of logs, and sheered off to make a dash over it. Cushing, who on these dangerous expeditions was like a schoolboy on a holiday, answered with ridicule all hails. "Go ashore for your lives," "Surrender yourselves, or I shall sink you," he cried, as the gunners on the ram trained a heavy gun on the little launch. Now she was headed straight for the ram, and had a run of thirty yards before striking the boom. She reached, and dashed over. Cushing, standing in the stern, held in one hand the tiller ropes, in the other the lanyard of the torpedo. He looked up, saw the muzzle of a heavy gun trained directly on his boat: one convulsive pull of the rope, and with a roar the torpedo exploded under the hull of the "Albemarle," just as a hundred-pound shot crashed through the bottom of his boat. In a second the launch had disappeared; her crew were struggling in the waves, or lying dead beneath them, and the "Albemarle" with a mortal wound was sinking to the bottom.

Cushing swam to the middle of the river, and headed down stream. Most of his companions were killed, captured, or drowned. In the middle of the stream he met Woodman, who had followed him on previous expeditions. Woodman was almost exhausted. Cushing supported him as long as he was able, but was forced to leave him, and the sailor sank to the bottom. The young lieutenant floated down the river until at last he reached the shore, exhausted and faint from a wound in his wrist. He lay half covered with water in a swamp until daylight. While there he heard two Confederate officers who passed say that the "Albemarle" was a total wreck. That news gave him new energy, and he set about getting safely away. Through the thick undergrowth of the swamp he crawled for

DESTRUCTION OF THE "ALBEMARLE."

some hours, until he found a negro who gave him shelter and food. Then he plunged again into the swamp, and walked on until he captured a skiff from a Rebel picket; and with this he safely reached the fleet, — the only one of the thirteen who set out two days before. So ended the most wonderful adventure of the war.

CHAPTER VII.

THE BLOCKADE-RUNNERS. — NASSAU AND WILMINGTON. — WORK OF THE CRUISERS.

WHILE it is undeniably true that the naval battles of the civil war were in many cases unimportant as compared with the gigantic operations of the mighty armies in Virginia and Tennessee, yet there was one service performed by the navy, alone and unaided, which probably, more than any thing else, led to the final subjugation of the South. This was the blockade.

To fully appreciate what a terrible weapon the blockade is when energetically pursued, one need only look at the condition of the South during the latter years of the war. Medicines were almost unattainable for love or money. Salt was more carefully hoarded than silver. Woollen goods for clothing were not to be had. Nothing that could not be produced by the people of the revolted States could be obtained at their markets. Their whole territory was in a state of siege, surrounded by a barrier only a little less unrelenting than the iron circle the Germans drew around besieged Paris.

Almost the first war measure of Abraham Lincoln was to declare the ports of the Confederacy in a state of blockade. At first this seemed a rash proclamation, and one which could not be sustained by the force at the command of the Federals. It is a rule of warfare, that "blockades, to be binding, must be effective;" that is, it is not lawful for a nation with a small fleet to declare an enemy's coast in a state of blockade, and then capture such trading-vessels as may happen to run in the way of its cruisers. The nation must have a large enough fleet to station vessels before each of the principal harbors of the enemy, and to maintain a constant and vigilant patrol up and down his coast. If this cannot be done, the blockade is called a "paper blockade," and merchantmen are justified in attempting to evade it. An instance of a "paper blockade" occurred during the early months of the civil war, which will illustrate this point. Wilmington, N.C., was throughout the war one of the favorite ports for blockade-runners. From its situation, the many entrances to its harbor, and other natural advantages, it was the most difficult of all the Southern ports to keep guarded. With the rest of the Confederate ports, Wilmington was declared blockaded; but it was long after, before a suitable blockading-fleet was stationed there. In July, 1861, the British brig "Herald" left Wilmington without molestation. When two days out, she ran across a United States man-of-war, that promptly captured her. The courts, however, decided that a port so little guarded as Wilmington was at that time could not be legally called blockaded, and the brig was therefore released.

But it did not take many months for the energetic men of the Navy Department to get together such a fleet of boats of all kinds as to enable them to effectually seal all the ports of the Confederacy. A blockading vessel need not be of great strength or powerful armament. All that is necessary is that she should be swift, and carry a gun heavy enough to overawe any merchantman that might attempt to run the blockade. And as such vessels were easy to improvise out of tug-boats, ferry-boats, yachts, and other small craft, it came about that by the last of 1861, the people of the seaport towns of the South, looking seaward from their deserted wharves, could see two or three Federal cruisers lying anchored off the outer bar, just out of reach of the guns of shore-batteries. It was a service of no little danger for the blue-jackets. The enemy were ever on the alert to break the blockade by destroying the ships with torpedoes. Iron-clad rams were built on the banks of the rivers, and sent down to sink and destroy the vessels whose watchfulness meant starvation to the Confederacy. The "Albemarle" and the "Merrimac" were notable instances of this course of attack. But the greatest danger which the sailors had to encounter was the peril of being wrecked by the furious storms which continually ravage the Atlantic coast. The sailor loves the open sea in a blow; but until the civil war, no captain had ever dared to lie tugging at his cables within a mile or two of a lee shore, with a stiff north-easter lashing the sea into fury. In the blockading service of our great naval war, the war of 1812, the method in vogue was to keep a few vessels cruising up and down the coast; and, when it came on to blow, these ships would put out into the open sea and scud for some other point. But in '61 we had hundreds of vessels stationed along the enemy's coast; and where a ship was stationed, there she stayed, to meet the fury of the wind and waves by putting out more anchors, and riding out at her cables storms that would have blown the blockader of 1812 hundreds of miles from her post.

In the earlier years of the war the blockade-runners were nearly all sailing-vessels, schooners, and brigs, that were easily captured. But when the supplies of the South became exhausted, and the merchants of England began building ships especially for this purpose, the duty of the blockading squadron became exciting and often very profitable. The business assumed such proportions that half the ship-yards in England were engaged in turning out fast steamers to engage in it. At first it was the custom to send goods in regular ocean-steamers from England to the blockaded port; but this was soon abandoned, as the risk of capture on the long run across the Atlantic was too great. Not until the plan was adopted of shipping the goods to some neutral port along our coast, and there transferring the cargo to some small, swift vessel, and making the run into the Confederate port in a few hours, did the business of blockade-running become very extensive. Goods shipped for a neutral point were in no danger of being captured by our cruisers, and therefore the danger of the long trans-Atlantic passage was done away with.

Of these neutral points which served as way-stations for the blockade-runners, there were four on or near our coast, — the Bermuda Islands, which lie about seven hundred miles east of Charleston; Nassau, which is off the coast of Florida, and a little more than five hundred miles southeast of Charleston; Havana; and the little Mexican town of Matamoras on the Rio Grande, opposite Brownsville, Texas. The Bermudas were to some extent used, but their distance from the coast made them inconvenient as compared with Nassau or Matamoras. Their chief trade was with Wilmington, which became a favorite port during the latter years of the war. Havana was popular for a time, and at first sight would appear to be admirably placed for a blockade-runners' rendezvous. But, though the coast of Florida was but one hundred miles distant, it was surrounded by dangerous reefs, its harbors were bad and far apart, and there were no railroads in the southern part of the State to transport the contraband goods after they were landed. Besides, Key West, the naval station of the Union forces in the South, was unpleasantly near, and the gulf blockade was maintained with more rigor than that on the Atlantic coast. Matamoras was peculiarly well situated for a blockade-running point. It is on the Mexican side of the Rio Grande River, about forty miles above its mouth. Goods once landed could be shipped in barges and lighters across the river in absolute safety, since heavy batteries prevented the cruisers of the gulf-squadron from entering the river. As a result of this trade, Matamoras became a thriving place. Hundreds of vessels lay in its harbor, where now it is unusual to see five at a time. For four years its streets were crowded with heavy freight vans, while stores and hotels reaped a rich harvest from the sailors of the vessels engaged in the contraband traffic. Now it is as quiet and sleepy a little town as can be found in all the drowsy land of Mexico.

But the true paradise of the blockade-runners was Nassau, the chief port of the Bahama Islands, and a colony of Great Britain. Here all the conditions necessary to successfully evade the blockade were to be found. The flag that waved over the island was that of a nation powerful enough to protect its citizens, and to enforce the laws relative to neutrality.

Furthermore, Great Britain was undoubtedly in sympathy with the Confederates; and so far from prohibiting the efforts of her citizens to keep up trade with the blockaded ports, she encouraged and aided them in every way in her power. And aside from her mere sympathy with the struggles

NASSAU: THE HAUNT OF THE BLOCKADE-RUNNERS.

of the young Confederacy, England had a most powerful incentive to break down the blockade. In Manchester the huge cotton-mills, employing thousands of hands, were shut down for lack of cotton, and the mill-hands were starving for lack of work; while shut up in the blockaded ports of the South were tons upon tons of the fleecy staple, that, once in England, would be worth its weight in gold. It was small wonder that the merchants of England set to work deliberately to fit out blockade-runners, that they might again get their mills running, and their people fed.

The years of the war were lively times for the little town of Nassau. Hardly had the proclamation of President Lincoln announcing the blockade of all Confederate ports been issued, when at a bound Nassau became prominent as the point of all most suitable for a blockade-runners' rendezvous. Its harbor and the surrounding waters were deep enough for merchant-vessels, but too shallow to allow much cruising about by warships of heavy armament. It was within a few hours' running of three Confederate ports, and it was protected by the flag of Great Britain. Early in the war the Confederates established a consulate in the little town, and the Stars and Stripes and the Stars and Bars waved within a few rods of each other. Then great shipping-houses of Liverpool sent over agents, and established branch houses. Great warehouses and wharves were built. Soon great ocean ships and steamers began unloading their cargoes at these wharves. Then swift, rakish schooners began to drop into the harbor, and after discharging heavy loads of cotton would take on cargoes of English goods, and slip out at nightfall to begin the stealthy dash past the watching gunboats. As the war went on, and the profits of the trade increased with its dangers, a new style of craft began to appear in the little harbor. These were the Clyde built blockade-runners, on which the workmen of the Clyde ship-yards had been laboring day and night to get them ready before the war should end. They were long, low, piratical looking craft, with two smoke-stacks raking aft, and with one or two masts for showing signals, for they never hoisted a sail. Two huge paddle-boxes towered above the deck amidships, the wheels being of enormous size. No structure of any kind encumbered the deck. Even the steersman stood unsheltered at a wheel in the bow. They were painted dark gray, and at night could slip unseen along the water within a stone's-throw of the most watchful lookout on a man-of-war. They burned great quantities of a kind of coal that gave out no smoke, and when steaming at night not a light was allowed on board. Many of these strange craft can be seen now along the levees at New Orleans, or at the wharves in Mobile, where they are used as excursion-steamers or for tug-boats. They were always the merest

COTTON SHIPS AT NASSAU.

shells, fitted only for carrying freight, as not many passengers were to be found who desired to be taken into the Confederate territory. Occasionally, however, some soldier of fortune from abroad would drift from Nassau, and thence to the mainland, to join the armies of the Confederacy. The Confederate agents on the island were always on the lookout for such adventurers, and were ever ready to aid them. Sometimes, too, returning agents of the Confederacy from Europe would make the run through the blockading-fleet; so that the blockade-runners were seldom without two or three passengers, poor though their accommodations might be. For the voyage from Nassau to Wilmington, three hundred dollars passage money was charged, or more than fifty cents a mile. To guard against treachery, passage could only be obtained through the Confederate consul, who carefully investigated the proofs of each applicant's identity before issuing to him a ticket.

When the blockade-runner had taken her cargo and passengers aboard, and was prepared for her voyage, every one in the little town came down to the docks to see her start. It was a populace strongly Southern in feeling that filled the streets of Nassau, and nothing but good wishes were to be heard on every side. Perhaps from a house on the hill-side, over which floated the Stars and Stripes, the United States consul might be watching through a spyglass the movements of the steamer, and wishing in his heart that she might fall in with some Yankee cruiser; but nevertheless, under his very eyes, the audacious racer slips out, and starts on her stealthy voyage. On leaving the harbor, a quick run of fifteen or twenty miles would be taken along the coast, to try the machinery. Great care would be taken to keep within British waters, lest some watchful gun-boat should seize the prize thus early in her career. When every thing proved in good working trim, the little vessel's prow would be turned northward, and the perilous voyage begun. For the first day, little danger was to be expected, and the voyage was generally so timed that the outer line of blockaders would be reached just after nightfall. A soldier going to enlist in one of the Confederate cavalry regiments thus tells the story of his evasion of the blockade.

"After a favorable voyage we reached the desired point off Wilmington at the proper time. A brief stoppage was made, when soon the final preparations were completed for running the gauntlet of the Federal blockaders, who would become visible shortly, as we approached nearer shore. All the lights in the steamer were extinguished, and all passengers ordered below, only the officers and crew being permitted to remain on deck. The furnaces were replenished with carefully selected coal, which would give the greatest amount of heat and the least smoke. The last orders were given, and every man was at his appointed place. Presently the boilers hissed, and the paddle-wheels began to revolve faster and faster, as the fleet little steamer rose higher and higher in the water from the immense force of the rapid strokes; she actually felt like a horse gathering himself up under you for a great leap. After a little while, the few faint sounds from the deck which we could hitherto faintly catch in the cabin ceased altogether, and there was the stillness of death except for the sounds necessarily made by the movements of the machinery. Then we realized that we were running for our lives past the line of cruisers, and that at any moment a big shell might come crashing through our cabin, disagreeably lighting up the darkness in which we were sitting. Our suspense was prolonged for some minutes longer, when the speed was slackened, and finally we stopped altogether. Even then we did not know whether we were safely through the lines, or whether we had been brought to under the guns of a hostile ship, for we could distinguish nothing whatever through the portholes. However, we were soon released from the cabin, and walked on deck, to find ourselves safely through the blockade. In the offing could be descried several of the now harmless blockaders, and near at hand lay the coast of North Carolina. Soon the gray dawn was succeeded by a brilliant, lovely sunrise, which lighted up cheerfully the low-lying shores and earthworks bristling with artillery, while from a fort near by floated the Southern Cross, the symbol of the glorious cause for which we had come to fight."

When the blockade-runner, after safely running the gauntlet of the war-ships, steamed leisurely up to the wharves of the blockaded town, every one rushed to the docks to greet her. Her captain and crew became at once people of great importance. They were beset on every side for news of the great world outside. The papers that they brought in were bought eagerly by the people, hungering for tidings of something else than the interminable war. The sailors of the steamer, on being paid off, rambled about the streets of the city, spending their money royally, and followed by a train of admiring hangers-on. The earnings of the sailors in case of a successful voyage were immense. A thousand dollars for the four or five days' trip was nothing unusual for common seamen, while the captain often received eight or nine thousand. But the risk of capture, with the confiscation of all property, and some months' imprisonment in a Federal fortress, rather marred the attractiveness of the nefarious trade. The profits of a successful voyage to the owner of the ship and cargo were enormous. One of the steamers, specially built for the trade, at large cost, has been known to pay for herself fully in one voyage. Indeed, the profits must have been huge to induce merchants to take the risk of absolutely losing a ship and cargo worth half a million of dollars. It is certain, too, that throughout the war the number of vessels captured, while trying to run the blockade, was far in excess of those that succeeded. Up to the end of 1863 the Federal Secretary of the Navy reported 1,045 vessels captured, classified as follows: schooners, 547; steamers, 179; sloops, 117; brigs, 30; barks, 26; ships, 15; yachts and boats, 117. Of course, most of these were small, coastwise vessels. Even among the steamers captured, there were but few of the fleet-going, English-built craft.

There was no small amount of smuggling carried on between the ports of the North and the blockaded ports. The patriotism of the Northern merchant was not always so great as to prevent his embarking in the traffic which he saw enriching his English competitor. Many of the schooners captured started from Northern ports and worked their way along the coast until that chain of inlets, sounds, and bayous was reached, which borders the coast south of Chesapeake Bay. Once inside the bar, the smuggler could run at his leisure for any of the little towns that stood on the banks of the rivers of Virginia and North Carolina. The chase of one of these little vessels was a dreary duty to the officers of the blockading-ships. The fugitives were fast clippers of the models that made Maine ship-builders famous, until the inauguration of steam-navigation made a gracefully modelled hull immaterial as compared with powerful machinery. Even when the great, lumbering war-ship had overhauled the flying schooner so as to bring a gun to bear on her, the little boat might suddenly dash into some inlet or up a river, where the man-of-war, with her heavy draught, could not hope to follow. And if captured, the prize was worth but little, and the prize-money, that cheers the sailors' hearts, was but small. But the chase and capture of one of the swift Clyde-built steamers was a different matter. Perhaps a lookout in the maintop of a cruiser, steaming idly about the Atlantic, between Nassau and Wilmington, would spy, far off on the horizon, a black speck, moving swiftly along the ocean. No curling smoke would tell of the blockade-runner's presence, and nothing could be seen until the hull of the steamer itself was perceptible. With the quick hail of the lookout, the man-of-war would head for the prize, and start in hot pursuit. Certain it is that the smuggler started to fly before the watchful lookout on the cruiser caught sight of her. The towering masts and capacious funnels of the man-of-war, with the cloud of black smoke from her furnaces, made her a conspicuous object at distances from which the smuggler would be invisible. With the blockade-runners the rule was to avoid any sail, no matter how innocent it might seem; and the appearance of a cloud of smoke on the horizon was the signal for an immediate change of course, and a flight for safety. When the chase began in this way, the cruiser had but little chance of making a capture, for the superior speed of the merchant-vessel would quickly carry her out of sight. Sometimes, however, a favorable wind would enable the pursuer to use her sails, and then the chase would become exciting. With a cloud of canvas set, the man-of-war would gradually overhaul the flying vessel; and when within range, the great bow-gun would be cleared, and with a roar a shell would be sent flying after the prize. All hands would watch its course anxiously. Generally it fell short. Then another and another messenger would be sent to the enemy, which seldom struck the mark, for gunnery on a rough sea is a difficult art. But the blockade-runner can't stand being used for target-practice long. The cool head of her captain begins to deliberate upon means of getting out of

BLOCKADE-RUNNER IN NORTH CAROLINA SOUNDS.

range. Mere running before the wind won't do it: so he makes a long detour, and doubles on his course, heading directly into the teeth of the breeze. Now the cruiser is at a disadvantage. Her sail-power gone, she stands no chance of capturing her game. Her shells begin to fall far short of the smuggler, and soon she ceases firing altogether; and the blockade-runner, driven hundreds of miles out of her course, but safe for the time, goes on her way rejoicing.

One of the most brilliant captures of the war was that of the blockade-runner "Young Republic," by the United States gunboat "Grand Gulf." The "Young Republic" succeeded in evading the watchfulness of the blockading-squadron about the mouth of the Cape Fear River, and under cover of the night ran in safely to the anchorage under the guns of the Confederate forts. The baffled blockaders saw her moving slowly up the river, while the cannon of the forts on either side thundered out salutes to the daring vessel that brought precious supplies to the Confederacy. But the blockading-squadron, though defeated for the time, determined to wait and catch her when she came out. Accordingly the "Grand Gulf," one of the fastest of the United States vessels, was stationed at the mouth of the river, with orders to watch for the "Young Republic." A week passed, and there was no sign of her. At last, one bright day, the lookout in the tops saw the mast and funnel of a steamer moving along above the forest which lined the river's bank. Soon the hull of the vessel came into view; and with a rattle of hawse-chains, her anchors were let fall, and she swung to beneath the protecting guns of the fort. It was clear that she was going to wait there until a dark or foggy night gave her a good chance to slip past the gunboat that watched the river's mouth as a cat watches the mouth of a mouse-hole. With their marine glasses the officers on the gunboat could see the decks of the "Young Republic" piled high with brown bales of cotton, worth immense sums of money. They thought of the huge value of the prize, and the grand distribution of prize-money, and determined to use every effort to make a capture. Strategy was determined upon, and it was decided to give the blockade-runner the chance to get out of the river that she was awaiting. Accordingly the gunboat steamed away up the coast a few miles, leaving the mouth of the river clear. When hidden by a projecting headland, she stopped and waited for the blockade-runner to come out. The stokers were kept hard at work making the great fires roar, until the steam-gauge showed the highest pressure the boilers could bear. The sailors got out additional sails, clewed up cordage and rigging, and put the ship in order for a fast run. When enough time had elapsed, she steamed out to see if the "Young Republic" had taken the bait. Officers and crew crowded forward to catch the first sight around the headland. The great man-of-war sped through the water. The headland was rounded, and a cheer went up from the crowd of jackies; for there, in the offing, was the blockade-runner, gliding through the water like a dolphin, and steaming for dear life to Nassau. Then the chase began in earnest. The "Young Republic" was one of those long, sharp steamers built on the Clyde expressly for running the blockade. Her crew knew that a long holiday in port, with plenty of money, would follow a successful cruise; and they worked untiringly to keep up the fires, and set every sail so that it would draw. On the cruiser the jackies saw visions of a prize worth a million and a half of dollars; and the thought of so much prize-money to spend, or to send home, spurred them on. For several hours the chase seemed likely to be a long, stern one; but then the freshening wind filled the sails of the gunboat, and she began to overhaul the fugitive. When within a mile or two, she began firing great shells with her pivot-gun. Then the flying blockade-runner began to show signs of fear; and with a good glass the crew could be seen throwing over bale after bale of the precious cotton, to lighten the vessel. In the last thirty miles of the chase the sea was fairly covered with cotton-bales. More than three hundred were passed floating in the water; and the jackies gnashed their teeth, and growled gruffly, at the sight of so much wealth slipping through their fingers. On the high paddle-wheel box of the blockade-runner, the captain could be seen coolly directing his crew, and now and again turning to take a look through his glass at the pursuer. As the chase continued, the certainty of capture became more and more evident. Then the fugitives began throwing overboard or destroying every thing of value: furniture,

PURSUING A BLOCKADE-RUNNER.

silver-ware, chronometers, the fittings of the cabin, every thing that could benefit their captors, the chagrined blockade-runners destroyed. The officers of the gunboat saw that if they wished to gain any thing by their capture, they must make haste. At the risk of an explosion, more steam was crowded on; and the gunboat was soon alongside the "Young Republic," and in a position to give her an enormous broadside. The blockade-runner saw that he was caught and must submit. For lack of a white flag, a pillow-case was run up to the masthead, and the beating of the great wheels stopped. The davits amidships of the "Grand Gulf" are swung out, and a boat's crew, with a lieutenant and dapper midshipman, climb in. A quick order, "Let fall there," and the boat drops into the water, and is headed for the prize. Another moment, and the stars and stripes supplant the pillow-case waving from the masthead of the "Young Republic." An officer who went into the boiler-room found that the captured crew had planned to blow up the vessel by tying down the safety-valve, so that an enormous pressure of steam strained the boilers almost to bursting. A quick blow of a hatchet, and that danger was done away with. Then, with a prize-crew on board, the "Young Republic" started on her voyage to New York; while the "Grand Gulf" returned to Wilmington to hunt for fresh game.

A curious capture was that of the British schooner "Francis," which was running between Nassau and the coast of Florida. On her last trip she was nearing the coast, when she fell in with a fishing-smack, and was warned that a Federal gunboat was not far away. Still she kept on her course until sundown, when the breeze went down, and she lay becalmed. The gunboat had been steaming into inlets and lagoons all day, and had not sighted the schooner. When night came on, she steamed out into the open sea, within a quarter of a mile of the blockade-runner, and, putting out all lights, lay to for the night. Those on the schooner could see the gunboat, but the lookout on the cruiser did not see the blockade-runner. Soon a heavy fog came up, and entirely hid the vessels from each other. The blockade-runners could only hope that a breeze might spring up, and enable them to escape. But now a curious thing occurred. It almost seems as if two vessels on the ocean exercise a magnetic attraction for each other, so often do collisions occur where there seems room for all the navies of the world to pass in review. So it was this night. The anxious men on the schooner soon found that the two vessels were drifting together, and they were absolutely powerless to prevent it. At midnight, though they could see nothing, they could hear the men on the gunboat talking. Two hours after, the schooner nestled gently up by the side of the gunboat; and a slight jar gave its crew their first intimation that a prize was there, simply waiting to be taken. All they had to do was to climb over the railing. This was promptly done, and the disgusted blockade-runners were sent below as prisoners. Half an hour later came a breeze that would have carried them safely to port.

The gray sea-fogs played many scurvy tricks with the blockading-fleets, often letting the runners in right under the muzzles of the great guns. It was far easier to spy out a vessel in the darkest night than in the thick gray fog that enveloped all objects like a blanket. One of the strangest of all the pranks played by the fog occurred in December, 1863, in Charleston Harbor. A wary blockade-runner was creeping out of the harbor, within easy range of the great guns of the fleet, and all hands were trembling, lest at any minute should come the flash of a gun, and shriek of a shell, bearing a peremptory command to heave to. Suddenly the flash came, and was followed by the bang! bang! of great guns from all quarters of the fleet. But the fire seemed pointed in another direction; and the runner made the best of her way out to sea, thinking that some less fortunate vessel, trying to come in on the other side of the fleet, had been captured or blown out of the water. It turned out that a small fog-bank had taken the form of a gray steamer moving swiftly over the water, and had been fiercely cannonaded by the whole Federal fleet. This occurrence gave the Confederates an idea; and they began sending out dummies to engage the fleet, while the true blockade-runners would slip out unobserved in the excitement. One night as the tide was running out with great force, an old hulk was cut adrift from a wharf, and drifted down rapidly upon the Federal fleet It was just after the exploits of the "Merrimac" had made Confederate rams famous, and the naval officers were a little nervous. The hulk drifted quite into the midst of the fleet before being observed; and when she was hailed she bore down on the largest of the men-of-war as though she were a powerful ram, steered by a commander of desperate bravery. The great gunboat's deck rang with the bo's'n's whistle, as the crew were piped to repel boarders, and to their quarters at the guns. A fierce fire was poured on the hostile craft, that came on sullenly, as if scorning to make reply. One by one the other vessels of the fleet drew near, and concentrated their fire on the wretched lumber schooner. It was too much for her; and she gave up the unequal combat, and sank to the bottom. For days after, the gallant tars of the squadron blockading Charleston rejoiced in the destruction of a "Rebel ram;" but none of them knew, that, while they were engaged in the desperate contest, two great blockade-runners, heavily laden with cotton, had slipped out of the harbor, and were well under way for Nassau.

Stories of adventure and of desperate pluck and dash abound in the records of the blockade. Both among the officers of the blockading-fleets, and the commanders of the runners, were found great courage and fine seamanship. One fact is particularly noticeable to the student of the blockade: an English captain running the blockade would never dare the dangers that a Confederate would brave without a tremor. A Confederate captain would rush his ship through the hostile fleet, and stick to her until she sunk; while an Englishman would run his ship ashore, and take to the woods. The cases of the "Hattie," commanded by H. S. Lebby, a Confederate, and the "Princess Royal," a fine, staunch, iron steamer, with an English commander and crew, are typical. The "Hattie" was the last runner to enter or leave Charleston Harbor. She was a small, swift steamer; but she made more successful trips than any other runner. Men living in Charleston to-day, who were interested in the work of this little vessel during the war, say that her cargoes were worth at least fifty millions of dollars. She had numerous narrow escapes, but was never captured. Her reputation was such that the Confederate authorities selected her as the vessel to bring in army supplies and ammunition, and at least three battles were fought with ammunition brought in her hold. Her last entrance to Charleston was one night in February, 1865. Eighteen Federal vessels lay anchored off the harbor, and for a runner to venture in seemed madness. But the captain of the "Hattie" was used to taking desperate chances, and he proposed to enter that harbor. The ship had been freshly painted a blue-white, and as she drifted along the water, with all lights out, looked like a bank of mist. She was within two hundred yards of the outer row of blockaders before her presence was detected. Suddenly fire was opened on her from the nearest gunboat, and in an instant the air was full of rockets announcing her presence. The little vessel had no means of retaliation: all there was for her to do was to dash through the fire and make for the city. Steam was crowded on; and she flew up the channel, running the gauntlet of the fleet, and escaping almost untouched. Then came the real peril. Just below Fort Sumter were two barges anchored in the channel, and filled with armed men. Past these she dashed, her great speed saving her from boarding; but she received the fire of both boats, which wounded several of her crew, and cut off the fingers of the pilot's hand resting on the wheel. This danger past, there was one more to be met. A large monitor lay anchored up the harbor, and the "Hattie" was running so close to her that the commands of the officers in the turret could be clearly heard. One after the other the two great guns were fired, both shots missing; and the "Hattie," safely past the gauntlet, sailed up to the dock in triumph. But by that time it was clear that the last days of the war were near at hand, and accordingly the work of unloading and reloading the vessel for her outward trip was pressed with the greatest vigor. All the time she lay at her dock, Charleston was being vigorously bombarded by the Federal men-of-war lying outside the harbor. The bay fairly swarmed with blockading cruisers; yet a week later the little steamer slipped out through a fleet of twenty-six cruisers without being hailed, and carried her cotton safely to market. When the news of Lee's surrender was received, she was lying safe at her dock in Nassau.

The "Princess Royal," to which we have alluded, was a large iron screw steamer, freighted with drugs, army supplies, guns, and two engines and boilers for two iron-clads in Charleston Harbor,—a most valuable and important cargo for the Confederates. She made the run from Nassau to a point near the coast without adventure, and in the early gray of the morning was stealing up the coast towards the harbor, when a blockader caught sight of her, and started in pursuit. The later began firing when a mile and a half away; and, though there was hardly a chance of the shots taking effect, the cannonade gave the captain of the runner the cold shakes. His boat was one of the fastest on the ocean, and he needed only to put on steam to escape all the blockaders on the coast. But he was a thorough paced coward; and, thinking only of his own safety, he headed the craft for the beach, and with his crew fled into the woods. The valuable ship and her cargo fell into the hands of the Federals.

Sometimes runners were captured through apparently the most trivial accidents. One ship, heavily laden with army supplies, and carrying a large number of passengers, was running through the blockading-fleet, and seemed sure of escape. All lights were out, the passengers were in the cabin, not a word was to be heard on deck, even the commands of the officers being delivered in whispers. Suddenly a prolonged cock-crow rent the air, and, with the silence of every thing surrounding, sounded like a clarion peal from a trumpet. The deck-hands rushed for a box of poultry on the deck, and dragged out bird after bird, wringing their necks. The true offender was almost the last to be caught, and avenged the deaths of his brothers by crowing vigorously all the time. The noise was enough to alarm the blockaders; and in a moment the hail, "Surrender, or we'll blow you out of water!" brought the unlucky runner to a standstill,—a prisoner. The "Southern Cross" narrowly escaped capture on account of the stupidity of an Irish deck-hand, whose craving for tobacco proved too strong for his discretion. The ship was steaming slyly by two cruisers, and in the darkness would have escaped unseen, when the deck-hand, who had been without a smoke as long as he could stand it, lit a match and puffed away at his pipe. The tiny flame was enough for the cruisers, and they began a spirited cannonade. The "Southern Cross" ran for her life. The shooting was guess-work, but the gunners on the cruisers showed all the proverbial Yankee skill at guessing. The first ball carried away the roof of the pilot-house, and the second ripped away the railing along the deck for thirty feet. But the captain was plucky, and made a run for it. He was forced to pass within a hundred feet of one of the cruisers; and as he saw the muzzles of the great guns bearing on his ship, he heard the command, "Heave to, or I'll sink you." But he took his chances, and escaped with only the damage caused by a solid shot crashing through the hull.

One of the strangest experiences of all was that of the captain of a blockade-runner putting in to Wilmington one bitter cold night, when the snow was blowing in clouds, and the fingers of the men at the wheel and the sailors on watch were frostbitten. The runner had reached the harbor safely; but there in channel lay a blockader in such a position that any ship coming in must pass within a hundred feet of her. The Confederate had a light-draught vessel, and tried to squeeze through. When he passed the gunboat, only twelve feet of space separated the two vessels; and he saw a lookout, with his arms on the rail, looking right at the passing vessel. The Confederate expected an immediate alarm, but it did not come. Wondering at the cause, but happy in his luck, he sped on, and gained the harbor safely. Some days after, he learned that the lookout was a dead man, frozen at his post of duty.

It will readily be understood that the inducements offered to blockade-runners must have been immense to persuade men to run such risks. The officers and sailors made money easily, and spent it royally when they reached Nassau. "I never expect to see such flush times again in my life," said a blockade-running captain, speaking of Nassau. "Money was as plentiful as dirt. I have seen a man toss up a twenty-dollar gold piece on "heads or tails," and it would be followed by a score of the yellow boys in five seconds. There were times when the bank-vaults could not hold all the gold, and the coins were dumped down by the bushel, and guarded by soldiers. Men wagered, gambled, drank, and seemed crazy to get rid of their money. I once saw two captains bet five hundred dollars each on the length of a certain porch. Again I saw a wager of eight hundred dollars a side as to how many would be at the dinner-table of a certain hotel. The Confederates were paying the English big prices for goods, but multiplying the figures by five, seven, and ten as soon as the goods were landed in Charleston. Ten dollars invested in quinine in Nassau would bring from four hundred to six hundred dollars in Charleston. A pair of four-dollar boots would bring from fourteen to sixteen dollars; a two-dollar hat would bring eight dollars, and so on through all the list of goods brought in. Every successful captain might have made a fortune in a year; but it is not believed that five out of the whole number had a thousand dollars on hand when the war closed. It was come easy, go easy."

CHAPTER VIII.

DUPONT'S EXPEDITION TO HILTON HEAD AND PORT ROYAL. — THE FIERY CIRCLE.

THE great joint naval and military expedition, which in August, 1861, had reduced the forts at Hatteras Inlet, and, continuing its progress, had, by successive victories, brought Roanoke Island, Newbern, Elizabeth City, and the Sounds of Pamlico and Albemarle under the sway of the Federal Government, was but the first of a series of expeditions intended to drive the Confederates from the Atlantic seaboard, and secure for the United States vessels safe harbors and coaling stations in the bays and inlets along the South Atlantic coast. The proper maintenance of the blockade made it necessary that the seaboard should be in the hands of the Federals. For a blockader off Charleston or Wilmington to be forced to return to Hampton Roads to coal or to make repairs, would entail the loss of weeks, perhaps months, of valuable time. Besides, the sounds and inlets with which that irregular coast is honey-combed were of great use to the Confederates, who could construct at their leisure great rams like the "Merrimac" or "Albemarle," and hurl them against the fleet with the hope of breaking the blockade. Such opportunities were eagerly seized by the Confederates whenever offered; and in many cases the defeating of their purposes seems almost providential, so great was the seeming disparity between the attacking ram and the forces which finally repulsed it.

In reviewing the part of the navy in the civil war, we find that it acted like a great iron band, ever drawing closer and closer about the Confederacy, forcing the Southern armies from one point after another, until at last the whole coast was in the hands of the Unionists, and the Confederates were driven into the interior, there to be dealt with by the Northern armies. One is reminded of that iron chamber in Poe's story, which day by day grows smaller and smaller, until the wretched prisoner within is forced into the pit yawning in the centre. So, during the war, the Confederates lost Hatteras Inlet, Roanoke Island, Hilton Head, Fernandina, Mobile, New Orleans, and Galveston comparatively early in the struggle. Wilmington, behind the almost impregnable bastions of Fort Fisher, and Charleston, surrounded by a cordon of defensive forts, remained the last strongholds of the Confederacy on the Atlantic coast, until the final downfall of the great uprising.

Shortly after the capture of the Hatteras Forts, the navy department saw the need of a harbor and base of naval operations farther south. Charleston, with its powerful defences, was deemed impregnable at that time; and elaborate descriptions of the Southern coast were prepared, setting forth the advantages and disadvantages of available Southern ports. Fernandina, Brunswick, Port Royal, and Bull's Bay, were duly considered; and, while the Navy Department was debating which point to seize, Admiral Dupont was diligently fitting out an expedition to be in readiness to attack any that should be determined upon. Up to the last moment it was thought that Fernandina would be selected. But finally, with the advice of Gen. Sherman, it was determined to make the attempt to wrest Port Royal from the Confederates.

Port Royal is the general name given to a broad body of water formed by the confluence of the Broad and Beaufort Rivers, and opening into the Atlantic Ocean on the South Carolina coast, about midway between Charleston and Savannah. No more beautiful region is to be found in the world. Far enough south to escape the rigors of the northern winters, and far enough north to be free from the enervating heat of the tropics; honeycombed by broad, salt-water lagoons, giving moisture and mildness to the air, — the country about Port Royal is like a great garden ; and even to-day, ravaged though it was by the storms of war, it shows many traces of its former beauty. It is in this region that are found the famous Sea Islands, on which grows cotton so much more fleecy and fine of fibre than the product of the interior, that it is known the world over as Sea Island cotton, and sells at the highest price in the markets of England. In '61 the islands bore the great hospitable manor-houses of the Southern planters; broad of rooms and wide of piazzas, and always open for the entertainment of travellers, were they friends or strangers. The planters living there were among the wealthiest in the South, at a time when all planters were wealthy. They numbered their slaves by thousands. Standing on the broad piazza of one of these Southern homes, one could see the rows of rough huts that made up the negro quarters, and hear faintly the sound of the banjo and rude negro melodies, mingling with the music of piano or harp within the parlor of the mansion-house. Refined by education and travel, the planters of the region about Port Royal made up a courtly society, until war burst upon them, and reduced their estates to wildernesses, and themselves to beggary.

At the head of the Beaufort River stood the little town of Beaufort. Before the war this was a thriving place; its magnificent harbor made it easily accessible for the largest merchant-ships, and the richly productive country round about furnished heavy cargoes of the fleecy staple that gave to the South the name of the "cotton kingdom." On Saturdays and holidays the broad streets of Beaufort would be crowded with carriages and horsemen from the neighboring plantations. The planters, in broad-brimmed hats and suits of snowy linen, thronged the broad piazzas of the hotel, or grouped together in the shade of the spreading trees that lined the streets, discussing the cotton crops and prices. Now all is changed. Beaufort is a sleepy little village, with no sign of trade, domestic or foreign; and the country round about, once dotted with handsome plantation homes, now seems a very wilderness, save where Northerners have erected for themselves winter homes on the Sea Islands.

It was late in October, 1861, when the final determination to attack the forts at Port Royal was reached. For weeks before, the squadron lying at Hampton Roads had been making preparations for a great naval movement, and all the newspapers of the North were filled with wise speculations as to its objective point. Reporters, correspondents, and editors were alike baffled in their efforts to secure accurate information; and even the commanders of the men-of-war were ignorant of their destination. But it seems that the Confederates were warned by some of their sympathizers in Washington, and the destination of the fleet was better known south of Mason and Dixon's line than in the North. On Tuesday, Oct. 29, the squadron was all ready for the voyage. It was by far the most powerful fleet ever gathered under the flag of the United States. Twenty-five vessels laden with coal had sailed the day before. On the placid waters of the bay, under the frowning walls of Fortress Monroe, floated fifty men-of-war and transports. The day was clear, and the breeze brisk, and the hearts of the jolly jack-tars bounded within them as they thought of escaping from the long inactivity of a season in port. Long-boats bearing despatches rowed from ship to ship; hucksters from the shore came off in dories, dingies, and all variety of queer craft, to drive a farewell bargain with the sailors. The transport vessels were crowded with soldiers in the gay uniforms of militia commands. (It was early in the war then, and they had not learned that a man could fight as well in dingy rags.) The "Wabash" was flag-ship, and aboard her was Admiral DuPont. When she made the signal for getting under way, all was bustle and animation on all the other vessels of the fleet, and on all sides could be heard the noise of preparation for the start. The boatswains piped away cheerily; and a steady tramp, tramp, from the deck of each ship, and the clicking of the capstan catches, told that the anchors were coming up. Soon from the black funnels of the steamers clouds of smoke began to pour, and in the rigging of the sail frigates were crowds of nimble sailors. The commands "All ready! Let fall!" rang sharply over the water from the ships. Broad sheets of snowy canvas appeared where before were but ropes and spars, and in a moment the whole squadron was under way. The steamers led off briskly, with much churning of the water by their paddle-wheels and "brazen-fins;" after them followed the magnificent sailing-frigates, with sail set, — lofty masses of canvas towering toward the skies, and moving with stately grace. At the very head of all went the flag-ship, the grand old "Wabash," with the flag of Admiral DuPont floating from the fore. None of the commanders knew whither they were bound. All were

FORTRESS MONROE.

to follow the flag-ship, and in event of separation to refer to sealed orders with which each was provided. For the first day all went well. The promise of fair weather given by the beautiful day of starting seemed about to be fulfilled. But on the second night, as they came near the terrible region of Cape Hatteras, the wind began to freshen, and continued increasing in fierceness until it fairly blew a gale. The night was pitchy dark, and the crews on the vessels could hardly see the craft by which they were surrounded. Great as was the danger of being cast on the treacherous shoals of Hatteras, the peril of instant destruction by collision was even more imminent. Fifty vessels, heavily freighted with human lives, were pitching and tossing within a few rods of each other, and within a few miles of a lee shore. It seemed that the destruction of a large number of the vessels was unavoidable; and the sailors may be pardoned, if, remembering the mishaps of the Burnside expedition, they conceived Hatteras to be tenanted by an evil spirit, determined to prevent the invasion of Confederate territory. To add to the danger, the Confederates had extinguished the warning light at the Cape, and the navigators of the fleet had nothing to guide them in their course. When morning came, the fleet was pretty well scattered, although still many vessels were near enough together to be in no small danger. The transport "Winfield Scott," which carried four hundred and fifty soldiers, besides a large crew, was observed to be rolling heavily, and flying signals of distress. From the decks of the "Bienville," the nearest steamer, the officers with their glasses could see the crew of the distressed vessel working like beavers, throwing overboard every thing of weight to lighten the ship. Notwithstanding all their efforts, she was clearly water-logged, and sunk so low in the water that wave after wave broke over her decks, every now and then sweeping a man away to sure death in the raging sea. It seemed folly to attempt to launch lifeboats in such a furious sea, but the captain of the "Bienville" determined to make the attempt to save the men on the doomed "Winfield Scott." The crew was piped to quarters, and the captain asked for volunteers to go to the rescue. Man after man stepped forward, until enough had been secured to man three boats with ten men each. Carefully the boats were dropped into the sea, and man after man swung into them; then they put off and started for the sinking ship. But while these preparations were being made, the two ships had been drifting closer and closer together. Soon it was seen that a collision was inevitable. Fortunately the boats were broadside on, so that the cutting effect of a blow from the bow was avoided. They were presently so near each other that the men began jumping from the deck of the "Winfield Scot" upon that

DU PONT'S EXPEDITION OFF CAPE HATTERAS.

of the "Bienville." The leap, though a perilous one, was made in safety by over thirty men. Suddenly a great wave lifted the ships up and dashed them together. Three poor wretches, just about to jump, were caught between the vessels and crushed to death. A few sharp cries of agony, and all was over; and the vessels, drifting apart, let their bodies, crushed beyond recognition, fall into the water. By this time the small boats, with their determined crews on board, had succeeded in getting around to the lee side of the sinking ship, and the work of getting the soldiers and sailors over the side was begun. By the most strenuous efforts all were saved, and the "Bienville" steamed away, leaving the "Winfield Scott" to her fate.

Night came on, with the gale blowing with still greater fury. The wind shrieked through the cordage, and now and again a great wave would sweep across the decks of the crowded vessels, making the men hang on to the rigging for dear life. Soon another ship began to go to pieces. The "Governor," which had been steaming along near the "Wabash" since the time of leaving Hampton Roads, had become separated from her consort during the gale of the first day. On the second night, those aboard her perceived that she was showing signs of weakness, and was likely to go down with all on board unless aid could be obtained. Not a sail, however, was in sight; and every wave seemed about to overwhelm or dash to pieces the frail craft. She labored heavily in the furious sea. By and by the strain on her timbers was such that the port hog-brace broke in two places, weakening the vessel so that her fate was apparent to all. Soldiers and sailors worked away with a frantic energy born by the fear of death, and succeeded in bracing up the timbers, so as to avoid, for a time, the breaking-up. Soon after, a heavy roll of the vessel broke the smokestack, and it was pitched overboard. Luckily it broke some three feet above the deck, so that the fires could still be kept up. Then the steampipe burst; and with this accident the fate of all on board seemed sealed, for they no longer could keep the vessel's head to the waves, and the great seas came rolling over her, sweeping her decks of every thing movable. They began sending up rockets, and, after some time of anxious waiting, saw an answering signal; so that, through the remainder of that fearful night, the men on the doomed ship felt that, whatever might occur, they had friends at hand. The night was spent in toil at the pumps; and in the morning a faint cheer went up as two vessels were seen, ready to lend assistance. A signal of distress, quickly hoisted, was answered from the nearer, which proved to be the "Isaac P. Smith." The "Smith" sent off a boat and made fast a hawser to the wreck, and took her in tow; but in a few minutes the hawser parted. It became clear that the men must be taken off the sinking ship; but how to do it, was the question. By this time a second ship, the "Young Rover," had arrived to assist in the rescue. A second cable was put aboard; but this, too, parted. Hope seemed lost, when the lookout reported a third ship, the frigate "Sabine," coming to the rescue. The "Sabine" came to anchor, and sent a hawser aboard the sinking "Governor." Then the hawser was gradually taken in until the two ships lay close together, stern to stern. Spars were rigged over the stern of the frigate, and some thirty men swung over the seething waters to safety. Then the two vessels came together with a crash, and about forty men sprang from the sinking ship to the deck of the frigate. But the damage done by the collision was so great that it was deemed prudent to slack up the hawser and let the "Governor" drop astern again. Those on board busied themselves throwing overboard all things movable, with the intention of lightening the vessel. After some hours of suspense, the work of getting the men off the sinking craft was recommenced, and boats were sent to their assistance. The sea was running too high for them to approach close to the steamer's guards, so they lay off some feet, and the soldiers jumped into them. It was a perilous leap, with the boats pitching one way, and the ship another, and a raging-sea of tossing waters between; but it was made bravely by every man, and but seven or eight were lost. Soon after the last man left the "Governor," she lurched to one side and sank, carrying with her the arms and ammunition of the troops she was transporting.

It was on Monday morning, Nov. 4, that the flag-ship "Wabash" cast anchor off Port Royal. In the offing were a few more sail headed for the same point, and during the day some twenty-five vessels of the scattered squadron came up. For the next day ships were constantly arriving, and by Tuesday night the whole squadron lay safely anchored in the broad harbor.

The defences which the Confederates had erected upon Hilton Head, a lofty bluff overlooking the harbor, were powerfully designed earthworks, poorly armed and manned. The forts were two in number, placed on a commanding elevation, and might have been made impregnable had the Confederates taken advantage of the warning sent them by their spies in Washington. Fort Walker had fourteen guns which could bear on an attacking fleet, and Fort Beauregard had twenty. When the fight began, the gunners found that most of their ammunition was either too large or too small for the guns. To support the forts in their fight, was a wretched little fleet of tugs and schooners, mounting a gun or two each, but absolutely powerless before the smallest of Du Pont's ships-of-war. Indeed, when the battle began, the Union navy gave its undivided attention to the forts, and did not even give battle to Tatnall's mosquito fleet.

Thursday morning dawned bright and mild as a morning in June. The shores of the beautiful bay were covered with woods, out of which rung the clear notes of Southern song-birds. The scene from the ships was one of the most charming imaginable. The placid bay, the luxuriant shores, the ocean showing across the low-lying ridge of white sand, the forts frowning from the steep headland, the fleet of majestic frigates mustered for the attack, and in the distance the flotilla of defenceless transports, safely out of range, their decks and rigging crowded with fifteen thousand men — all this presented a panorama of life and beauty which few eyes have ever beheld.

Du Pont, in the majestic "Wabash," moved down the bay, and, as he came in range of Fort Walker, sent a shell shrieking from a bow-gun, as signal that the action was begun. The old frigate moved on slowly, making play with the bow-guns until abreast of the fort, when with a crash she let fly her whole broadside. On she went for a few yards, then turning in a grand circle came back, giving the other broadside to the forts as she passed. The other ships fell in behind; and round and round before the forts the fiery circle revolved, spitting out fire and ponderous iron bolts, and making the peaceful shores of the bay tremble with the deep reverberations of the cannon.

The Confederates, for their part, went into the action with the utmost coolness. They had been assured that their position was impregnable, and

THE OPENING GUN.

had been cautioned to be deliberate and determined in their defence. For a time their artillery service was admirable. But soon they found certain discouraging features about the affair. Their guns were too light to have any effect on the fleet, and their powder was of such bad quality that many of their shots fell short. Two great guns dismounted themselves,

THE FIGHT AT HILTON HEAD.

seriously injuring the men who were handling them, and the very first broadside from the fleet dismounted several more. Then it was found that the shells for the great Parrott guns were too large, and that the shells from other cannon failed to explode, owing to defective fuses. Soon the fleet found a point of fire from which it could enfilade the forts, and thereafter a perfect hail of shell and grape-shot fell in the trenches. One shell disabled eleven men. A solid shot struck a gun thought to be perfectly protected, and hurled it, with the men serving it, over the parapet. Every twenty minutes a gun was dismounted in Fort Walker, and at the end of the conflict Fort Beauregard had but nine serviceable guns.

For about four hours there was no cessation of fire on the part of the fleet. Round and round the circle the vessels steamed, giving one fort a broadside on the way up, and the other a broadside on the way down. The bombs rose from them in a majestic sweep through the air, and plunged into the fort, exploding with a roar equal to that of a cannon. One ship was commanded by Capt. Drayton, who rained shot and shell mercilessly against the forts, although one of them was in command of his own brother.

At half-past one Fort Walker was found untenable, and the work of abandoning it was begun. The evacuation was completed in great haste, many valuables were left behind, and not even the guns were spiked. Still the entire garrison escaped to mainland, although the Federals had three thousand troops who might have made them all prisoners. Not long thereafter, Fort Beauregard also yielded to fate, and the day was won by the Federals.

The landing of the troops was at once begun. Thirty large boats bore a Connecticut regiment of one thousand men to the beach. Their bright, fresh uniforms, their muskets glittering in the sun, and their regular, swaying stride as they marched up the sandy beach to the martial strains of the regimental band, made a striking picture. They clambered over the ramparts, and in a few moments the stars and stripes floated from the staff which had but lately upheld the flag of the young Confederacy. Within the forts, all was carnage and confusion: dismounted cannon, surrounded by the dead bodies of the gunners, heaps of shells, and fragments of wood-work, were piled about the parade-ground and in the trenches. The story of the terrific bombardment was graphically told by those horrible evidences of death and destruction. And well might the scene be a horrible one. For over five hours, fifty shot a minute had been discharged at the forts, and most of them did execution. When one recollects that each shot of the great guns cost eight dollars, we get a vivid idea of the money spent in war.

Immediately upon the capture of Hilton Head, the victors began making it a great naval and military station. Great storehouses were built, wharves constructed, and vast intrenchments thrown up for the defence of the spot. The slaves, escaping from the neighboring plantations, came in droves, begging to be allowed to work; but they received but a cold welcome, for they were still looked upon as property, and the officers did not wish to be charged with enticing them away from their masters.

The news of the occupation of Hilton Head by the Northern armies caused the greatest consternation in the cities of Charleston and Savannah. From both places people fled into the interior, expecting an immediate advance of the Union troops. But the armies were set to digging, not to marching, and soon the affrighted citizens returned to their homes. Port Royal was held by the Northern forces until the end of the war, and proved of great value for the proper maintenance of the blockade. Its greatest disadvantage was its unhealthiness. Of fifteen thousand men landed there in November, five thousand were on the sick-list within a month.

CHAPTER IX.

THE FIRST IRON-CLAD VESSELS IN HISTORY.—THE "MERRIMAC" SINKS THE "CUMBERLAND," AND DESTROYS THE "CONGRESS."—DUEL BETWEEN THE "MONITOR" AND "MERRIMAC."

IT will be remembered that when the Union forces, alarmed by the threatening attitude of the inhabitants of Norfolk and the vicinity, fled from the Norfolk navy-yard, leaving every thing there in flames, they left behind them a fine United States frigate, "Merrimac," a ship of thirty-five hundred tons, carrying forty guns. The departing Federals did their work of destruction fairly well; for the great ship was burnt to the upper edge of her copper sheathing, and sank to the bottom of the river. Three or four months after the occupation of the Norfolk navy-yard by the Confederates, Lieut. George M. Brooke, an ex-officer of the United States navy, who had resigned that he might follow the fortunes of his State, while looking at the hulk lying in the river-channel, was suddenly inspired with the thought that she might be raised and converted into a formidable vessel-of-war. He carefully matured his plans, and after due consideration proposed to the Confederate secretary of the navy, that the "Merrimac" be raised and converted into an iron-clad. His plans were approved, and orders were given that they should be carried out. The "Merrimac," as originally built, was one of the grand old types of war-vessels. Her solid oak sides rose high above the water, and were pierced by a long row of gaping port-holes. Her masts towered high in the air; and when her great sails were set, her hull seemed crushed beneath so vast an expanse of canvas. When she had been remodelled, her entire appearance was changed. She had no longer the appearance of a ship, but seemed like a house afloat; and tradition says that the old salt on the "Cumberland," who first sighted her, reported gravely to the officer of the deck, "Quaker meetin'-house floating down the bay, sir."

When the hulk had been raised and placed in the dry-dock, the first thing done was to cut it down to the level of the berth-deck; that is, to the level of the deck below the gun-deck in the old rig. Then both ends of the ship were decked over for a distance of seventy feet; while the midship section was covered by a sort of roof, or pent-house, one hundred and seventy feet long, and extending about seven feet above the gun-deck. This roof was of pitch pine and oak, twenty-four inches thick, and covered with iron plates two inches thick. The upper part of the roof, being flat, was railed in, making a kind of promenade deck. In the great chamber formed by this roof were mounted ten guns, two of which, the bow and stern guns, were seven-inch rifles, and fairly powerful guns for those days. A strange feature of this ship, and one that was not discovered until she was launched, was that the weight of the iron-plating and the heavy guns she carried sunk her so deep in the water that the low deck forward and aft of the gun-room was always under water; so much so that the commander of another ship in the Confederate navy writes that he was obliged always to give the "Merrimac" a wide berth, lest he should run his ship on some part of the ram which lay unseen beneath the surface of the water. Powerful as this ship was, she had some serious defects. The greatest of these were her engines. They were the same that had been in her as a United States vessel, and had been condemned by a naval board as very defective. Naturally several weeks under water had not improved them; but the Confederates could not be particular about machinery just then, and the old engines were left in the new ram. It was quickly found that they could not be depended upon more than six hours at a time; and one of the ship's officers, in writing years afterwards, remarks, "A more ill-contrived or unreliable pair of engines could only have been found in some vessels of the United States navy." The second faulty feature about the "Merrimac" was that her rudder and propeller were entirely unprotected. The ram which was so much dreaded, and which made the "Merrimac" a forerunner of a new class of war-vessels, was of cast-iron, projecting four feet, and so badly secured that it was loosened in ramming the "Cumberland," and started a bad leak in the Confederate ship.

When this formidable vessel was completed, she was christened by her new owners the "Virginia;" but the name of the old United States frigate of which she was built stuck to her, and she has ever since been known as the "Merrimac," and so we shall speak of her in this narrative. She received as commander Commodore Franklin Buchanan, an ex-Union officer of ability and daring, to whom the cadets of the naval academy at Annapolis owe the beautiful situation of the academy, and many of its admirable features; for he it was, who, in 1845, under a commission from Mr. Bancroft, Secretary of the Navy, organized and located the naval academy, and launched that institution upon its successful career. Of officers the "Merrimac" had no lack, and good ones they were; but in her crew she was lamentably deficient. Most of the crew was made up of men from the army, who knew nothing of seamanship, but who could at any rate fire a gun. A few good sailors were obtained from those who escaped to Norfolk after the destruction of the Confederate flotilla at Elizabeth City by Capt. Rowan's squadron. They had but little chance for drills and exercise on the new ship, for up to the very hour of sailing she was crowded with workmen getting her ready for the task of breaking down the Yankee blockade. When she finally set out to do battle for the South, she was a new and untried ship: not a gun had been fired, and hardly a revolution of her engines had been made. And so she started down the river on her trial trip, but intending, nevertheless, to do battle with the strongest ships of the United States navy. Accompanying her were four small Confederate gunboats,—the "Beaufort," the "Yorktown," the "Jamestown," and the "Teaser." Soon rounding out into Hampton Roads, the little squadron caught sight of the Northern fleet at anchor, and made for them. An officer on the "Congress" thus tells the story of the events that followed: —

"The 8th of March was a fine mild day, such as is common in Southern Virginia during the early spring; and every one on board our ship was enjoying the weather, and pleasing himself with the prospect of going North in a day or two at farthest, and being relieved from the monotony of a blockade at anchor. Some of us were pacing the poop, basking in the sun, and watching the gulls, which here, as all over the world, wherever a man-of-war is anchored, manage to find out when it is dinner-time, appearing regularly when the mess-tins are being washed, and the cooks are taking the buckets of broken victuals to the head to throw overboard. Then they chatter and scream, and fight for the remnants as they drift astern, until all is consumed, when they betake themselves to fresh fields out of sight until we pipe to dinner again.

"One bell had struck some 'time, when the attention of the quartermaster on watch was drawn to an unusual appearance against the fringe of woods away over in the Norfolk Channel. After gazing intently some time, he approached the officer of the deck, and presenting him the glass said, 'I believe *that thing* is a-comin' down at last, sir.'

"Sure enough! There was a huge black roof, with a smokestack emerging from it, creeping down towards Sewall's Point. Three or four satellites, in the shape of small steamers and tugs, surrounded and preceded her. Owing to the intervening land, they could not be seen from Hampton Roads until some time after we had made them out; but, when they did show themselves clear of the point, there was a great stir among the shipping. But they turned up into the James River channel instead of down toward the fort, approaching our anchorage with ominous silence and deliberation.

"The officers were by this time all gathered on the poop, looking at the strange craft, and hazarding all sorts of conjectures about her; and when it was plain that she was coming to attack us, or to force the passage, we beat to quarters, the "Cumberland's" drum answering ours.

"By a little after four bells, or two o'clock, the strange monster was close enough for us to make out her plating and ports; and we tried her with a solid shot from one of our stern-guns, the projectile glancing off her forward casemate like a drop of water from a duck's back. This opened our eyes. Instantly she threw aside the screen from one of her forward ports, and answered us with grape, killing and wounding quite a number. She then passed us, receiving our broadside and giving one in return, at a distance of less than two hundred yards. Our shot had apparently no effect upon her, but the result of her broadside on our ship was simply terrible. One of her shells dismounted an eight-inch gun, and either killed or wounded every one of the gun's crew, while the slaughter at the other guns was fearful. There were comparatively few wounded, the fragments of the huge shells she threw killing outright as a general thing. Our clean and handsome gun-deck was in an instant changed into a slaughter-pen, with lopped-off legs and arms, and bleeding, blackened bodies, scattered about by the shells; while blood and brains actually dripped from the beams. One poor fellow had his chest transfixed by a splinter of oak as thick as the wrist; but the shell-wounds were even worse. The quartermaster, who had first discovered the approach of the iron-clad, — an old man-of-war's man, named John Leroy, — was taken below with both legs off. The gallant fellow died in a few minutes, but cheered and exhorted the men to stand by the ship, almost with his last breath. The 'Merrimac' had, in the mean time, passed up stream; and our poor fellows, thinking she had had enough of it, and was for getting away, actually began to cheer. For many of them it was the last cheer they were ever to give. We soon saw what her object was; for standing up abreast of the bow of the 'Cumberland,' and putting her helm aport, she ran her ram right into that vessel. The gallant frigate kept up her splendid and deliberate, but ineffectual, fire, until she filled and sank, which she did in a very few minutes. A small freight-steamer of the quartermaster's department, and some tugs and boats from the camp-wharf, put off to rescue the survivors, who were forced to jump overboard. In spite of shot from the Confederate gunboats, one of which pierced the boiler of the freight-boat, they succeeded in saving the greater number of those who were in the water. Seeing the fate of the 'Cumberland,' which sank in very deep water, we set our topsails and jib, and slipped the chains, under a sharp fire from the gunboats, which killed and wounded many. With the help of the sails, and the tug 'Zouave,' the ship was now run on the flats which make off from Newport News Point. Here the vessel keeled over as the tide continued to fall, leaving us only two guns which could be fought, — those in the stern ports. Two large steam-frigates and a sailing-frigate, towed by tugs, had started up from Hampton Roads to our assistance. They all got aground before they had achieved half the distance; and it was fortunate that they did so, for they would probably have met the fate of the 'Cumberland,' in which case the lives of the twelve or thirteen hundred men comprising their crews would have been uselessly jeopardized.

"After the 'Merrimac' had sunk the 'Cumberland,' she came down the channel and attacked us again. Taking up a position about one hundred and fifty yards astern of us, she deliberately raked us with eighty-pounder shell; while the steamers we had so long kept up the river, and those which had come out with the iron-clad from Norfolk, all concentrated the fire of their small rifled guns upon us. At this time we lost two officers, both elderly men. One was an acting master, who was killed on the quarter-deck by a small rifle-bolt which struck him between the shoulders, and went right through him. The other was our old coast pilot, who was mortally wounded by a fragment of shell. We kept up as strong a fire as we could from our two stern-guns; but the men were repeatedly swept away from them, and at last both pieces were disabled, one having the muzzle knocked off, and the other being dismounted. Rifles and carbines were also used by some of our people to try to pick off the 'Merrimac's' crew when her ports were opened to fire, but of course the effect of the small-arms was not apparent to us.

"It is useless to attempt to describe the condition of our decks by this time. No one who has not seen it can appreciate the effect of such a fire in a confined space. Men were being killed and maimed every minute, those faring best whose duty kept them on the spar deck. Just before our stern-guns were disabled, there were repeated calls for powder from them; and, none appearing, I took a look on the berth-deck to learn the cause. After my eyes had become a little accustomed to the darkness, and the sharp smoke from burning oak, I saw that the line of cooks and wardroom servants stationed to pass full boxes had been raked by a shell, and the whole of them either killed or wounded, — a sufficient reason why there was a delay with the powder. (I may mention here that the officer who commanded our powder division was a brother of the captain of the 'Merrimac.') The shells searched the vessel everywhere. A man previously wounded was killed in the cock-pit where he had been taken for surgical aid. The deck of the cock-pit had to be kept sluiced with water from the pumps, to extinguish the fire from the shells, although dreadfully wounded men were lying on this deck, and the water was icy cold; but the shell-room hatch opened out of the cock-pit, and fire must be kept out of there at all hazards, or the whole of us would go into the air together. In the wardroom and steerage, the bulkheads were all knocked down by the shells, and by the axe-men making way for the hose, forming a scene of perfect ruin and desolation. Clothing, books, glass, china, photographs, chairs, bedding, and tables were all mixed in one confused heap. Some time before this, our commanding officer, a fine young man, had been instantly killed by a fragment of shell which struck him in the chest. His watch, and one of his shoulder-straps (the other being gone), were afterwards sent safely to his father, a veteran naval officer.

"We had now borne this fire for nearly an hour, and there was no prospect of assistance from any quarter, while we were being slaughtered without being able to return a shot. Seeing this, the officer who had succeeded to the command of the ship, upon consultation with our former captain (who was on board as a guest), ordered our flag to be struck. It is not a pleasant thing to have to strike your flag; but I did not see then, and do not see now, what else we were to do.

"A boat now boarded us with an officer from the 'Merrimac,' who said he would take charge of the ship. He did nothing, however, but gaze about a little, and pick up a carbine and cutlass, — I presume as trophies.

One of the small gunboats then came alongside, and the officer from the 'Merrimac' left. The commander of the gunboat said that we must get out of the ship at once, as he had orders to burn her. Some of our people went on board of his craft as prisoners, but not many. As her upper deck was about even with our main-deck ports, our surgeon stepped out of one, and told the commanding officer that we had some dreadfully wounded men, and that we must have time to collect them, and place them on board his vessel, and, moreover, that our ship was on fire with no possibility of saving her. The reply was, 'You must make haste: those scoundrels on shore are firing at me now.' In fact, the rifle-balls were 'pinging' about very briskly, scarring the rusty black sides of the poor old frigate; for the Twentieth Indiana Regiment had come down from the camp to the point, and opened fire on the gunboat as she lay alongside of us. Our doctor having no desire to be killed, especially by our own people, jumped back into the port, just as the steamer, finding it too hot, shoved off and left us. As soon as she did so, they all opened upon us again; although we had a white flag flying to show we were out of action, and we certainly could not be held responsible for the action of the regiment on shore. After ten or fifteen minutes, however, they all withdrew, and went down the channel, to bestow their attentions upon the frigate 'Minnesota' which was hard aground. Fortunately the 'Merrimac' drew too much water to come near the 'Minnesota' at that stage of tide, and the small-fry were soon driven off by the latter ship's battery. Night now approaching, the whole Rebel flotilla withdrew, and proceeded up the Norfolk Channel.

"Although relieved from the pressure of actual battle, we still had the unpleasant consciousness that the fire was making progress in the vicinity of our after-magazine; and we felt as I suppose men would feel who are walking in the crater of a volcano on the verge of eruption. Fortunately for us, the 'Merrimac' and her consorts had not fired much at our upper works and spars, the principal damage being inflicted upon our lower decks. We had, therefore, the launch and first cutter, — large boats, — which, with a little stuffing of shot-holes, were fit to carry us the short distance between our ship and the shore. The yard and stay-tackles were got up, and the boats put into the water, as soon as possible; the fire gaining, and the sun going down, in the mean time.

"By successive boatloads the survivors were all landed; the launch being brought up under the bill port, and the wounded, in cots, lowered into her by a whip from the fore yard, which was braced up for the purpose. This boat was nearly filled with water on her last trip, being a good deal damaged; obliging some of the officers, who had stayed until the last, to jump overboard into the icy cold water, and lean their hands on the gunwale, so as to relieve the boat of a part of their weight. She grounded in water about waist-deep; and the soldiers from the camp waded out and assisted our men in bearing on shore, and to the log hospital of the Twentieth Indiana, those who were in cots. We had managed to get the body of our gallant young commander on shore in one of the cots, as a wounded man. The mass of the men were so 'gallied,' to use a sailor phrase, by the time the action was over, what with enduring so severe a fire without being able to respond, and also with the knowledge that an explosion of the magazine might occur at any time, that I doubt whether they could have been induced to bring off a man whom they knew to be dead. The officers repeatedly went about the decks looking for wounded men; and I firmly believe that all who were alive were brought off. Our poor old ship, deserted by all but the dead, burned till about midnight, when she blew up."

The final destruction of the "Congress" must have been a most imposing spectacle. A member of the Confederate army, who was stationed in one of the batteries near the scene of action, thus describes it: "Night had come, mild and calm, refulgent with all the beauty of Southern skies in early spring. The moon, in her second quarter, was just rising over the rippling waters; but her silvery light was soon paled by the conflagration of the 'Congress,' whose lurid glare was reflected in the river. The burning frigate four miles away seemed very much nearer. As the flames crept up the rigging, every mast, spar, and rope glittered against the dark sky in dazzling lines of fire. The hull, aground upon the shoal, was plainly visible; and upon its black surface each port-hole seemed the mouth of a fiery furnace.

For hours the flames raged, with hardly a perceptible change in the wondrous picture. At irregular intervals, loaded guns and shells, exploding as the flames reached them, sent forth their deep reverberations, re-echoed over and over from every headland of the bay. The masts and rigging were still standing, apparently intact, when about two o'clock in the morning a monstrous sheet of flame rose from the vessel to an immense height. The ship was rent in twain by the tremendous flash. Blazing fragments seemed to fill the air; and, after a long interval, a deep, deafening report announced the explosion of the ship's powder-magazine. When the blinding glare had subsided, I supposed that every vestige of the vessel would have disappeared; but apparently all the force of the explosion had been upward. The rigging had vanished entirely, but the hull seemed hardly shattered; the only apparent change in it was that in two or three places, two or three of the port-holes had been blown into one great gap. It continued to burn until the brightness of its blaze was effaced by the morning sun."

In the great drama of the first day's fight at Hampton Roads, the heroic part was played by the frigate "Cumberland." On the morning of that fateful 8th of March, she was swinging idly at her moorings, her boats floating at the boom, and her men lounging about the deck, never dreaming of the impending disaster. It was wash-day, and from the lower rigging of the ship hung garments drying in the sun. About noon the lookout saw a cloud of smoke, apparently coming down the river from Norfolk, and at once notified the officer of the deck. It was surmised that it might be the new and mysterious iron-clad "Merrimac," about which many rumors were current, but few facts known. Quickly the ship was set in trim for action, and the men sent to quarters. . All the stern preparations for battle were made — the guns all shotted, the men in position, the magazines opened; shot, shell, cartridges, all in place; the powder-boys at their stations; swords, pistols, boarding-pikes, in the racks. Down in the cock-pit the surgeons spread out upon their tables the gleaming instruments, which made brave men shudder with the thought of what a few minutes would bring.

The sailors prepared for the fight gayly, never doubting for a moment that victory would be on their side. So paltry had been the resistance that the Confederates had heretofore been able to oppose to the Northern arms, by sea, that the blue-jackets felt that they had only to open a fight in order to win it. The officers were more serious. Rumors had reached them that the "Merrimac" was a most powerful vessel, destined to annihilate the navy of the North; and they looked on this first battle with the monster with many misgivings. Their fears were somewhat lessened by an article printed in the Norfolk papers, a few days previous, denouncing the "Merrimac" as a bungling bit of work, absolutely unseaworthy, and unable to stand against the powerful vessels of the North. As it turned out, however, this article was published as a *ruse* to deceive the Northern authorities.

The iron ship came steaming sullenly down the bay. The "Congress" was the first ship in range, and a puff of smoke from the "Merrimac's" bow-gun warned the crew of the frigate that danger was coming. All held their breath an instant, until, with a clatter and whiz, a storm of grape-shot rattled against her sides, and whistled through the rigging. Then came a sigh of relief that it was no worse. When the enemy was within a quarter of a mile, the "Congress" let fly her whole broadside, and the crew crowded the ports to see the result. The great iron shot rattled off the mailed sides of the monster, like hailstones from a roof. Then came the return fire; and the "Congress" was riddled with shells, and her decks ran with blood. The "Merrimac" passed sullenly on.

Now it was the turn of the "Cumberland." Her officers and crew had seen the results of the fire of the "Congress," and, with sinking hearts, felt how hopeless was their own position. There was no chance for escape, for no wind filled the sails of the frigate. She lay helpless, awaiting the attack of the iron battery that bore down upon her, without firing a shot or opening a port. At a little past two the mailed frigate had approached the "Cumberland" within grape-shot distance. Fire was opened upon her with the heaviest guns; and officers and men watched breathlessly the course of their shot, and cried aloud with rage, or groaned in despair, as they saw them fall harmlessly from the iron ship. Still they had no thought of surrender. The fire of the "Cumberland" was received silently by the "Merrimac;" and she came straight on, her sharp prow cutting viciously through the water, and pointed straight for her victim. A second broadside, at point-blank range, had no effect on her. One solid shot was seen to strike her armored sides, and, glancing upward, fly high into the air, as a baseball glances from the bat of the batsman; then, falling, it struck the roof of the pilot-house, and fell harmlessly into the sea. In another instant the iron ram crashed into the side of the "Cumberland," cutting through oaken timbers, decks, and cabins. At the same time all the guns that could be brought to bear on the Northern frigate were discharged; and shells crashed through her timbers, and exploded upon her decks, piling splinters, guns, gun-carriages, and men in one confused wreck. Had not the engines of the ram been reversed just before striking the frigate, her headway would have carried her clear to the opposite side of the doomed ship, and the "Cumberland," in sinking, would have carried her destroyer to the bottom with her. As it was, the "Merrimac," with a powerful wrench, drew out of the wreck she had made, loosening her iron prow, and springing a serious leak in the operation. She drew off a short distance, paused to examine the work she had done, and then, as if satisfied, started to complete the destruction of the "Congress."

And well might the men of the "Merrimac" be satisfied with their hour's work. The "Cumberland" was a hopeless wreck, rapidly sinking. Her decks were bloodstained, and covered with dead men, and scattered arms and legs, torn off by the exploding shells. And yet her brave crew stuck to their guns, and fought with cool valor, and without a vestige of confusion. They had had but a few moments to prepare for action; and the long rows of clothes, drying in the rigging, told how peaceful had been their occupation before the "Merrimac" appeared upon the scene. Yet now that the storm of battle had burst, and its issue was clearly against them, these men stood to their guns, although they could feel the deck sinking beneath them. Every man was at his post; and even when the waters were pouring in on the gun-deck, the guns were loaded and fired. Indeed, the last shot was fired from a gun half buried in the waves. Then the grand old frigate settled down to the bottom, carrying half her crew with her, but keeping the stars and stripes still floating at the fore.

"MERRIMAC" AND "CUMBERLAND."

The destruction of the "Cumberland" being completed, the "Merrimac" steamed over to the "Congress." This frigate fought well and valorously, but was soon pounded into a helpless condition by the shells of the "Merrimac," as shown by the story of her officer, already quoted. When a white flag, floating at her peak, told of surrender, the "Merrimac" left her to the attention of the smaller vessels in the Confederate flotilla, and set out to find further victims. But by this time the remainder of the Federal fleet had taken alarm, and fled into a safe position under the shelter of the Federal batteries on shore. The "Minnesota" only had been unfortunate in her attempted flight, and was aground on a bar near the scene of the fight. But now only two hours of daylight remained, and the tide was low, and still on the ebb. The heavy iron frigate could not get within effective distance of the "Minnesota," her crew were weary with a day's fighting, and so she turned away and headed up the river for Norfolk.

In taking account of injuries on the ram that night, it was found that the injured numbered twenty-one; many of whom had been shot while alongside the surrendered "Congress." Not an atom of damage was done to the interior of the vessel, and her armor showed hardly a trace of the terrible test through which it had passed. But nothing outside had escaped: the muzzles of two guns had been shot off; the ram was wrenched away in withdrawing from the "Cumberland;" one anchor, the smoke-stack, steam-pipe, railings, flag-staff, boat-davitts—all were swept away as though a hugh mowing-machine had passed over the deck. But, so far as her fighting qualities were concerned, the "Merrimac" was as powerful as when she started out from Norfolk on that bright spring morning.

It can easily be understood that the news of the engagement caused the most intense excitement throughout this country, and indeed throughout the whole world. In the South, all was rejoicing over this signal success of the Confederate ship. Bells were rung, and jubilees held, in all the Southern cities. An officer of the "Merrimac," who was despatched post-haste to Richmond with reports of the engagement, was met at every station by excited crowds, who demanded that he tell the story of the fight over and over again. At last the starving people of the Confederacy saw the way clear for the sweeping away of the remorseless blockade.

In the North, the excitement was that of fear. The people of seaboard cities imagined every moment the irresistible iron ship steaming into their harbors, and mowing down their buildings with her terrible shells. The Secretary of War said, at a hastily called cabinet meeting in Washington: "The 'Merrimac' will change the whole character of the war: she will destroy every naval vessel; she will lay all the seaboard cities under contribution. Not unlikely we may have a shell or cannon-ball from one of her guns, in the White House, before we leave this room."

In this excited state, wild with joy, or harassed with fear, the whole country went to sleep that March night, little dreaming that the morrow would change the whole face of the naval situation, and that even then a little untried vessel was steaming, unheralded, toward Hampton Roads, there to meet the dreaded "Merrimac," and save the remnants of the Federal fleet. Then no one knew of the "Monitor;" but twenty-four hours later her name, and that of her inventor Ericsson, were household words in all the States of the Union and the Confederacy.

Capt. John Ericsson was a Swedish engineer, residing in this country, who had won a name for himself by inventing the screw-propeller as a means of propulsion for steamships. He and a Connecticut capitalist, C. S. Bushnell by name, had ever since the opening of the war been trying to induce the Government to build some iron-clads after a pattern designed by Ericsson, and which afterwards became known as the "monitor" pattern. Their labors at Washington met with little success. After a long explanation of the plan before the wise authorities of the Naval Board, Capt. Ericsson was calmly dismissed with the remark, "It resembles nothing in the heavens above, or the earth beneath, or the waters under the earth. You can take it home, and worship it without violating any Commandment." Finally, however, leave was obtained to build a monitor for the Government, provided the builders would take all financial risks in case it proved a failure. So, with this grudging permission, the work of building the warship that was destined to save the Federal navy was begun. Work was prosecuted night and day, and in one hundred days the vessel was ready for launching. Great was the discussion over her. Distinguished engineers predicted that she would never float; and many attended the launch expecting to see the vessel plunge from the ways to the bottom of the river, like a turtle from a log. So general was this opinion, that boats were in readiness to rescue her passengers if she went down. But Capt. Ericsson's plans were well laid. The great vessel glided with a graceful dip into the river, and floated at her cables buoyantly. She was a strange-looking craft. All that was to be seen of her above water was a low deck about a foot above the water, bearing in the centre a large round iron turret pierced with two great port-holes. Besides the turret, the smooth surface of the deck was broken by two other elevations, — a small iron pilot-house forward, made of iron plates about ten inches thick, and with iron gratings in front; aft of the turret was a low smoke-stack. Beneath the water-line this vessel had some strange features. The upper part of her hull, forming the deck, projected beyond her hull proper about four feet on every side. This projection was known as the "overhang," and was designed as a protection against rams. It was made of white oak and iron, and was impenetrable by any cannon of that day; although now, when steel rifled cannon are built that will send a ball through twenty inches of wrought iron, the original "Monitor" would be a very weak vessel.

The turret in this little vessel, which held the two guns that she mounted, was so arranged as to revolve on a central pivot, thus enabling the gunners to keep their guns continually pointed at the enemy, whatever might be the position of the vessel. When the time for the first battle actually arrived, it was found that the turret would not revolve properly; but in later ships of the same class this trouble was avoided.

It was at two o'clock on the morning after the day on which the "Merrimac" had wrought such havoc among the ships of the North, that this queer-looking little vessel steamed into Hampton Roads. As the gray dawn began to break, she passed under the quarter of the "Minnesota," and cast anchor. The tars on the great frigate looked curiously at the strange craft, and wondered if that insignificant "cheese-box on a raft" was going to do battle with the dreaded "Merrimac." Small hopes had they that their noble frigate would be saved by any such pygmy war-ship.

In the mean time, the men of the "Merrimac" up at Norfolk were working energetically to prepare her for the destruction of the rest of the Union ships. Her ram was tightened in its place, her steering apparatus overhauled, and some changes made, and her rickety engine was patched up. At daybreak all was bustle as the ram prepared to move down on the Union fleet. But just as she was about to start, her officers saw the queer craft lying by the "Minnesota," which they at once knew to be the Ericsson "Monitor." Her appearance was not very terrible; but, nevertheless, the Confederates felt that she had appeared at a most inopportune moment for them. Still they raised anchor, and started down the bay to meet their mysterious enemy.

It was Sunday morning, and the sun rose in a cloudless blue sky. A light breeze stirred the surface of the water, and played lazily with the long streaming pennants of the men-of-war. The batteries on both sides of the bay were crowded with men waiting for the great naval battle of the day. Up at Norfolk a gay holiday party was embarking on steam-tugs, to accompany the Confederate ship and witness the total destruction of the Union fleet. No thought of defeat ever entered the minds of the proud believers in the new iron-clad of the Confederacy.

At the first sign of life on board the "Merrimac," the "Monitor" began her preparations for the battle. In fifteen minutes she was in battle trim. The iron hatches were closed, the dead-light covers put on, and obstructions removed from the main deck, so as to present a smooth surface only twenty-four inches above the water, unbroken, save by the turret and pilot-house. In the pilot-house was Lieut. Worden, who was to command the "Monitor" in this her first battle.

Leisurely the "Merrimac" came down the bay, followed by her attendant tugs; and, as she came within range, she opened fire on the "Minnesota," which was still aground. The frigate responded with a mighty broadside, which, however, rattled off the mailed sides of the ram like so many peas.

BATTLE OF THE "MONITOR" AND "MERRIMAC."

Clearly, every thing depended upon the "Monitor;" and that little craft steamed boldly out from behind the "Minnesota," and sent two huge iron balls, weighing one hundred and seventy pounds each, against the side of the "Merrimac." The shot produced no effect beyond showing the men of the "Merrimac" that they had met a foeman worthy of their steel. The "Merrimac" slowed up her engines, as though to survey the strange antagonist thus braving her power. The "Monitor" soon came up, and a cautious fight began; each vessel sailing round the other, advancing, backing, making quick dashes here and there, like two pugilists sparring for an opening. The two shots of the "Monitor" would come banging one after the other against the "Merrimac's" armor, like the "one, two" of a skilled boxer. In this dancing battle the "Monitor" had an enormous advantage, on account of her size, greater speed, and the way in which she answered her helm. The "Merrimac" was like a huge hawk being chased and baited by a little sparrow. Her heavy broadsides found nothing to hit in the almost submerged hull of the "Monitor." When a ball struck the turret, it glanced off, unless striking fair in the centre, when it fell in fragments, doing no greater damage than to dent the iron plates, and sometimes knocking down the men at the guns inside. The first manœuvre tried by the "Merrimac" was to run down her little antagonist; and she did strike her with a force that dented the iron overhang of the "Monitor," and dashed the men in the "Merrimac" to the deck, with blood streaming from their nostrils. For a moment it seemed as though the "Monitor" must go under; but gradually the terrible ram glanced off, and the little vessel, righting, sent again her terrible two shots at her enemy. In the action of the day before, shot and shell had beaten against the sides of the ram so rapidly that one could not count the concussions. Now it was a series of tremendous blows about a minute apart; and, if the men had not been working away at their guns, they could have heard the oak timbers splintering behind the iron plating. At a critical moment in the fight the "Merrimac" ran aground; and the "Monitor" steamed around her several times, seeking for weak places in which to plant a shot. Once Worden dashed at his adversary's screw, hoping to disable it, but missed by perhaps two feet. Two shots from the "Monitor" struck the

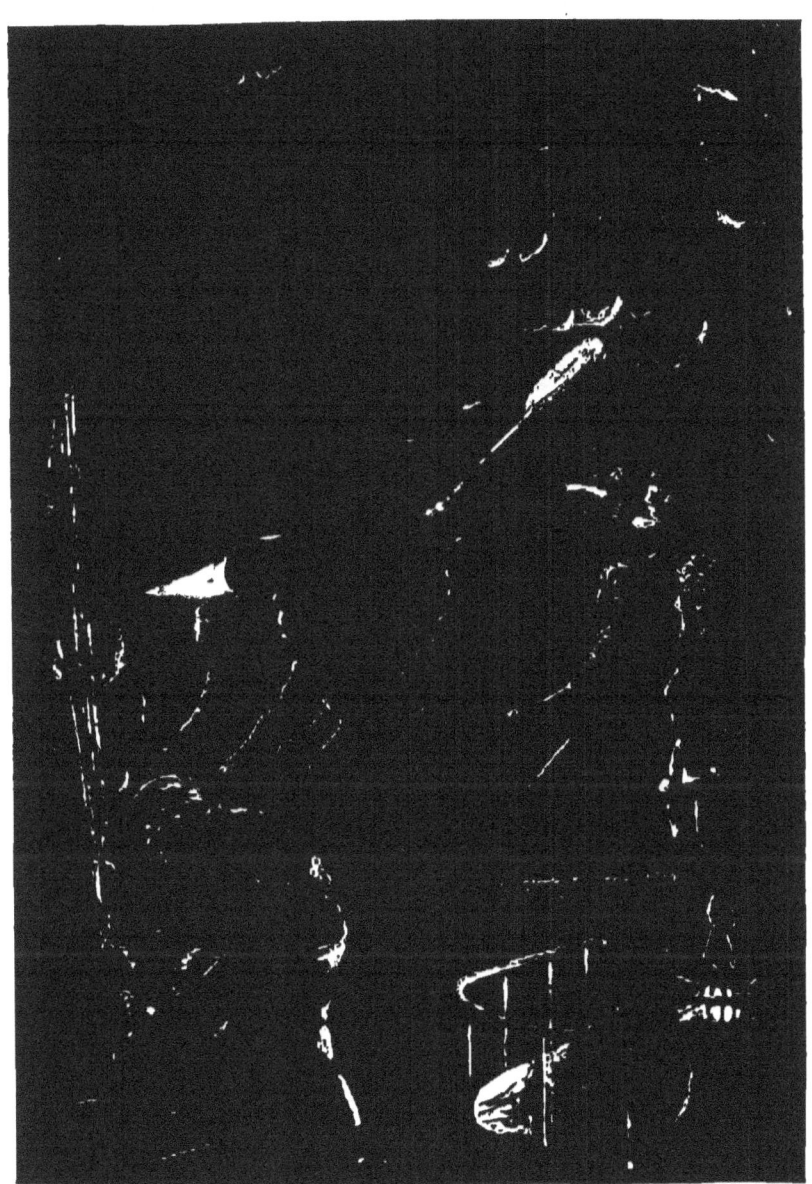

HANDLING A GUN.

muzzles of two cannon protruding from the port-holes of the "Merrimac," and broke them off, throwing huge splinters of iron among the gunners inside. And so the battle continued until about noon : gun answered gun with thunderous reports, that echoed back from the batteries on shore in rolling reverberations. The pleasure-seeking tugs from Norfolk had scuttled back again out of the way of the great cannon-balls that were skipping along the water in every direction. Neither of the combatants had received any serious injury. On board the "Monitor" the only hurt was received by a gunner, who was leaning against the iron wall of the turret just as a shot struck outside; he was carried below, disabled. But at last one lucky shot fired from one of the disabled guns of the "Merrimac" ended this gigantic contest ; sending each contestant to her moorings, without an actual victory for either side. This shot struck full and fair against the gratings of the pilot-house, through which Lieut. Worden was looking as he directed the course of his ship. The concussion knocked him senseless. Flakes of iron and powder were driven into his eyes and face, blinding him completely for the time. He fell back from the wheel, and the "Monitor" was left for a moment without her guiding spirit. All was confusion; but in a few moments Worden recovered, and gave the order to sheer off. The "Monitor" then drew away, while Worden was moved to the cabin, and the second officer sent to his station in the turret. Lying on a sofa in the cabin, his eyes bandaged, and the horror of life-long blindness upon him, Worden asked faintly, " Have I saved the ' Minnesota' ? " — " Yes," answered the surgeon. "Then," said he, "I die happy."

While these scenes were transpiring on the "Monitor," the "Merrimac" lay quietly awaiting her return. The Confederate officers say that she waited an hour, and then, concluding that the "Monitor" had abandoned the fight, withdrew to Norfolk. The Northern officers and historians say that the "Merrimac" was in full retreat when the decisive shot was fired. It is hard to decide, from such conflicting statements, to which side the victory belonged. Certain it is, that not a man on the "Merrimac" was injured, and that all damages she sustained in the fight were remedied before sunrise the next day. Later, as we shall see, she challenged the

Union fleet to a new battle, without response. But with all these facts in view, it must be borne in mind that the purpose of the "Merrimac," that bright March Sunday, was to destroy the frigate "Minnesota:" in that purpose she was foiled by the "Monitor," and to that extent at least the "Monitor" was the victor.

Lieut. Worden, after the fight, went directly to Washington. President Lincoln was at a cabinet meeting when he heard of Worden's arrival in the city, and hastily rising said, "Gentlemen, I must go to *that fellow.*" Worden was lying on a sofa, his head swathed in bandages, when the President entered. "Mr. President," said he, "you do me great honor by this visit." — "Sir," replied Mr. Lincoln, while the tears ran down his cheeks, "I am the one who is honored in this interview."

Among his crew Worden was very much beloved. The following letter, sent him while on a bed of pain, is all the more touching for the rude form in which their affection for their commander is expressed:—

TO CAPTAIN WORDEN.

HAMPTON ROADS, April 24, 1862.
UNITED STATES MONITOR.

TO OUR DEAR AND HONORED CAPTAIN.

Dear Sir, — These few lines is from your own crew of the Monitor, with their kindest Love to you their Honored Captain, hoping to God that they will have the pleasure of welcoming you back to us again soon, for we are all ready able and willing to meet Death or any thing else, only give us back our Captain again. Dear Captain, we have got your Pilot-house fixed and all ready for you when you get well again; and we all sincerely hope that soon we will have the pleasure of welcoming you back to it. . . . We are waiting very patiently to engage our Antagonist if we could only get a chance to do so. The last time she came out we all thought we would have the Pleasure of sinking her. But we all got disappointed, for we did not fire one shot, and the Norfolk papers says we are cowards in the Monitor — and all we want is a chance to show them where it lies with you for our Captain We can teach them who is cowards. But there is a great deal that we would like to write to you but we think you will soon be with us again yourself. But we all join in with our kindest love to you, hoping that God will restore you to us again and hoping that your sufferings is at an end now, and we are all so glad to hear that your eyesight will be spaired to you again. We would wish to write more to you if we have your kind Permission to do so but at present we all conclude by tendering to you our kindest Love and affection, to our Dear and Honored Captain.

We remain untill Death your Affectionate Crew

THE MONITOR BOYS.

The "Merrimac," after being repaired and altered to some extent, sailed down the bay on the 11th of April, for the purpose, as her officers said, of meeting the "Monitor" again. She steamed into the Roads, and exchanged a few shots with the Union batteries at the rip-raps; but the "Monitor," and other Union vessels, remained below Fortress Monroe, in Chesapeake Bay, out of the reach of the Confederate vessel. Again, a few days later, the "Merrimac" went to Hampton Roads, and tried to lure the "Monitor" to battle; but again the challenge passed unanswered. It is probable that the Federal naval authorities did not care to imperil the only vessel that stood between them and destruction, out of mere bravado. Had the "Monitor" come out, an attempt would have been made to carry her by boarding. The crew of the "Merrimac" were prepared for the attack; and four gunboats accompanying her were crowded with men, divided into squads, each with its specified duty. Some were to try and wedge the turret, some were to cover the pilot-house and all the openings with tarpaulin, others were to try to throw shells and gunpowder down the smoke-stack. But all these preparations proved useless, as the "Monitor" still remained quietly at her anchorage. On May 8 a third trip was made by the "Merrimac." When she came down the bay, she found the Union fleet, including the "Monitor," hard at work shelling the Confederate batteries at Sewall's Point. As she came towards them, they ceased their cannonade, and retired again to the shelter of Fortress Monroe. The "Merrimac" steamed up and down the Roads for some hours; and finally Commodore Tatnall, in deep disgust, gave the order, "Mr. Jones, fire a gun to windward, and take the ship back to her buoy."

Back to Norfolk she went, never again to leave that harbor. On the 9th of May the officers of the "Merrimac" noticed that the Confederate flag was no longer floating over the shore-batteries. A reconnoissance proved that the land forces had abandoned Norfolk, and it was necessary to get the ship away before the Union troops arrived and hemmed her in. Her pilots declared that if the ship was lightened they could take her up the James River; and accordingly all hands threw overboard ballast and trappings, until she was lightened three feet. Then the pilots claimed that with the prevalent wind they could not handle her. It was now useless to try to run her through the Union fleet, for the lightening process had exposed three feet of her unarmed hull to the fire of the enemy. It was accordingly determined that she should be destroyed. She was run ashore on Craney Island, and trains of powder laid all over her, and fired. Every gun was loaded, and the doors of the magazine were left open. Her crew then started on the march for the interior. It was just in the gray of the morning that a rumbling of the earth was felt, followed by a shock that made all stagger. A column of smoke and flame shot into the air; huge cannon were hurled high above the tree-tops, discharging in mid-air. One shot fell in the woods some distance ahead of the marching crew, and all knew that it marked the end of the mighty "Merrimac."

CHAPTER X.

THE NAVY IN THE INLAND WATERS.—THE MISSISSIPPI SQUADRON.—SWEEPING THE TENNESSEE RIVER.

WE will now leave for a time the blue-water sailors, whose battles, triumphs, and defeats we have been considering, and look at the work done by the tars of both North and South on the great waterways which cut up the central portion of the United States, known as the Valley of the Mississippi. It was in this section that the navy of the North did some of its most effective work against the Confederacy, and it was there that the sailor boys of the South did many deeds of the most desperate valor. There is much of romance about service on the blue ocean which is not to be found in routine duty along the yellow muddy streams that flowed through the territory claimed by King Cotton. The high, tapering masts, the yards squared and gracefully proportioned, the rigging taut, and with each rope in its place, of an ocean-frigate, are not seen in the squat, box-like gunboats that dashed by the batteries at Vicksburg, or hurled shot and shell at each other in the affair at Memphis. But Farragut, stanch old sea-dog as he was, did much of his grandest fighting on the turbid waters of the Mississippi; and the work of the great fleet at Port Royal was fully equalled by Porter's mortar-boats below New Orleans.

Let us follow the fortunes of the Union fleet on their cruises about the great rivers of the interior, and first discover what the work was that they set out to perform.

The rivers making up the Mississippi system flow for the greater part of their length through the States that had joined the new Confederacy. The northern Confederate battle-line was along the south bank of the Ohio River, and there they had erected batteries that controlled the passage of that river. South of the mouth of the Ohio, every river was lined with Confederate batteries, and bore on its placid bosom fleets of Confederate gunboats. At Columbus on the Mississippi, not far south of the mouth of the Ohio, were strong batteries over which floated the stars and bars of the Confederacy. Farther down was Island Number 10, bearing one of the most powerful fortifications the world has ever seen. Then came Fort Pillow, guarding the city of Memphis; then at Vicksburg frowned earthworks, bastions, and escarpments that rivalled Gibraltar for impregnability. Lower down were fortifications at Grand Gulf, Port Hudson, and Baton Rouge. Fort Henry guarded the Tennessee River, and Fort Donelson the Cumberland, and both of these rivers were very important as waterways for the transportation of supplies to the Union armies marching into Tennessee. It was absolutely necessary that all these fortifications should be swept away, and the rivers opened for navigation down to the Gulf of Mexico. It was necessary that the work should be done from above; for the forts below New Orleans were thought to be impassable, and Farragut's passage of them late in the war made all the world ring with his name.

It became evident, very early in the war, that no great progress could be made in the task of crushing the powerful insurrection until telling blows had been struck at the Confederate control of the inland waterways. When the attention of the war department was turned in that direction, they found but little to encourage them in the prospect. Along the thousands of miles of the banks of the Mississippi and its tributaries, there was not one gun mounted belonging to the United States, not one earthwork over which floated the starry flag of the Union. The

Confederate positions on this great chain of waterways were, as we have seen, of great strength. To attack them, the armies of the North must first fight their way through whole States populated by enemies. Obviously, the war department alone could not complete so gigantic a task, and the services of the navy were called into requisition. So energetically did the navy department prosecute its task, that, by the end of the war, over one hundred Federal war-vessels floated on those streams, on which, three years before, no craft dared sail under the American flag. It was a strange navy in looks, but in actions it showed itself worthy of the service in which it was enlisted.

Many of the steamers built for the river marine were wooden gunboats, hastily remodelled from the hulks of old craft. They were seldom plated with iron, and their machinery was feebly protected by coal bunkers, while their oaken sides were barely thick enough to stop a musket-ball. But the true iron-clad war-vessel made its appearance on the rivers even before it was to be seen in the ocean squadrons.

It was as early in the war as July, 1861, that the quartermaster-general advertised for bids for the construction of iron-clad gunboats for service on the Mississippi and tributary rivers. The contract was given to James B. Eads, an engineer, who during the war performed much valuable service for the United States Government, and who in later years has made himself a world-wide fame by the construction of the jetties at the mouth of the Mississippi River, by which the bar at the mouth of the great stream is swept away by the mighty rush of the pent-up waters. Mr. Eads was instructed to build seven iron-clad gunboats with all possible expedition. They were to be plated two and a half inches thick, and, though of six hundred tons burden, were not to draw more than six feet of water. They were to carry thirteen heavy guns each.

These river-gunboats, like the little "Monitor," had none of the grace and grandeur of the old style of sailing-frigate, in which Paul Jones fought so well for his country. The tapering masts of the mighty frigate, the spidery cordage by which the blue-jackets climbed to loosen the snowy sheets of canvas — these gave way in the gunboat to a single slender flagstaff for signalling, and two towering smoke-stacks anchored to the

A RIVER-GUNBOAT.

deck by heavy iron cables, and belching forth the black smoke from roaring fires of pitch-pine or soft coal. Instead of the gracefully curved black sides, with two rows of ports, from which peeped the muzzles of great cannon, the gunboat's sides above water sloped like the roof of a house, and huge iron shutters hid the cannon from view. Inside, all was dark and stuffy, making battle-lanterns necessary even in daylight fights. The broad white gundeck, scrubbed to a gleaming white by hollystone and limejuice, on which the salt-water sailors gathered for their mess or drill, was replaced by a cramped room, with the roof hardly high enough to let the jolly tars skylark beneath without banging their skulls against some projecting beam. Truly it may be said, that, if the great civil war made naval architecture more powerful, it also robbed the war-vessels of all their beauty.

It is hard to appreciate now the immense difficulty experienced in getting those first seven river-gunboats built by the appointed time. The war had just begun, and a people accustomed to peace had not yet found out that those not actually at the seat of war could continue their usual course of life unmolested. Rolling-mills, machine-shops, founderies, sawmills, and shipyards were all idle. Working-men were enlisting, or going to the Far West, away from the storm of war that was expected to sweep up the Mississippi Valley. The timber for the ships was still standing in the forests. The engines that were to drive the vessels against the enemy were yet to be built. Capt. Eads's contract called for the completion of the seven vessels in sixty-five days, and he went at his work with a will. His success showed that not all the great services done for a nation in time of war come from the army or navy. Within two weeks four thousand men were at work getting the gunboats ready. Some were in Michigan felling timber, some in the founderies and machine-shops of Pittsburg, and others in the shipyards at St. Louis, where the hulls of the vessels were on the stocks. Day and night, week-days and Sundays, the work went on; and in forty-five days the first vessel was completed, and christened the "St. Louis." The others followed within the appointed time. Before the autumn of 1861, the river navy of the United States numbered nearly a score of vessels, while nearly forty mortar-boats were in process of construction. Of this flotilla, Capt. A. H. Foote, an able naval officer, was put in command, and directed to co-operate with the land forces in all movements.

The first service to which the gunboats were assigned was mainly reconnoitring expeditions before the front of the advancing Union armies. They were stationed at the junction of the Ohio and Mississippi Rivers; and the country about Cairo was occupied by a large body of Union troops under the command of Gen. Grant, then a young officer little known. The opening fight of the river campaign was little more than a skirmish; but it proved the superiority of the gunboats over a land-force for the purpose of opening the river. One bright day in September, the "Lexington" and "Conestoga" were ordered to proceed down the river eight or ten miles, and dislodge a Confederate battery that had taken a position on Lucas Point. The two vessels steamed cautiously down the stream, without encountering any resistance until within easy range of the battery, when the Confederates opened with sixteen cannon. The shot and shells fell all about the vessels; but neither was hit, showing that the Confederate gunners were not yet used to firing at a moving mark. But the fire of the gunboats was admirably directed; the shells falling among the Confederates, dismounting the guns, and driving the gunners from their pieces. It was too hot a spot for any man to hold; and a cavalry corps quickly attached their horses to the guns, and drew them down the river to the shelter of the Confederate works at Columbus. Then the defeated party sent up the gunboat "Yankee" to attack the two victors, but this vessel was quickly disposed of. She opened fire at long range, but without success. The first shot from the "Conestoga" struck the water a few feet from the "Yankee," and, ricochetting, plunged into her hull. The discomfited vessel immediately put about, and started down stream, followed by a heavy fire from the two Northern ships. Just as she was passing out of range, an eight-inch shell from the "Lexington" struck her starboard wheel-house, and shattered the paddle-wheel, totally disabling the vessel, so that she drifted sidelong to her anchorage like a wounded duck.

On the return of the Northern vessels up the river, they first encountered the form of warfare that proved the most perilous for the sailors of the river navy. Confederate sharp-shooters lined the banks, perched in the trees, or hidden in the long, marshy grass; and any unwary tar who showed his head above the bulwarks was made a target for several long rifles in the hands of practised shots.

The next active service performed by the gunboats was at the battle of Belmont, directly opposite the Confederate batteries at Columbus. The Union troops, landing in force, had driven the Confederates from their camp, and were engaged in securing the spoils, when the gunners at Columbus, seeing that the camp was in the hands of the enemy, turned their heavy guns on it, and soon drove out the Yankees. The Confederates had rallied in the woods, and now came pouring out, in the hope of cutting off the Union retreat to the boats. On all sides the dark gray columns could be seen marching out of the woods, and pouring down upon the retreating army of the North. Batteries were wheeling into position, and staff-officers in travelling carriages were dashing to and fro carrying orders. It seemed a black day for the three or four thousand Unionists who were making for their transports with all possible speed. But now was the time for the gunboats to take a hand in the fight. Three of them dropped into position, and began a deadly fire upon the Confederate line. The huge shells ploughed their way through whole platoons of men. Bursting, they would mow down soldiers like saplings before a cyclone. One shell exploded directly beneath an officers' carriage, and threw horses, carriage, and men high in the air. The Confederates hastened to get their field-batteries into position, and replied to the deadly fire from the ships, but to no avail. Their light artillery was of no effect upon the plated sides of the gunboats, and they saw their cannon dismounted or shattered by the solid shot from the big guns of the iron-clads. They fought bravely, but the conflict was unequal. It was sheer madness for any body of men, with muskets and light artillery, to stand against the fire of the gunboats. The gunboats saved the day. The retreat of the Union army was unchecked; and, covered by the war-vessels, the transports returned safely to Cairo.

On the Tennessee River, near the northern boundary of Tennessee, the Confederates had thrown up certain earthworks to which they gave the name of Fort Henry. This, with Fort Donelson, situated near by, formed the principal Confederate strongholds in Tennessee. Gen. Grant determined to strike a heavy blow by capturing these two forts; and Commodore Foote, with his seven gunboats, was ordered to co-operate with the land-forces in the expedition. They started from Cairo on Feb. 2, 1862. When a few miles below the fort, the troops were landed and ordered to proceed up the back country, and attack the fort in the rear, while Foote should engage it from the river with his gunboats. While the troops were being landed, Gen. Grant boarded the "Essex," and went up the river to get a view of the fort they were about to attack. Had it been completed in accordance with the plans of the engineers, it would have been most formidable. Time, however, had been short, and the earthworks were far from being completed. There were many points on the river or on the opposite bank, from which a well-directed artillery fire would make them untenable. The Confederate commander, Gen. Tilghman, fully appreciated this fact, and, at the approach of the gunboats, had sent four-fifths of his garrison across the country to Fort Donelson, being determined to sacrifice as few men as possible in the defence of so untenable a position. While Grant and Foote were examining the works through their field-glasses, the sullen boom of a great gun came over the waters, and a heavy rifled shot crashed through the stateroom of Capt. Porter on the "Essex." The two commanders concluded that the Confederate gunners, though new to war, understood something of artillery practice; and the "Essex" was accordingly taken down the river, out of range.

The following night was chill and rainy; and the Union forces, bivouacking on shore, grumbled loudly over their discomforts. The morning dawned dark; but soon the sun came out, and the preparations for battle were begun. The troops were first despatched on their cross-country march; and, as they departed, Commodore Foote remarked coolly, that his gunboats would have reduced the fort before the land forces came within five miles of it. This proved to be the fact.

The gunboats formed in line of battle, and advanced up the river. The four iron-clads led, steaming abreast. About a mile in the rear, came the three wooden vessels. The fort was soon in range; but both parties seemed anxious for a determined conflict, and no shot was fired on either side as the gunboats came sullenly on. How different must have been the feelings of the two combatants! Tilghman, with his handful of men, hardly able to work eight of the eleven guns mounted in his fort, and knowing that his defeat was a mere question of time; Foote, with his iron-clads and supporting gunboats, his seventy-two guns, and his knowledge that six thousand men were marching upon the rear of the Confederate works. On the one side, all was absolute certainty of defeat; on the other, calm confidence of victory.

When the flotilla was within a third of a mile of the fort, the fire began. The gunners on the ships could see the muzzles of the Confederate guns, the piles of shells and cannon-balls, and the men at their work. The firing on both sides was deliberate and deadly. The Confederates were new to the work, but they proved themselves good marksmen. The first shot was fired from the shore, and, missing the "Essex" by but a few feet, plumped into the water, so near the next ship in line as to throw water over her decks. Within five minutes, the "Essex" and the "Cincinnati" were both hit. The armor of the gunboats proved no match for the shots of the Confederates, and in many cases it was penetrated. In some instances, shells, entering through the port-holes, did deadly damage.

On the shore, the shells from the gunboats were doing terrible work. Banks of solid earth, eight feet thick, were blown away by the terrible explosions. One, bursting in front of a ten-inch columbiad, filled that powerful gun with mud almost to the muzzle, disabling it for the remainder of the fight. A shot from the "Essex" struck the muzzle of a great gun, ripped off a splinter of iron three feet long, and crushed a gunner to pulp. The gun was just about to be fired, and burst, killing or wounding every man of the crew. At the same moment a shell crashed through the side of the "Essex," killing men right and left: took off the head of a sailor standing by Capt. Porter, wounded the captain, and plunged into the boiler. In an instant the ship was filled with scalding steam. The men in the pilot-house were suffocated. Twenty men and officers were killed or scalded. The ship was disabled, and drifted out of the fight. While withdrawing, she received two more shots, making twenty in all that had fallen to her share in this hot engagement. But by this time the fort was very thoroughly knocked to pieces. The big twenty-four pounder was dismounted, and five of its crew killed. Gun after gun was keeled over, and man after man carried bleeding to the bomb-proofs, until Gen. Tilghman himself dropped coat and sword, and pulled away at a gun by the side of his soldiers. Receiving ten shots while they could only fire one, this little band held out for two long hours; and only when the crew of the last remaining piece threw themselves exhausted on the ground, did the flag come fluttering down. Gen. Tilghman went to the fleet and surrendered the fort to Commodore Foote, and Grant's army came up more than an hour after the battle was over. To the navy belongs the honor of taking Fort Henry, while to Gen. Tilghman and his plucky soldiers belongs the honor of making one of the most desperate fights under the most unfavorable circumstances recorded in the history of the civil war.

The fall of Fort Henry opened the way for the Union advance to Fort Donelson, and marked the first step of the United States Government toward regaining control of the Mississippi. It broke the northern battle-line of the Confederacy, and never again was that line re-established.

With Fort Henry fallen, and Gen. Tilghman and his little garrison prisoners on the Union gunboats, Grant's soldier-boys and Foote's blue-jackets began active preparations for continuing the conquest of Tennessee by the capture of Fort Donelson. No time was lost. The very night that the stars and stripes were first hoisted over the bastion of Fort Henry saw three of Foote's gunboats steaming up the river on a reconnoitring expedition. Before them the Confederates fled in every direction. After several hours' advance, they came to a heavy railroad-bridge spanning the river, and effectually preventing further progress. Beyond the bridge were several Confederate steamers, black with men, and heavily laden with valuable military stores. With all steam on, they were dashing up stream, and rapidly leaving the gunboats behind. Enraged at seeing such valuable prizes slipping through their hands, the Union gunners sent shell after shell shrieking after the flying boats, but to no avail. A party was hastily landed for the purpose of swinging the draw of the bridge, but found the machinery broken, and the ways on which the bridge swung twisted and bent out of shape. An hour's hard work with axes and crowbars, and the draw was swung far enough to let pass the "Conestoga" and the "Lexington." They dashed forward like greyhounds slipped from the leash; and, after several hours' hard steaming, a smoke over the tree-tops told that the Confederate fugitives were not far ahead. Soon a bend in the river was passed; and there, within easy range, were two of the flying steamers. A commotion was visible on board, and boat after boat was seen to put off, and make for the shore; on reaching which the crews immediately plunged into the woods, and were out of sight before the gunboats could get within range. Soon light blue smoke curling from the windows of the steamers told that they had been fired; and as the last boats left each vessel, she ceased her onward course, and drifted, abandoned and helpless, down the stream. When within about a thousand yards of the two gunboats, the deserted steamers blew up with such force, that, even at that great distance, the glass was shattered in the "Conestoga," and her woodwork seriously damaged.

The two gunboats leisurely continued their excursion into the heart of the enemy's country. Little or no danger was to be feared. At that time, the Confederates had not learned to plant torpedoes in their rivers, to blow the enemy's vessels into fragments. There was no artillery stationed in that section to check their progress, and the only resistance found was an occasional rifle-shot from some concealed sharp-shooter in the bushes on the shore. On the 7th of February the gunboats reached Cerro Gordo, Tenn.; and here they made a valuable capture. The Confederates had been at work for weeks converting the steamer "Eastport" into an iron-clad ram; and, as the Union vessels came up, they found her almost completed, and absolutely without defence. Besides the new vessel, there was in the shipyard a large quantity of lumber and ship-timber, which was of the greatest value to the builders of the river navy. The two gunboats promptly captured all this property; and waiting until the "Tyler," which had been detained at the drawbridge, came up, they left her in charge, and continued their raid into the enemy's country. Little incident occurred until they reached the head of navigation of the river, where they found all the Confederate vessels which had been flying before them for two days. These were burned, and the two gunboats started back down the river, stopping for the "Eastport" on the way. The captured vessel was afterwards completed, and served the cause of the Union for two years, when she was blown up on the Red River.

When the raiding expedition reached Cairo, the officers found Foote getting his squadron together for the attack on Fort Donelson. This fortification was one strongly relied upon by the Confederates for the maintenance of their northern line of battle. It was on the bank of the Cumberland River, nearly opposite the site of Fort Henry on the Tennessee. A garrison of at least fifteen thousand men manned the works, and were commanded by no less than three generals; and the fact that there were *three* generals in command had much to do with the fall of the fort. Its strength was rather on its river-front. Here the river winds about between abrupt hillsides, and on the front of one of these hills stood Fort Donelson. The water-batteries were made up of heavy guns, so mounted as to command the river for miles. On the landward side were heavy earthworks, abatis, and sharp pointed *chevaux-de-frise*.

Against this fortification marched Grant with an army of eighteen thousand men, and Foote with his flotilla of gunboats. The Sunday before the start, Foote, who was a descendant of the old Puritans, and ever as ready to pray as to fight, attended church in a little meeting-house at Cairo. The clergyman did not appear on time; and the congregation waited, until many, growing weary, were leaving the church. Then the bluff old sailor rose in his pew, and, marching to the pulpit, delivered a stirring sermon, offering thanks for the victories of the Union arms, and imploring divine aid in the coming struggles. The next day he was on his way to hurl shot and shell at the men in the trenches of Fort Donelson.

While the capture of Fort Henry was a feather in the caps of the sailor-boys of the North, Fort Donelson must be credited to the valor of the soldiers. Against the heavy wall of the water-batteries, the guns of Foote's little flotilla pounded away in vain, while the heavy shells from the Confederate cannon did dreadful work on the thinly armored gunboats. It was on the 13th of April that the assault was opened by the "Carondelet." This vessel had reached the scene of action before the rest of the flotilla, and by order of the army commander tested the strength of the fort by a day's cannonade. She stationed herself about a mile from the batteries, at a spot where she would be somewhat protected by a jutting point, and began a deliberate cannonade with her bow-guns. One hundred and thirty shots went whizzing from her batteries against the front of the Confederate batteries, without doing any serious damage. Then came an iron ball weighing one hundred and twenty pounds, fired from a heavy gun, which burst through one of her portholes, and scattered men bleeding and mangled in every direction over the gundeck. She withdrew a short distance for repairs, but soon returned, and continued the fire the remainder of the day. When evening fell, she had sent one hundred and eighty shells at the fort, with the result of killing one man. This was not promising.

The next day the attack was taken up by all the gunboats. The distance chosen this time was four hundred yards, and the fight was kept up most stubbornly. It was St. Valentine's Day; and as the swarthy sailors, stripped to the waist, begrimed with powder, and stained with blood, rammed huge iron balls down the muzzles of the guns, they said with grim pleasantry, "There's a valentine for the gray-coats." And right speedily did the gray-coats return the gift. Shot and shell from the batteries came in volleys against the sides of the gunboats. In the fort the condition of affairs was not serious. The shells chiefly fell in the soft earth of the hilltop above, and embedded themselves harmlessly in the mud. One of the gunners after the fight said: "We were more bothered by flying mud than any thing else. A shell bursting up there would throw out great clots of clay, that blocked up the touch-holes of our guns, spoiled the priming of our shells, and plastered up the faces of our men.

Of course, now and then a bit of shell would knock some poor fellow over; but, though we were all green hands at war, we expected to see lots more blood and carnage than the Yankee gunboats dealt out to us."

The gunboats, however, had put themselves in a hot place. Twenty heavy guns on the hillside high above were hurling solid shot down on the little fleet. The sailors stuck to their work well; and though the vessels were in a fair way of being riddled, they succeeded in driving the enemy from his lower battery. But the upper battery was impregnable; and the gunners there, having got the correct range, were shooting with unpleasant precision. Two of the vessels were disabled by being struck in the steering-chains. On the "Carondelet" a piece burst, hurling its crew bleeding on the deck. No vessel escaped with less than twenty wounds, while the flag-ship was hit fifty-nine times. Commodore Foote was wounded in the foot by a heavy splinter; a wound from which he never fully recovered, and which for some years debarred him from service afloat.

That afternoon's bombardment showed clearly that Fort Donelson could never be taken by the navy. When Foote ordered his gunboats to cease firing and drop back out of position, the Confederates swarmed back into the lower battery that they had abandoned; and, after a few hours' work, the fort was as strong as before the fight. It was the first case in the history of the war in which the navy had failed to reduce the fortifications against which it had been ordered. The Hatteras forts, the works at Roanoke Island and at Hilton Head, Fort Henry — all had fallen before the cannon of the Union sailors; and Foote may well be pardoned if he yielded to Gen. Grant with great reluctance the honor of reducing Fort Donelson. For two days Grant's army invested the fort, and kept up a constant cannonade; then the defenders, despairing of escape, and seeing no use of further prolonging the defence, surrendered.

The capture of Fort Donelson was an important success for the Union arms. In addition to the large number of prisoners, and the great quantity of munitions of war captured, the destruction of the fort left the Cumberland River open to the passage of the Union gunboats, and the Confederate battle-line was moved back yet another point. But now was to come a most heroic test of the power of the river-navy and the army of the North.

Some sixty miles below Cairo, the rushing, tawny current of the mighty Mississippi turns suddenly northward, sweeping back, apparently, toward its source, in a great bend eight or ten miles long. At the point where the swift current sweeps around the bend, is a low-lying island, about a mile long and half a mile wide. This is known as Island No. 10; and at the opening of the war, it was supposed to hold the key to the navigation of the Mississippi River. Here the Confederates had thrown up powerful earthworks, the heavy guns in which effectually commanded the river, both up and down stream. The works were protected against a land bombardment by the fact that the only tenable bit of land, New Madrid, was held by Confederate troops. The shores of the Mississippi about Island No. 10 present the dreariest appearance imaginable. The Missouri shore is low and swampy. In 1811 an earthquake-shock rent the land asunder. Great tracts were sunk beneath the water-level of the river. Trees were thrown down, and lie rotting in the black and miasmatic water. Other portions of the land were thrown up, rugged, and covered with rank vegetation, making hills that serve only as places of refuge for water-moccasons and other noxious reptiles. Around this dreary waste of mud and water, the river rushes in an abrupt bend, making a peninsula ten miles long and three wide. Below this peninsula is New Madrid, a little village in the least settled part of Missouri; here the Confederates had established an army-post, and thrown up strong intrenchments. It was not, however, upon the intrenchments that they relied, but rather upon the impassable morasses by which they were surrounded on every side. In New Madrid were posted five or six thousand men; a small fleet of Confederate gunboats lay in the stream off the village; and higher up the river was Island No. 10, with its frowning bastions and rows of heavy siege-guns, prepared to beat back all advances of the Union troops.

In planning for the attack of this stronghold, the first difficulty found by Commodore Foote lay in the fact that his gunboats were above the batteries. In fighting down stream in that manner, the ships must be kept at long range: for, should a shot from the enemy injure the engine or boiler of a gunboat, the vessel is doomed; for the rapid current will rush her down under the enemy's guns, and her capture is certain. But the peril of running the batteries so as to carry on the fight from below seemed too great to be ventured upon; and besides, even with Island No. 10 passed, there would still be the batteries of New Madrid to cope with, and the gunboats of the Confederates to take the ships in the rear. So it was determined that the navy should begin a bombardment of the Confederate works, while the army under Gen. Pope should attend to New Madrid. Accordingly, on March 15, the whiz of a rifled shell from the flag-ship "Benton" announced to the Confederates that the North wanted the Mississippi opened for travel.

In this engagement use was made for the first time of a new style of vessel known as mortar-boats, which in later conflicts on the rivers did great service. These boats were simple floats, heavily built, and calculated to stand the most terrible shocks. On the float was raised a sort of sheet-iron fort or wall, about five feet high; and in the centre stood one thirteen-inch mortar. The mortar is the earliest of all forms of cannon, and was in use in Europe in 1435. Its name is derived from its resemblance to an ordinary druggist's mortar. The great thirteen-inch mortars used in the civil war weighed seventeen thousand pounds, and threw a shell thirteen inches in diameter. These shells were so heavy that it took two men to bring them up to the cannon's mouth. In the river-service, the mortar-boats were moored to the bank, and a derrick was set up in such a position that the shells could be hoisted up, and let fall into the yawning iron pot below. Foote had fourteen of these monsters pounding away at the Confederates, and the roar was deafening.

A correspondent of the "Chicago Times," who was with the fleet at the time of the bombardment, thus describes the manner of using these immense cannon: "The operation of firing the mortars, which was conducted when we were near by, is rather stunning. The charge is from fifteen to twenty-two pounds. The shell weighs two hundred and thirty pounds. For a familiar illustration, it is about the size of a large soup-plate. So

MORTAR-BOATS AT ISLAND NO. 10.

your readers may imagine, when they sit down to dinner, the emotions they would experience if they happened to see a ball of iron of those dimensions coming toward them at the rate of a thousand miles a minute. The boat is moored alongside the shore, so as to withstand the shock firmly, and the men go ashore when the mortar is fired. A pull of the string does the work, and the whole vicinity is shaken with the concussion. The report is deafening, and the most enthusiastic person gets enough of it with two or three discharges. There is no sound from the shell at this point of observation, and no indication to mark the course it is taking; but in a few seconds the attentive observer with a good glass will see the cloud of smoke that follows its explosion, and then the report comes back with a dull boom. If it has done execution, the enemy may be seen carrying off their killed and wounded."

And so from mortar-boats and gunboats, the iron hail was poured upon the little island, but without effect. When Foote with his flotilla first opened fire, he thought that the Confederate works would be swept away in a day or two. His ordnance was the heaviest ever seen on the Mississippi, and in number his guns were enough to have battered down a mountain. But his days grew to weeks, and still the flag of the Confederacy floated above Island No. 10. The men on the mortar-boats were giving way under the tremendous shocks of the explosions. Many were rendered deaf for days at a time. The jar of the explosions brought to the surface of the river hundreds of old logs and roots that had lain rotting in the soft ooze of the bottom. When all the mortars were engaged, the surface of the river was covered with foam and bubbles; and men by the thousand went about with their ears stuffed with tow, to protect them against the sound. Yet, after weeks of such firing, Gen. Beauregard telegraphed to Richmond, that the Yankees had "thrown three thousand shells, and burned fifty tons of gunpowder," without injuring his batteries in the least.

The Confederates remained passive in their trenches. They had no guns that would carry far enough to reply to Foote's mortars, and they did not wish to waste powder. It was galling to stand fire without replying; but, fortunately for them, the fire was not very deadly, and but few were injured. When, however, a shell did fall within the works, it made work enough to repair damages, as by its explosion a hole as large as a small house would be torn in the ground. But for every one that fell within the batteries, twenty fell outside. Some strange freaks are recorded of the shells. One fell on a cannon, around which eight or ten men were lying. The gun-carriage was blown to pieces, but not a man was hurt. Another fell full on the head of a man who was walking about distributing rations, and not so much as a button from his uniform was ever found.

But while the navy was thus playing at bowls with great guns, the army had marched through the interior, captured New Madrid, and obtained a foothold below Island No. 10. Thus the Confederates were surrounded; and the very impassability of the land, that had been an advantage to them, now told against them, for it cut off all hope of re-enforcements. Gen. Pope's position was such that he could not get at the island, nor secure a commanding position, without aid from the navy. He begged Foote to try to run the batteries; but the commodore replied, that the risk was greater than the prospective gain, and continued his cannonade. Then a new idea was broached. By cutting a canal through the bayous, swamps, and woods of the peninsula, the lighter vessels could be taken by the fort without risk, and Foote would then dare the dangers of a dash by in the gunboats. Every one said that such a canal was impossible; but the men of the North were given to doing impossible things in those days, and while Foote's mortar-boats continued their thunder, fifteen hundred men were set to work cutting a way through the noisome swamps. A channel forty feet wide must be made. First gangs of men with axes and saws, working in three feet of water, went ahead, cutting down the rank vegetation. As fast as a little space was cleared, a small steamer went in, and with dredge and steam-capstan hauled out the obstructions. In some places the surveyed channel was so filled with drift-wood, fallen trees, and tangled roots, that the labor of a thousand men for a day seemed to make no impression. When the canal was pretty well blocked out, the levee was cut; and the rush of the waters from the great river undermined trees, and piled up new obstacles for the steamers to tow away. Amid the foulest vapors the men worked, and more than a thousand were sent to the hospital with chills and fever, and rheumatism. The most venomous snakes lurked in the dark recesses of the swamp; on cypress-stumps or floating logs the deadly water-moccason lay stretched out, ready to bite without warning. Wherever there was a bit of dry ground, the workers were sure to hear the rattle of the rattlesnake. Sometimes whole nests of these reptiles would be uncovered.

The work was continued day and night. When the failing daylight ceased to make its way through the thickly intwined branches of trees and climbing vines, great torches would be lighted, and by their fitful glare the soldiers and sailors worked on in the water and mud. The light glared from the furnaces of the steamers, lighting up the half-naked forms of the stokers. Now and then some dry vine or tree would catch a spark from a torch, and in an instant would be transformed into a pillar of fire. After eight days of work the canal was finished, and was found to be of sufficient depth for the passage of the transports. And now Commodore Foote saw that the time had come when he must attempt to run his gunboats past the forts, be the danger what it might.

On April 1, Foote ordered a reconnoissance of the batteries, and this order evoked one of the most daring deeds in the history of the war. The night was pitchy dark, and heavy clouds were driven across the sky by a strong, damp wind, that told of a coming storm. In five boats a party of fifty sailors and fifty soldiers put off from the fleet, prepared to go down and beard the Confederate lion in his den. Hardly had they started on their perilous expedition, when the rain began falling in sheets, and now and again flashes of lightning made the dark shores visible for an instant, then the black night hid every thing again from view. It was midnight, and the fierceness of the wind added to the terror of the moment. On the banks, the great forest-trees were bending and groaning before the blast, while the broad surface of the river was lashed into foaming billows. Under cover of the darkness the little band passed rapidly down the river; past the shore-batteries and past the Confederate picket-boats, they sped unseen. When they were within a few feet of the shore, a flash of lightning revealed them for just an instant to the sentries. Then all was black, save for the quick flashes of the sentries' guns as they gave the alarm and fell back. The Federals landed rapidly, and drove the confused Confederates from the battery. Then began the work of spiking the guns. Every fifth man carried a number of rat-tail files, which were to be driven into the vents of the cannon, and then broken off. While the raiders were engaged in this work, the Confederates rallied, and soon drove back the blue-jackets to their boats, with a slight loss in killed and captured. How many guns they had disabled, it is hard to say. In the excitement and glory of successful adventure, the reports were much exaggerated. Histories of that date depict the men as calmly spiking *every* gun, and then retiring deliberately. One writer claims that only one gun was spiked. However, testimony from Confederates on duty in the batteries goes to show that four guns were totally disabled. But the true value of the adventure to the Union forces was the dash and valor it disclosed, and the encouragement the people received from its success.

The next day after this successful exploit, a gunboat, the "Carondelet," was made ready to try the dash past the batteries of Island No. 10. Again the weather was favorable to the plans of the Federals, for the night was as dark and wild as the one before. The day had been clear, and the night opened with so bright a moon that for a time it was thought that the project would have to be abandoned; but toward ten o'clock a heavy thunder-storm came up, and soon the black sky, the wildly waving tree-tops, and the sheets of rain scudding across the river, gave promise of a suitable night.

All day the sailors on the "Carondelet" had been working busily, getting their vessel in trim for the trip. Heavy planks were laid along the deck, to ward off plunging shot. Chain cables were coiled about all weak points, cord-wood was piled around the boilers, and the pilot-house was wrapped round and about with heavy hawsers. On the side toward the battery was tied a large barge, piled high with cotton-bales. When the time for starting drew nigh, all lights were extinguished. The guns were run in, and the ports closed. The sailors, heavily armed, were sent to their stations. Muskets, revolvers, and sabres were in the racks. Down in the boiler-room the stokers were throwing coal upon the roaring fires; and in the engine-room the engineer stood with his hand on the throttle, waiting for the signal to get under way.

Towards eleven o'clock the time seemed propitious for starting. The storm was at its height, and the roll of the thunder would drown the beat of the steamer's paddles. The word was given; and the "Carondelet," with her two protecting barges, passed out of sight of the flotilla, and down towards the cannon of the enemy. For the first half-mile all went well. The vessel sped along silently and unseen. The men on the gun-deck, unable to see about, sat breathlessly, expecting that at any moment a cannon-ball might come crashing through the side into their midst. Suddenly from the towering smoke-stacks, burst out sheets of flame five feet high, caused by the burning soot inside, and lighting up the river all about. Quickly extinguished, they quickly broke out again; and now from the camp of the alarmed enemy came the roll of the drum, and the ringing notes of the bugle sounding the alarm. A gunboat was bearing down on the works, and the Confederates sprang to their guns with a will. The men on the "Carondelet" knew what to expect, and soon it came. Five signal rockets rushed up into the sky, and in an instant thereafter came the roar of a great gun from one of the batteries. Then all joined in, and the din became terrible. With volley after volley the Confederates hurled cannon-balls, shells, musket, and even pistol-bullets at the flying ship, that could only be seen an instant at a time by the fitful flashes of the lightning. On the "Carondelet" all was still as death. The men knew the deadly peril they were in, and realized how impossible it was for them to make any fight. In the black night, threading the crooked and ever-changing channel of the Mississippi River, it was impossible to go more than half-speed. In the bow men were stationed casting the lead, and calling out the soundings to the brave old Capt. Hoel, who stood on the upper deck unprotected from the storm of bullets, and repeated the soundings to Capt. Walker. So through the darkness, through the storm of shot and shell, the "Carondelet" kept on her way. Past the land-batteries, past the rows of cannon on the island, and past the formidable floating battery, she swept uninjured. Heavy and continuous as was the fire of the Confederates, it was mainly without aim. The hay-barge was hit three times, but not a scar was on the gunboat when she stopped before the water-front of New Madrid after twenty minutes' run through that dreadful fire.

And now the roar of the great guns had died away, and the men on the vessels of the flotilla up the river were all anxiety to know what had been the fate of their gallant comrades on the "Carondelet." All the time the battle raged, the decks of the ships at anchor were crowded with sailors looking eagerly down the river, and trying to make out by the blinding flashes of the cannon the dark form of a gunboat speeding by the hostile camp. Now all is silent; the roar of battle is over, the flash of gunpowder no more lights up the night. But what has become of the gallant men who braved that tempest of steel and iron? Are they floating down the troubled waters beneath the wreck of their vessel? It was a moment of suspense. After a few minutes' silence, there comes through the strangely quiet air the deep boom of a heavy gun. It had been agreed, that, if the "Carondelet" made the passage of the batteries safely, she should fire six heavy guns. The old tars on the decks say softly to themselves, "One." Then comes another, and a third, and still more, until suddenly a ringing cheer goes up from the flotilla, louder than the thunder itself. Men dance for joy; grizzled tars fall into each other's arms, sing, shout, cry. An answering salute goes booming back, rockets scud up into the clouds; and Commodore Foote, with a heart too full for talking, goes down into his cabin to be alone.

That night's work by the "Carondelet" terminated Confederate domain on Island No. 10. The next night another gunboat came down, and the two set to work carrying the troops across the river, protecting artillerymen engaged in erecting batteries, and generally completing the investment of the island. In two days every loop-hole of escape for the Confederates is closed, — gunboats above and below them, batteries peering down from every bluff, and regiments of infantry, all prepared to move upon the works. They made one or two ineffectual but plucky attempts to ward off capture. One private soldier swam ashore, skulked past the Union pickets, and made his way to one of the Union mortar-boats. He succeeded in getting to the mortar, and successfully spiked it, thus terminating its usefulness. A second Confederate succeeded in reaching the deck of the mortar-boat, but while making his way across the deck tripped and fell. The rat-tail file he was carrying was driven into his side, making a wound from which he died in two hours. A third man, reckless of life, set out in a canoe to blow up a gunboat. He carried with him a fifty-pound keg of gunpowder, which he proposed to strap on the rudder-post of the vessel. He succeeded in getting under the stern of the vessel; but the gleam of his lighted match alarmed the sentry, who fired, hitting him in the shoulder. The Confederate went overboard, and managed to get ashore; while his keg of powder, with the fuse lighted, went drifting down stream. Soon it exploded, throwing up an immense column of water, and showing that it would have sent the stoutest vessel to the bottom had it been properly placed.

But such struggles as these could not long avert the impending disaster. The Confederates were hemmed in on every side. It was true that they had a strong position, and could make a desperate resistance; but they were separated from their friends, and their final downfall was but a question of time. Appreciating this fact, they surrendered two days after the "Carondelet" had passed the batteries; and Foote made his second step (this time one of sixty miles) toward the conquest of the Mississippi.

To-day nothing remains of the once extensive island, save a small sand-bank in the middle of the great river. The rushing current of the Father of Waters has done its work, and Island No. 10 is now a mere tradition.

CHAPTER XI.

FAMOUS CONFEDERATE PRIVATEERS, — THE "ALABAMA," THE "SHENANDOAH," THE "NASHVILLE."

LET us now desert, for a time, the progress of the Union forces down the Mississippi River, and turn our attention toward the true home of the sailors, — the blue waters of the ocean. We have heard much, from many sources, of the exploits of the Confederate commerce-destroyers, privateers, or, as the Union authorities and the historians of the war period loved to call them, the "Rebel pirates." In the course of this narrative we have already dealt with the career of the "Sumter," one of the earliest of these vessels. A glance at the career of the most famous of all the Confederate cruisers, the "Alabama," will be interesting.

This vessel was built in England, ostensibly as a merchant-vessel, although her heavy decks and sides, and her small hatchways, might have warned the English officials that she was intended for purposes of war. Before she was finished, however, the customs-house people began to suspect her character; and goaded on by the frequent complaints of the United States minister, that a war-vessel was being built for the Confederates, they determined to seize her. But customs-house officials do things slowly; and, while they were getting ready for the seizure, Capt. Semmes, who had taken command of the new ship, duped them, and got his vessel safely out of English waters. Private detectives and long-shore customs officers had been visiting the ship daily on visits of examination; but, by the aid of champagne and jolly good-fellowship, their inexperienced eyes were easily blinded to the manifest preparations for a war-like cruise. But finally came a retired naval officer who was not to be humbugged. A sailor on board thus tells the story of his visit: "He was evidently a naval officer, alert and resolute, and soon silenced the officer's explanations. He looked at the hatchways, shot-racks, and magazines; and, surveying the hammock-hooks on the berth-deck, said, 'You'll have a large crew for a merchant-steamer.' We had taken on board some heavy oak plank, that lay on the main deck; the officer remarked that they were for anchor-stocks, and was shortly answered, 'Wouldn't make bad gun-platforms, sir,' which, indeed, was just what they were intended for. With a 'Good-morning, sir,' our visitor mounted the side and was gone." This visit alarmed the Confederates; and immediate preparations were made to run the ship, which still went by the name of the "No. 290," out of the British waters the next day. To disarm suspicion, a large party of ladies and gentlemen were invited aboard; and the ship started down the Mersey, ostensibly on her trial trip, with the sounds of music and popping corks ringing from her decks. But peaceful and merry as the start seemed, it was the beginning of a voyage that was destined to bring ruin to hundreds of American merchants, and leave many a good United States vessel a smoking ruin on the breast of the ocean. When she was a short distance down the river, two tugs were seen putting off from the shore; and in a moment the astonished guests were requested to leave the ship, and betake themselves homeward in the tugs. It is unnecessary to follow the voyage of the "No. 290" to Nassau, and detail the way in which cannon, ammunition, and naval stores were sent out from Portsmouth in a second vessel, and transferred to her just outside of Nassau. It is enough to say that on a bright, clear Sunday morning, in the latter part of August, 1862, Capt. Rafael Semmes, late of the Confederate cruiser "Sumter," a gentleman of middle height, wearing a uniform of gray and gold, his dark mustache waxed to such sharp points that one would think him a Frenchman rather than a Southerner, stood on the quarter-deck of the "No. 290," with his crew mustered before him, reading out his commission from Jefferson Davis, as commander of the Confederate States' steam-sloop "Alabama." As he read, an old master's-mate, standing at the peak-halyards, begins pulling at the ropes. The British ensign, carried through the ship's anonymous days, comes fluttering down, and in its place runs up the white naval ensign of the Confederacy, with the starry Southern cross in the red field of the corner. Then the reading is ended. Boom! goes the starboard forecastle-gun. The band bursts forth with the stirring notes of Dixie; and the sailors, after three ringing cheers, crowd forward to wait for further developments. Soon the sailors are summoned aft again, and Capt. Semmes addresses them. He tells them that, as the "Alabama" is to be a ship-of-war, they are released from their shipping contracts, but are invited to ship under the new plan. He briefly details the purpose of the cruise. The "Alabama" is to be a bird of passage, flitting from port to port, and hovering about the highways of travel, to lie in wait for the merchant-vessels of the North. Armed vessels she will avoid as much as possible, confining her warfare to the helpless merchant-men. It is hardly a glorious programme, but it seems to bear the promise of prize-money; and before the day is over Capt. Semmes has shipped a crew of eighty men, and with these the "Alabama" begins her cruise. The remainder of the sailors are sent ashore, and the "Alabama" starts off under sail, in search of her first capture.

Let us look for a moment at this vessel, perhaps the most famous of all cruisers. She was a fast screw-steamer, of a little more than a thousand tons' burden. Her screw was so arranged that it could be hoisted out of the water; and, as the saving of coal was a matter of necessity, the "Alabama" did most of her cruising under sail. Her hull was of wood, with no iron plating, and her battery consisted of but eight light guns; two facts which made it necessary that she should avoid any conflicts with the powerful ships of the United States navy. Her lines were beautifully fine; and, as she sped swiftly through the water, Capt. Semmes felt that his vessel could escape the Northern cruisers as easily as she could overhaul the lumbering merchantmen. The crew was a turbulent one, picked up in the streets of Liverpool, and made up of men of all nationalities. Terrific rows would arise in the forecastle, and differences between the sailors were often settled by square stand-up fights. The petty officers seldom interfered; one old boatswain remarking, when he heard the noise of blows in the forecastle, "Blast them, let 'em slug one another's heads off; it will keep 'em out of mischief." And it generally did, for the combatants were usually fast friends the next day.

As soon as the new ship was cleaned up, and put in order, drill began. The men were all green; and hard, steady work at the guns, and with the cutlasses, was necessary to fit them for service. The decks resounded with "right," "left," "head protect," "right overcut." The men were slow in learning; but the officers were Southerners, devoted to their cause, and were tireless in getting the crew into shape.

After several days of cruising and drill, a vessel was sighted which was unmistakably American. One of the sailors tells the story of her capture graphically. "On the morning of the 5th of September the cry of 'ship ahoy!' from the masthead brought all hands on deck. Sure enough, about two miles to the leeward of us was a fine barque, at once pronounced a 'spouter' (whaler), and an American. In order to save coal, — of which very essential article we had about three hundred tons aboard, — we never used our screw unless absolutely necessary. We were on the starboard tack, and with the fresh breeze soon came alongside. We had the American flag set, and the chase showed the stars and stripes. A gun was fired; and, as we came within hail, we gave the order, 'Back your mainsail; I'll send a boat on board of you.'

"'Cutter away,' and the boat came down from the davits, and we pulled for our first prize. It soon became a vain thing, and tiresome; but this our first essay was a novelty, and we made the stretches buckle with our impatience to get aboard. The bowman hooked on to the chains, and we went up the side like cats. When we got aft, the captain asked in a dazed sort of manner, 'Why — why — what does this mean?' The master,

Fullam, replied, 'You are prize to the Confederate steamer "Alabama," Capt. Semmes commanding. I'll trouble you for your papers.' Now, this man had been four years out, and had no doubt heard of the trouble at home; but he couldn't realize this, and he stared, and said, 'Confederate government — Alabama — why, that's a State,' and then was sternly told to get his papers. We were ordered to put the crew in irons, and they, too, seemed utterly dumbfounded; and one poor fellow said to me, 'Must I lose all my clothes?' I answered, 'Yes,' but advised him to put on all he could, and if he had any money to slip it in his boot. 'Money! I h'aint seen a dollar for three years; but I'm obliged to ye all the same.'"

Then, after searching the vessel for valuables, the captives were taken back to the "Alabama," while one boat's-crew remained behind to fire the vessel.

"She was loaded with oil," writes sailor Haywood; "and, when it caught, a high column of dense black smoke poured out of the hatchways, and spread in vast involutions to the leeward. Soon the red forked flames began to climb her masts, and her spars glowed with light; with a crash her mainmast fell, carrying the foremast with it, and sending a shower of sparks high in the air; her stout sides seemed to burst open; and what was a stately ship was now a blackened hulk, the rising sea breaking in white-caps over it, and at last, with a surge and wallow, sinking out of sight." Alone, by one of the lee-ports, the ruined American captain stood, looking sadly upon the end of all his long four years' labor. For this he had borne the icy hardships of the Arctic seas. The long, dreary four years of separation from wife and home had been lightened by the thought, that by a prosperous voyage he might bring home enough money to stay always in the little shingled cottage in the narrow street of some New England fishing-village; but now all that was over. When he should arrive home he would be penniless, with nothing but the clothes on his back, and all because of a war of the very existence of which he knew nothing. It was hard to bear, but war brings nothing but affliction.

After this capture, the "Alabama" had a lively season for several weeks, capturing often two or three vessels a day. Generally they met with no

LOOTING A PRIZE.

resistance; but occasionally the blood of some old sea-dog would boil, and he would do the best in his power to injure his captors. A story of one such incident was thus told by one of the "Alabama's" crew: —

"When we ran around in search of whalers, we came upon a Yankee skipper who didn't know what surrender meant. We were just well to the west of the stormy cape, when one morning after breakfast we raised a whaler. He was headed up the coast, and about noon we overhauled him. He paid no attention to the first shot, and it was only when the second one hulled him that he came into the wind. It was then seen that he had fifteen or sixteen men aboard, and that all were armed with muskets, and meant to defend the ship. The lieutenant was sent off with his boat; but no sooner was he within fair musket-range, than the whaler opened on him, killing one man, and wounding two, at the first volley. The officer pushed ahead, and demanded a surrender; but he got another volley, and the reply that the whaler 'would go to the bottom before he would surrender to a Rebel!'

"The boat was recalled, and our gunners were instructed to hull the whaler with solid shot. We approached him within rifle-range, and opened fire. Every one of the balls plumped through his side at and above the water-line, and he answered with his muskets, severely wounding two men. He was repeatedly hailed to surrender, but in reply he encouraged his men to maintain their fire. We soon had the sea pouring into his starboard side through a dozen holes; and when it was seen that he would soon go down, we ceased firing, and again demanded his surrender. I can remember just how he looked as he sprang upon the rail, — tall, gaunt, hair flying, and eyes blazing, — and shouted in reply, —

"'The "Ben Scott" don't surrender! Come and take us — if you can.'

"Five minutes later his craft settled down, bow first. We lowered the boats to save his crew, and, strangely enough, not a man was lost. When we brought them aboard, the Yankee skipper walked up to Semmes, bareheaded, barefooted, and coatless, and said, —

"'If I'd only have had one old cannon aboard, we'd have licked ye out of yer butes! Here we are, and what are ye going to do with us?'

"He was voted a jolly good fellow, and the crew were better treated than any other ever forced aboard. In order to give them their liberty, the very next capture we made was bonded, and they were put aboard to sail for home."

But now the decks of the "Alabama" were getting rather uncomfortably crowded with prisoners, and it became necessary to put into some port where they could be landed. Accordingly the ship was headed for Martinique, and soon lay anchored in the harbor of that place, where she began coaling. While she lay there, a Yankee schooner put into the port, and was about to drop anchor near the dangerous cruiser, when some one gave the skipper a hint; and, with a startled "b'gosh," he got his sails up, and scudded out to sea. The "Alabama" lay in port some days. The first set of the sailors who received permission to go ashore proceeded to get drunk, and raised so great a disturbance, that thereafter they were obliged to look on the tropical prospect from the deck of the vessel. The next day a United States war-vessel was seen standing into the harbor, and Capt. Semmes immediately began to make preparations to fight her. But as she came nearer she proved to be the "San Jacinto," a vessel mounting fourteen heavy guns, and altogether too powerful for the "Alabama." So thinking discretion the better part of valor, the Confederate ship remained safe in the neutral harbor. The "San Jacinto" quietly remained outside, thinking that at last the fox was caught. But that same night, with all lights extinguished, and running under full steam, the "Alabama" slipped right under the broadside of her enemy, getting clean away, so quietly that the "San Jacinto" remained for four days guarding the empty trap, while the "Alabama" was off again on another voyage of destruction, and the tuneful souls in the forecastle were roaring out the chorus, —

"Oh, our jolly privateer
Has left old England's shore!
Lord, send us lots of prizes,
But no Yankee man-of-war."

Soon after leaving Martinique, the "Alabama" made a capture which embarrassed the captain not a little by its size. It was Sunday (which

Capt. Semmes calls in his journal "the 'Alabama's' lucky day"), when a bit of smoke was seen far off on the horizon, foretelling the approach of a steamer. Now was the time for a big haul; and the "Alabama's" canvas was furled, and her steam-gear put in running order. The two vessels approached each other rapidly; and soon the stranger came near enough for those on the "Alabama" to make out her huge walking-beam, seesawing up and down amidships. The bright colors of ladies' dresses were visible; and some stacks of muskets, and groups of blue-uniformed men, forward, told of the presence of troops. The "Alabama" came up swiftly, her men at the guns, and the United States flag flying from the peak, — a rather dishonorable ruse habitually practised by Capt. Semmes. In a moment the stranger showed the stars and stripes, and then the "Alabama" ran up the white ensign of the Confederacy, and fired a blank cartridge. But the stranger had no thought of surrendering, and crowded on all steam and fled. The "Alabama" was no match for her in speed, so a more peremptory summons was sent in the shape of a shell that cut the steamer's foremast in two. This hint was sufficient. The huge paddles ceased revolving, and a boat's-crew from the "Alabama" went aboard to take possession. The prize proved to be the mail steamer "Ariel," with five hundred passengers, besides a hundred and forty marines and a number of army and navy officers. Now Capt. Semmes had an elephant on his hands, and what to do with that immense number of people he could not imagine. Clearly the steamer could not be burned like other captures. For two days Capt. Semmes kept the prize near him, debating what was to be done, and then released her; exacting from all the military and naval officers their paroles that they would not take up arms against the Confederacy.

After this exploit the "Alabama" went into port for a few days, and then headed into the Gulf of Mexico. Here she steamed about, capturing and burning a few United States merchantmen, until on the 11th of January she found herself off the port of Galveston, where a strong blockading fleet was stationed. And here she fought her first battle.

About four o'clock of a clear afternoon, the lookout in the cross-trees of the United States sloop-of-war "Hatteras," stationed off the port of Galveston, hailed the officer of the deck, and reported a steamer standing up and down outside. The stranger was watched closely through marine glasses, and finally decided to be a blockade-runner trying to make the port; and the "Hatteras" immediately set out in pursuit. This was just what Capt. Semmes desired. He knew that the ships stationed off Galveston were not heavily armed, and he felt sure that if he could entice one away from the rest of the fleet he would be able to send her to the bottom. Accordingly he steamed away slowly, letting the "Hatteras" gain on him, but at the same time drawing her out of the reach of any aid from her consorts. When about twenty miles away from the fleet, the "Alabama" slowed down and finally stopped altogether, waiting for the "Hatteras" to come up. The latter vessel came within two hundred yards, and hailed, "What ship's that?"—"Her Majesty's ship 'Petrel,'" answered Semmes, pursuing the course of deception that brings so much discredit on his otherwise dashing career. The captain of the "Hatteras" answered that he would send a boat aboard; but, before the boat touched the water, a second hail announced, "We are the Confederate ship 'Alabama,'" and in an instant a heavy broadside crashed into the "Hatteras." Every one of the shots took effect; and one big fellow from the one hundred and five pounder rifle peeled off six feet of iron plating from the side of the "Hatteras," and lodged in the hold. Dazed by this unexpected fire, but plucky as ever, the blue-jackets sprang to their guns and returned the fire. The two ships were so close together that a good shot with a revolver could have picked off his man every time, and the sailors hurled taunts at each other between the volleys. Not a shot missed the "Hatteras:" in five minutes she was riddled with holes, and on fire, and a minute or two later the engineer came up coolly and reported, "Engine's disabled, sir;" followed quickly by the carpenter, who remarked, "Ship's making water fast; can't float more than ten minutes, sir." There was nothing for it but surrender, and the flag came down amid frantic yells from the "Alabama" sailors. Semmes got out his boats with wonderful rapidity, and picked up all the men on the "Hatteras;" and the defeated vessel sank in ten minutes. One of the strange things about this battle was the small number of men injured. Nothing but shells were fired, and they searched every part of the vessels; yet when the fight was over the "Alabama" had but one man wounded, while the "Hatteras" had two men killed and three wounded. The shells played some strange pranks in their course. One ripped up a long furrow in the deck of the "Alabama," and knocked two men high in the air without disabling them. Another struck a gun full in the mouth, tore off one side of it, and shoved it back ten feet, without injuring any of the crew. One man who was knocked overboard by the concussion was back again and serving his gun in two minutes. A shell exploded in the coal of the "Hatteras," and sent the stuff flying all about the vessel, without injuring a man.

With her prisoners stowed away in all available places about her decks, the "Alabama" headed for Jamaica, and cast anchor in the harbor of Port Royal. There were several English men-of-war there, and the officers of the victorious ship were lionized and feasted to their hearts' content. The prisoners were landed, the "Alabama's" wounds were bound up, and she was made ready for another cruise.

After five days in port, she set out again on her wanderings about the world. Week after week she patrolled the waters in all parts of the globe where ships were likely to be met. Sometimes she would go a fortnight without a capture, and then the men in the forecastle would grow turbulent and restive under the long idleness. Every bit of brass-work was polished hour after hour, and the officers were at their wits' end to devise means for "teasing-time." The men made sword-knots and chafing-gear enough to last the whole navy, and then looked longingly at the captain's mustache, as the only thing left in which a "Turk's head" could be tied. Music enlivened the hours for a time; but the fiddler was soon voted a bore, and silenced by some one pouring a pint of molasses into the f-holes of his instrument. The enraged musician completed the job by breaking it over the head of the joker. After several weeks, they put into Cape Town. Here the practical joker of the crew made himself famous by utterly routing an inquisitive old lady, who asked, "What do you do with your prisoners?" The grizzled old tar dropped his voice to a confidential whisper, and, with a look of the utmost frankness, replied, "We biles 'em, mum. We tried a roast, but there ain't a hounce of meat on one o' them Yankee carkages. Yes, mum, we biles 'em." The startled old lady gasped out, "Good lordy," and fled from the ship.

Putting out from Cape Town, the "Alabama" continued her weary round of cruising. Many vessels were captured, and most of them were burned. One Yankee captain proved too much for Semmes, as his story will show. His ship was chased by the "Alabama" in heavy weather all day, and occasionally fired upon. When the steamer was abeam, "she closed up with us," the captain says, "as near as safety would permit, and, hailing us, asked where we were bound, and demanded the surrender of the ship to the Confederate Government. I answered through my trumpet, 'Come and take me.' Conversation being too straining for the lungs amid the howling of the wind and rolling of the huge billows, and the proximity of the vessels too dangerous, we separated a little, and had recourse to blackboards to carry on our conversation. Semmes asked where we were bound. I answered, without a blush, 'Melbourne,' thinking that possibly he might try to intercept me if he knew that I was to pass through the Straits of Sunda. Then he had the check to order me to 'haul down your flag and surrender, escape or no escape,'—on a kind of parole, I suppose he meant. I wrote on the board: 'First capture, then parole.' This answer vexed him, I am sure, for he immediately wrote: 'Surrender, or I will sink you.' I wrote: 'That would be murder, not battle.'—'Call it what you will, I will do it,' he wrote. 'Attempt it, and by the living God, I will run you down, and we will sink together,' I wrote in reply. I knew his threat was vain; for in that heavy sea, rolling his rails under, he did not dare to free his guns, which were already double lashed. They would have carried away their tackles, and gone through the bulwarks overboard. Conscious that he had made empty threats, we said no more, but doggedly kept on our course. Sail was still further reduced on both vessels, as the wind kept increasing and was now blowing a gale. We were now gradually and surely drawing ahead of the steamer.

It was growing dark. Rejoicing at my fortunate escàpe, I gave the valiant Semmes a parting shot by hoisting the signal 'Good-by.' Dipping the star-spangled banner as a salute, I hauled it down, and the steamer was soon lost to sight in the darkness. . . . I never saw her after our escape; but, indirectly, she forced me to sell my ship in China soon after."

But we cannot follow the "Alabama" in her career about the world. A full account of her captures would fill volumes; and in this narrative we must pass hastily by the time that she spent scouring the ocean, dodging United States men-of-war, and burning Northern merchantmen, until, on the 11th of June, she entered the harbor of Cherbourg, France, and had hardly dropped anchor when the United States man-of-war "Kearsarge" appeared outside, and calmly settled down to wait for the Confederate to come out and fight. Capt. Semmes seemed perfectly ready for the conflict, and began getting his ship in shape for the battle. The men, too, said that they had had a "plum-pudding voyage" of it so far, and they were perfectly ready for a fight. The forecastle poet was set to work, and soon ground out a song, of which the refrain was, —

> "We're homeward bound, we're homeward bound!
> And soon shall stand on English ground;
> But, ere our native land we see,
> We first must fight the 'Kearsargee.'"

This was the last song made on board the "Alabama," and the poet was never more seen after the fight with the "Kearsargee."

The "Kearsarge" had hardly hove in sight when Capt. Semmes began taking in coal, and ordered the yards sent down from aloft, and the ship put in trim for action. Outside the breakwater, the "Kearsarge" was doing the same thing. In armament, the two vessels were nearly equal; the "Alabama" having eight guns to the "Kearsarge's" seven, but the guns of the latter vessel were heavier and of greater range. In the matter of speed, the "Kearsarge" had a slight advantage. The great advantage which the "Kearsarge" had was gained by the forethought of her commander, who had chains hung down her sides, protecting the boilers and machinery. Semmes might easily have done the same thing had the idea occurred to him.

It was on Sunday, June 19, that the "Alabama" started out to the duel that was to end in her destruction. Though Sunday was Capt. Semmes's lucky day, his luck this time seemed to have deserted him. The "Alabama" was accompanied in her outward voyage by a large French iron-clad frigate. The broad breakwater was black with people waiting to see the fight. The news had spread as far as Paris, and throngs had come down by special trains to view the great naval duel. A purple haze hung over the placid water, through which could be seen the "Kearsarge," with her colors flying defiantly, steaming slowly ahead, and ready for the "Alabama" to come up. Small steamers on every side followed the "Alabama," as near the scene of conflict as they dared. One English yacht, the "Deerhound," with her owner's family aboard, hung close to the combatants during the fight. No duel of the age of chivalry had a more eager throng of spectators.

Now the "Alabama" has passed the three-mile line, and is on the open sea. The big French iron-clad stops; the pilot-boats, with no liking for cannon-balls, stop too. The "Deerhound" goes out a mile or so farther, and the "Alabama" advances alone to meet the antagonist that is waiting quietly for her coming. The moment of conflict is at hand; and Capt. Semmes, mustering his men on the deck, addresses them briefly, and sends them to their quarters; and now, with guns shotted, and lanyards taut, and ready for the pull, the "Alabama" rushes toward her enemy. When within a distance of a mile, the first broadside was let fly, without avail. The "Kearsarge," more cool and prudent, waits yet awhile; and, when the first shot does go whizzing from her big Dahlgren guns, it strikes the "Alabama," and makes her quiver all over. Clearly it won't do to fight at long range; and Capt. Semmes determines to close in on his more powerful antagonist, and even try to carry her by boarding, as in the glorious days of Paul Jones. But the wary Winslow of the "Kearsarge" will have none of that; and he keeps his ship at a good distance, all the time pouring great shot into the sides of the "Alabama." Now the two

RESCUE OF CAPTAIN SEMMES.

vessels begin circling around each other in mighty circles, each trying to get in a raking position. The men on the "Alabama" began to find that their gunpowder was bad and caky; while at the same moment one of the officers saw two big solid shot strike the "Kearsarge" amidships, and fall back into the water, revealing the heretofore unsuspected armor. This was discouraging. Then came a big shot that knocked over the pivot-gun, and killed half its crew. One sailor saw a shot come in a port, glide along the gun, and strike the man at the breach full in the breast, killing him instantly.

The "Kearsarge," too, was receiving some pretty heavy blows, but her iron armor protected her vulnerable parts. One shell lodged in her stern-post, but failed to explode. Had it burst, the "Kearsarge's" fighting would have been over.

After an hour the officers of the "Alabama" began coming to Capt. Semmes with grave faces, and reporting serious accidents. At last the first lieutenant reported the ship sinking, and the order was given to strike the flag. She was sinking rapidly, and the time had come for every man to save himself. The "Kearsarge" was shamefully slow in getting out her boats; and finally when the "Alabama," throwing her bow high in the air, went down with a rush, she carried most of her wounded with her, and left the living struggling in the water. Capt. Semmes was picked up by a boat from the yacht "Deerhound," and was carried in that craft to England away from capture. For so escaping, he has been harshly criticised by many people; but there seems to be no valid reason why he should refuse the opportunity so offered him. Certain it is, that, had he not reached the "Deerhound," he would have been drowned; for none of the boats of the "Kearsarge" were near him when he was struggling in the water.

So ended the career of the "Alabama." Her life had been a short one, and her career not the most glorious imaginable; but she had fulfilled the purpose for which she was intended. She had captured sixty-four merchant-vessels, kept a large number of men-of-war busy in chasing her from one end of the world to the other, and inflicted on American commerce an almost irreparable injury.

THE END OF A PRIVATEER.

Although the "Alabama" was by all means the most noted and the most successful of all the Confederate cruisers, there were others that entered upon the career of privateering, and followed it for a while with varying degrees of success. Some were captured revenue-cutters, which the Confederates armed with a single heavy gun, and turned loose on the ocean in search of Yankee schooners. Others were merely tugs or pilot-boats. Generally their careers were short. In one instance a fine privateer, from which the Confederates expected great things, attempted to capture a United States man-of-war, under the delusion that it was a merchant-vessel. The captain of the man-of-war saw the mistake under which the Confederate labored, and allowed the privateer to come up within short range, when, with a sudden broadside, he sent her to the bottom, abruptly terminating her career as a commerce destroyer. Some quite formidable iron-clad cruisers were built abroad; but in most cases all the diplomacy of the Confederate agents proved unavailing to prevent the confiscation of the ships by the neutral governments in whose territory they were built. Two iron-clad rams built at Liverpool, ostensibly for private parties, but really for the Confederate Government, were seized by the British authorities. Six splendid vessels were built in France, but only one succeeded in getting away to join the Confederate service. This one was a ram with armored sides, and was named the "Stonewall." The war was nearly over when she was put in commission, and her services for the Confederacy amounted to nothing. She made one short cruise, during which she fell in with two United States men-of-war, that avoided a fight with her on account of her superior strength. At the end of her cruise the war was over, and she was sold to the Mikado of Japan, whose flag she now carries.

The "Nashville" was an old side-wheel passenger-steamer, of which the Confederates had made a privateer. Her career was a short one. She made one trip to England as a blockade-runner, and on her return voyage she burned three or four United States merchantmen. She then put into the Great Ogeechee River, where she was blockaded by three Union men-of-war. The Confederates protected her by filling the river with torpedoes, and anchoring the ship at a point where the guns of a strong fort could

THE "NASHVILLE" BURNING A PRIZE.

beat back all assailants. Here she lay for several weeks, while the men on the blockaders were fuming at the thought that they were to be kept idle, like cats watching a rat-hole. At last Capt. Worden, who was there with his redoubtable monitor "Montauk," determined to destroy the privateer, despite the torpedoes and the big guns of the fort. He accordingly began a movement up the river, picking his way slowly through the obstructions. The fort began a lively cannonade; but Worden soon found that he had nothing to fear from that quarter, as the guns were not heavy enough to injure the iron sides of the little monitor. But, as he went up the river, the "Nashville" took the alarm and fled before him; and it seemed that the most the Union fleet could do would be to keep her from coming down again, for with her light draught she could keep well out of range of the monitor's guns. But one morning Worden perceived a strange commotion on the "Nashville;" and, looking carefully through his glass, he saw that she was aground. Now was his time; and at once he pushed forward to a point twelve hundred yards from her, and directly under the guns of Fort MacAllister. From this point he began a deliberate fire upon the doomed privateer. The great guns of the fort were roaring away, and their shells came crashing against the sides of the "Montauk;" but to this Worden paid no heed. It was splendid long-distance practice for his gunners; and, when they got the range, not a shot missed the stranded Confederate vessel. From his pilot-house Worden could see the crew of the "Nashville" escaping in boats, leaping into the water over the sides, — doing any thing to escape from that terribly destructive fire. All the time the great fifteen-inch shells were dropping into the vessel with fearful precision. By and by a heavy fog fell upon the scene; but the gunners on the "Montauk" knew where their enemy was, and kept up their steady fire, though they could see nothing. When the fog lifted, they saw the "Nashville" a mass of flames; and in a moment she blew up, covering the placid surface of the river with blackened fragments. Then the "Montauk" returned to her consorts, well satisfied with her day's work.

The last of the Confederate privateers to ravage the ocean was the "Shenandoah," originally an English merchant-vessel engaged in the East

India trade. She was large, fast, and strongly built; and the astute agent of the Confederacy knew, when he saw her lying in a Liverpool dock, that she was just calculated for a privateer. She was purchased by private parties, and set sail, carrying a large stock of coal and provisions, but no arms. By a strange coincidence, a second vessel left Liverpool the same day, carrying several mysterious gentlemen, who afterwards proved to be Confederate naval officers. The cargo of this second vessel consisted almost entirely of remarkably heavy cases marked "machinery." The two vessels, once out of English waters, showed great fondness for each other, and proceeded together to a deserted, barren island near Madeira. Here they anchored side by side; and the mysterious gentlemen, now resplendent in the gray and gold uniform of the Confederacy, stepped aboard the "Shenandoah." Then the cases were hoisted out of the hold of the smaller vessel; and, when the "machinery" was mounted on the gun-deck of the "Shenandoah," it proved to be a number of very fine steel-rifled cannon. Then the crew was mustered on the gun-deck, and informed that they were manning the new Confederate ship "Shenandoah;" and with a cheer the flag was hoisted at the peak, and the newly created ship-of-war started off in search of merchantmen to make bonfires of. From Madeira the cruiser made for the Southern Ocean, — a fresh field not yet ravaged by any Confederate vessel. This made the hunting all the better for the "Shenandoah," and she burned vessels right and left merrily. In the spring of 1865, she put into the harbor of Melbourne, Australia, where her officers were lavishly entertained by the citizens. Thence she proceeded to the northward, spending some time in the Indian Ocean, and skirting the Asiatic coast, until she reached Behrings Straits. Here she lay in wait for returning whalers, who in that season were apt to congregate in Behrings Sea in great numbers, ready for the long voyage around Cape Horn to their home ports on the New England coast. Capt. Waddell was not disappointed in his expectations, for he reached the straits just as the returning whalers were coming out in a body. One day he captured eleven in a bunch. With one-third his crew standing at the guns ready to fire upon any vessel that should attempt to get up sail, Waddell kept the rest of his men rowing from

"SHENANDOAH" BURNING WHALERS.

ship to ship, taking off the crews. Finally all the prisoners were put aboard three of the whalers, and the eight empty ships were set afire. It was a grand spectacle. On every side were the towering icebergs, whose glassy sides reflected the lurid glare from the burning ships. Great black volumes of smoke arose from the blazing oil into the clear blue northern sky. The ruined men crowded upon the three whalers saw the fruits of their years of labor thus destroyed in an afternoon, and heaped curses upon the heads of the men who had thus robbed them. What wonder if, in the face of such apparently wanton destruction as this, they overlooked the niceties of the law of war, and called their captors pirates! Yet for the men of the "Shenandoah" it was no pleasant duty to thus cruise about the world, burning and destroying private property, and doing warfare only against unarmed people. More than one has left on record his complaint of the utter unpleasantness of the duty; but all felt that they were aiding the cause for which their brothers at home were fighting, and so they went on in their work of destruction.

For two months more Waddell continued his depredations in the northern seas. Many a stout bark from New London or New Bedford fell a prey to his zeal for a cause that was even then lost. For the Confederacy had fallen. The last volley of the war had been discharged three months before. Of this Capt. Waddell was ignorant, and his warlike operations did not end until the captain of a British bark told him of the surrender of Lee and Johnston, and the end of the war. To continue his depredations longer would be piracy: so Capt. Waddell hauled down his Confederate flag, and heading for Liverpool surrendered his ship to the British authorities, by whom it was promptly transferred to the United States. So ended the last of the Confederate privateers.

CHAPTER XII.

WORK OF THE GULF SQUADRON.—THE FIGHT AT THE PASSES OF THE MISSISSIPPI.—DESTRUCTION OF THE SCHOONER "JUDAH."—THE BLOCKADE OF GALVESTON, AND CAPTURE OF THE "HARRIET LANE."

THE naval forces of the United States during the war may be roughly classified as the Atlantic fleets, the river navy, and the Gulf squadron. The vessels comprising the latter detachment enjoyed some light service during the opening months of the war; but, as the time went on, the blue-jackets of the Gulf squadron found that they had no reason to congratulate themselves on securing an easy berth. Their blockading duty was not so arduous as that of their brothers along the rugged Atlantic coast; but they were harassed continually by Confederate rams, which would make a dash into the fleet, strike heavy blows, and then fly up some convenient river far into the territory of the Confederacy. One such attack was made upon the squadron blockading the Mississippi in October, 1861.

Some eighty miles below New Orleans, the Mississippi divides into three great channels, which flow at wide angles from each other into the Gulf of Mexico. These streams flow between low marshy banks hardly higher than the muddy surface of the river, covered with thick growths of willows, and infested with reptiles and poisonous insects. The point from which these three streams diverge is known as the "Head of the Passes," and it was here that the blockading squadron of four vessels was stationed. The ships swung idly at their moorings for weeks. The pestilential vapors from the surrounding marshes were rapidly putting all the crews in the sick bay, while the clouds of gnats and mosquitoes that hung about made Jack's life a wretched one. They did not even have the pleasurable excitement of occasionally chasing a blockade-runner, for the wary merchants of New Orleans knew that there was absolutely no hope of running a vessel out through a river so effectually blockaded. And so the sailors idled away their time, smoking, singing, dancing to the music of a doleful fiddle, boxing with home-made canvas gloves that left big spots of black and blue where they struck, and generally wishing that "Johnny Reb" would show himself so that they might have some excitement, even if it did cost a few lives.

But while the blue-jackets at the mouth of the river were spending their time thus idly, the people in the beleaguered city higher up were vastly enraged at being thus cooped up, and were laying plans to drive their jailers away. Occasionally they would take a small fleet of flat boats, bind them together, and heap them high with tar, pitch, and light wood. Then the whole would be towed down the river, set on fire, and drifted down upon the fleet. The light of the great fire could be seen far off, and the war-ships would get up steam and dodge the roaring mass of flames as it came surging down on the swift current. So many trials of this sort failed, that finally the people of the Crescent City gave up this plan in disgust.

Their next plan seemed for a time successful. It was at four o'clock one October morning that the watch on the sloop-of-war "Richmond" suddenly saw a huge dark mass so close to the ship that it seemed fairly to have sprung from the water, and sweeping down rapidly. The alarm was quickly given, and the crew beat to quarters. Over the water from the other ships, now fully alarmed, came the roll of the drums beating the men to their guns. The dark object came on swiftly, and the word was passed from man to man, "It's a Confederate ram." And indeed it was the ram "Manassas," which the Confederates had been hard at work building in the New Orleans ship-yards, and on which they relied to drive the blockading squadron from the river. As she came rushing towards the "Richmond," two great lights higher up the river told of fire-rafts bearing down upon the fleet, and by the fitful glare three smaller gun-boats were seen coming to the assistance of the "Manassas." Clearly the Confederates were attacking in force.

The first volley from the fleet rattled harmlessly from the iron-clad sides of the "Manassas;" and, not heeding it, she swept on and plunged into the side of the "Richmond." The great iron prow cut deep into the wooden sides of the Union vessel. Heavy oaken timbers were splintered like laths, and the men were violently hurled to the deck. As the ram drew away, the blue-jackets sprang to their guns and gave her a volley. Some of the shots must have penetrated her armor, for she became unmanageable. But the darkness prevented the officers of the "Richmond" from seeing how much damage they had done, and they did not follow up their advantage. The strange panic that the sight of a ram so often brought upon sailors of the old school fell on the officers of this squadron, and they began hastily getting their ships out of the river. By this time four more Confederate steamers had come to the aid of the ram, and were cannonading the Northern fleet at long range. In their hurried attempt to escape, the "Richmond" and the "Vincennes" had run aground. The captain of the latter vessel, fearing capture, determined to fire his vessel and escape with his crew to the "Richmond." Accordingly he laid a slow-match to the magazine, lighted it, and then, wrapping his ship's colors about his waist in the most theatrical manner, abandoned his ship. But the plan was not altogether a success. As he left the ship, he was followed by a grizzled old sailor, who had seen too much fighting to believe in blowing up his own ship; and, when he saw the smoking slow-match, he hastily broke off the lighted end, and without saying a word threw it into the water. No one observed the action, and the crew of the "Vincennes" watched mournfully for their good ship to go up in a cloud of smoke and flame. After they had watched nearly an hour, they concluded something was wrong, and returned to their old quarters. By this time the enemy had given up the conflict, and the United States navy was one ship ahead for the old sailor's act of insubordination. The Confederate flotilla returned to New Orleans, and reported that they had driven the blockaders away.

There was great rejoicing in the city: windows were illuminated, and receptions were tendered to the officers of the Confederate fleet. But, while the rejoicing was still going on, the Union ships came quietly back to their old position, and the great river was as securely closed as ever.

About a month before the fight with the "Manassas," the blue-jackets

FORT PENSACOLA.

of the North scored for themselves a brilliant success in the harbor of Pensacola. The frigate "Colorado" was lying outside the harbor of that city, within clear view of the city front. For some weeks the sailors had been greatly interested in watching the activity of people on shore around a small schooner that was lying in a basin near the navy-yard. With a harbor so thoroughly blockaded as was that of Pensacola, there seemed really no need of new vessels; and the haste of the Confederates seemed inexplicable, until they saw through their glasses men at work mounting a heavy pivot-gun amidships. That made it clear that another privateer was being fitted out to ravage the seas and burn all vessels flying the United States flag. The gallant tars of the "Colorado" determined to go in and burn the privateer before she should have a chance to escape. It was an undertaking of great peril. The schooner was near the navy-yard, where one thousand men were ready to spring to her assistance at the first alarm. On the dock fronting the navy-yard were mounted a ten-inch columbiad and a twelve-pounder field-piece, so placed as to command the deck of the schooner and the wharf to which she was moored. Fort Pensacola, not far distant, was full of Confederate troops. But the Union sailors thought that the destruction of the privateer was of enough importance to warrant the risk, and they determined to try the adventure.

Accordingly, on the first dark night, four boats, containing one hundred officers, sailors, and marines, put off from the side of the "Colorado," and headed for the town. All was done with the most perfect silence. The tholes of the oars were wrapped in cloth to deaden their rattle in the rowlocks. No lights were carried. Not a word was spoken after the officers in muffled tones had given the order, "Give way." Through the darkness of the night the heavy boats glide on. Every man aboard has his work laid out for him, and each knows what he is to do. While the main body are to be engaged in beating back the guards, some are to spike the guns, and others to fire the schooner in several places. When within a hundred yards of the schooner, they are discovered by the sentry. As his ringing hail comes over the water, the sailors make no reply, but bend to the oars, and the boats fairly leap toward the wharf. Bang! goes the sentry's rifle; and the men in the hold of the schooner come rushing up just as the two boats dash against her side, and the sailors spring like cats over the bulwarks. One man was found guarding the guns on the wharf, and was shot down. Little time is needed to spike the guns, and then those on the wharf turn in to help their comrades on the schooner. Here the fighting is sharp and hand to hand. Nearly a hundred men are

DESTRUCTION OF THE SCHOONER "JUDAH."

crowded on the deck, and deal pistol-shots and cutlass-blows right and left. Several of the crew of the schooner have climbed into the tops, and from that point of vantage pour down on the attacking party a murderous fire. Horrid yells go up from the enraged combatants, and the roar of the musketry is deafening. The crew of the schooner are forced backward, step by step, until at last they are driven off the vessel altogether, and stand on the wharf delivering a rapid fire. The men from the navy-yard are beginning to pour down to the wharf to take a hand in the fight. But now a column of smoke begins to arise from the open companionway; and the blue-jackets see that their work is done, and tumble over the side into their boats. It is high time for them to leave, for the Confederates are on the wharf in overwhelming force. As they stand there, crowded together, the retiring sailors open on them with canister from two howitzers in the boats. Six rounds of this sort of firing sends the Confederates looking for shelter; and the sailors pull off through the darkness to their ship, there to watch the burning vessel, until, with a sudden burst of flame, she is blown to pieces.

Considering the dashing nature of this exploit, the loss of life was wonderfully small. Lieut. Blake, who commanded one of the boats, was saved by one of those strange accidents so common in war. As he was going over the side of the "Colorado," some one handed him a metal flask filled with brandy, to be used for the wounded. He dropped it into the lower pocket of his overcoat, but, finding it uncomfortable there, changed it to the side pocket of his coat, immediately over his heart. When the boats touched the side of the schooner, Blake was one of the first to spring into the chains and clamber aboard. Just as he was springing over the gunwale, a Confederate sailor pointed a pistol at his heart, and fired it just as Blake cut him down with a savage cutlass-stroke. The bullet sped true to its mark, but struck the flask, and had just enough force to perforate it, without doing any injury to the lieutenant.

The first death in the fight was a sad one. A marine, the first man to board the schooner, lost his distinguishing white cap in his leap. His comrades followed fast behind him, and, seeing that he wore no cap, took him for one of the enemy, and plunged their bayonets deep in his breast, killing him instantly. He was known to his comrades as John Smith, but on searching his bag letters were found proving that this was not his own name. One from his mother begged him to return home, and give up his roving life. He proved to be a well-educated young man, who through fear of some disgrace had enlisted in the marines to hide himself from the world.

Another dashing event occurred on the Gulf Coast some months later, although in this instance the Confederates were the assailants and the victors. Galveston had for some time been in the hands of the Union forces, and was occupied by three regiments of United States troops. In the harbor lay three men-of-war, whose cannon kept the town in subjection. It had been rumored for some time that the Confederates were planning to re-capture the city, and accordingly the most vigilant lookout was kept from all the ships. On the 1st of January, 1863, at half-past one A.M., as the lookout on the "Harriet Lane" was thinking of the new year just ushered in, and wondering whether before the end of that year he could see again his cosey Northern home and wife and friends, he saw far up the river a cloud of black smoke, that rose high in the air, and blotted from sight the shining winter stars. He rubbed his eyes, and looked again. There was no mistake: the smoke was there, and rapidly moving toward him. Clearly it was a steamer coming down the river; but whether an armed enemy or a blockade-runner, he could not say. He gave the alarm; and in a moment the roll of the drums made the sailors below spring from their hammocks, and, hastily throwing on their clothes, rush on deck. The drums beat to quarters, and the crew were soon at their guns. Over the water came the roll of the drums from the other ships, and from the troops on shore, now all aroused and in arms For thirty hours the Federals had been expecting this attack, and now they were fully prepared for it.

The attacking vessels came nearer, and the men on the Union ships strained their eyes to see by the faint starlight what manner of craft they had to meet. They proved to be two large river-steamships, piled high with cotton-bales, crowded with armed men, and provided with a few field-

CAPTURE OF THE "HARRIET LANE."

pieces. Clearly they were only dangerous at close quarters, and the
"Lane" at once began a rapid fire to beat them back. But the bad light
spoiled her gunners' aim, and she determined to rush upon the enemy, and
run him down. The Confederate captain managed his helm skilfully, and
the "Lane" struck only a glancing blow. Then, in her turn, the "Lane"
was rammed by the Confederate steamer, which plunged into her with a
crash and a shock which seemed almost to lift the ships out of water. The
two vessels drifted apart, the "Lane" hardly injured, but the Confederate
with a gaping wound in his bow which sent him to the bottom in fifteen
minutes. But now the other Confederate came bearing down under a full
head of steam, and crashed into the "Lane." Evidently the Confederates
wanted to fight in the old style; for they threw out grappling-irons, lashed
the two ships side to side, and began pouring on to the deck of the
Federal ship for a hand-to-hand conflict. Cries of anger and pain, pistol-
shots, cutlass blows, and occasional roars from the howitzers rose on the
night air, and were answered by the sounds of battle from the shore, where
the Confederates had attacked the slender Union garrison. The sinking
steamer took up a position near the "Lane," and poured broadside after
broadside upon the struggling Union ship. But where were the other three
Union vessels all this time? It seemed as though their commanders had
lost all their coolness; for they ran their vessels here and there, now trying
to do something to help their friends on shore, now making an ineffectual
attempt to aid the "Harriet Lane." But on board that vessel matters
were going badly for the Federals. The Confederates in great numbers
kept pouring over the bulwarks, and were rapidly driving the crew from the
deck. Capt. Wainwright lay dead at the door of the cabin. Across his
body stood his young son, his eyes blazing, his hair waving in the wind.
He held in his right hand a huge revolver, which he was firing without
aim into the tossing mass of struggling men before him, while he called on
his dead father to rise and help him. A stray bullet cut off two of his
fingers, and the pain was too much for the little hero only ten years old;
and, dropping the pistol, he burst into tears, crying, "Do you want to kill
me?" The blue-jackets began to look anxiously for help toward the other

vessels. But, even while they looked, they saw all hope of help cut off; for with a crash and a burst of flame the "Westfield" blew up. It turned out later, that, finding his ship aground, the captain of the "Westfield" had determined to abandon her, and fire the magazine; but in fixing his train he made a fatal error, and the ship blew up, hurling captain and crew into the air. The men on the "Harriet Lane" saw that all hope was gone, and surrendered their ship. When the captains of the two remaining gunboats saw the stars and stripes fall from the peak, they turned their vessels' prows toward the sea, and scudded out of danger of capture. At the same moment, cheers from the gray-coats on shore told that the Confederates had been successful both by land and sea, and the stars and bars once more floated over Galveston.

CHAPTER XIII.

THE CAPTURE OF NEW ORLEANS.—FARRAGUT'S FLEET PASSES FORT ST. PHILIP AND FORT JACKSON.

WHILE Commodore Foote, with his flotilla of gunboats and mortar-boats, was working his way down the Mississippi River, making occasional dashes into the broad streams that flow from either side into the father of waters, Admiral Farragut, with his fleet of tall-sparred, ocean-going men-of-war, was laying his plans for an expedition up-stream. But Farragut's first obstacle lay very near the mouth of the broad, tawny river that flows for a thousand miles through the centre of the United States. New Orleans, the greatest city of the Confederacy, stands on the river's bank, only ninety miles from the blue waters of the Gulf of Mexico. The Confederate authorities knew the value of this great city to their cause, and were careful not to let it go unprotected. Long before any thought of civil war disturbed the minds of the people of the United States, the Federal Government had built below the Crescent City two forts, that peered at each other across the swift, turbid tide of the Mississippi River. Fort St. Philip and Fort Jackson they were called, the latter being named in honor of the stubborn old military hero who beat back the British soldiers at the close of the war of 1812 on the glorious field of Chalmette near New Orleans. Fort Jackson was a huge star of stone and mortar. In its massive walls were great cavernous bomb-proofs in which the soldiers were secure from bursting shells. It stood back about a hundred yards from the levee, and its casemates just rose above the huge dike that keeps the Mississippi in its proper channel. When the river was high from the spring floods of the north, a steamer floating on its swift tide towered high above the bastions of the fort. In the casemates and on the parapets were mounted seventy-five guns of all calibres. By its peculiar shape and situation on a jutting point of land, the fort was able to bring its guns to bear upon the river in three directions.

When the storm of civil war burst upon the country, the Confederates of New Orleans were prompt to seize this and Fort St. Philip, that stood on the other side of the river. They found Fort Jackson in the state of general decay into which most army posts fall in times of peace, and they set at work at once to strengthen it. All over the parapet, bomb-proofs, and weak points, bags of sand were piled five or six feet deep, making the strongest defence known in war. Steamers plied up and down the river, bringing provision, ammunition, and new cannon, and soon the fort was ready to stand the most determined siege. Fort St. Philip, across the river, though not so imposing a military work, was more powerful. It was built of masonry, and heavily sodded over all points exposed to fire. It was more irregular in shape than Fort Jackson, and with its guns seemed to command every point on the river. Both were amply protected from storming by wide, deep moats always filled with water.

In these two forts were stationed troops made up of the finest young men of New Orleans. For them it was a gay station. Far removed from the fighting on the frontier, and within an easy journey of their homes, they frolicked away the first year of the war. Every week gay parties of pleasure-seekers from New Orleans would come down; and the proud defenders would take their friends to the frowning bastions, and point out how easily they could blow the enemy's fleet out of water if the ships ever came within range of those heavy guns. But the ships did not come within range of the guns for many months. They contented themselves with lying at the Head of the Passes, and stopping all intercourse with the outer world,

LEVEE AT NEW ORLEANS BEFORE THE WAR.

until New Orleans began to get shabby and ragged and hungry, and the pleasure-parties came less often to the forts, and the gay young soldiers saw their uniforms getting old and tattered, but knew not where to get the cloth to replace them.

In the city no rumble of commerce was heard on the streets. Grass grew on the deserted levee, where in times of peace the brown and white cotton-bales were piled by the thousand, waiting for strong black hands to seize and swing them upon the decks of the trim Liverpool packets, that lay three or four deep along the river front. The huge gray custom-house that stood at the foot of Canal Street no longer resounded with the rapid tread of sea-captains or busy merchants. From the pipes of the cotton-presses, the rush of the escaping steam, as the ruthless press squeezed the great bale into one-third its original size, was no longer heard. Most of the great towering steamboats that came rushing down the river with stores of cotton or sugar had long since been cut down into squat, powerful gunboats, or were tied up idly to the bank. Across the river, in the ship-yards of Algiers, there seemed a little more life; for there workmen were busy changing peaceful merchant vessels into gunboats and rams, that were, the people fondly hoped, to drive away the men-of-war at the river's mouth and save the city from starvation. From time to time the streets of the city resounded with the notes of drum and fife, as one after the other the militia companies went off to the front and the fighting. Then the time came when none were left save the "Confederate Guards," old gray-haired men, judges, bankers, merchants, gentlemen of every degree, too old for active service at the front, but too young not to burn for the grasp of a gun or sword while they knew that their sons and grandsons were fighting on the blood-stained soil of Virginia and Tennessee.

But, while the city was gradually falling into desolation and decay, preparations were being made by the Federal navy for its capture. On the 2d of February, 1862, Admiral Farragut sailed from Hampton Roads in his stanch frigate the "Hartford," to take command of a naval expedition intended to capture New Orleans. The place of rendezvous was Ship Island, a sandy island in the Gulf of Mexico. Here he organized his squadron, and started for his post in the Mississippi, below the forts.

The first obstacle was found at the mouth of the river, where the heavy war-vessels were unable to make their way over the bar. Nearly two weeks were occupied in the work of lightening these ships until they were able to pass. The frigate "Colorado" was unable to get over at all. The "Pensacola" was dragged through the mud by the sheer strength of other vessels of the expedition. While they were tugging at her, a huge hawser snapped with a report like a cannon, and the flying ends killed two men and seriously wounded five others. But at last the fleet was safely past all obstacles, and Admiral Farragut found himself well established in the lower Mississippi, with a force of twenty-five men-of-war, and twenty mortar-schooners; one of the most powerful armadas ever despatched against an enemy. Farragut lost no time in getting his ships prepared for the baptism of fire which was sure to come. While he was diligently at work on his preparations, he was visited by some French and English naval officers, who had carefully examined the defences of the Confederates, and came to warn him that to attack the forts with wooden vessels, such as made up his fleet, was sheer madness, and would only result in defeat. "You may be right," answered the brave old sailor, "but I was sent here to make the attempt. I came here to reduce or pass the forts, and to take New Orleans, *and I shall try it on.*" The foreigners remarked that he was going to certain destruction, and politely withdrew.

In the mean time, the tars on the mortar-fleet were working industriously to get their ships in fighting-trim. The topmasts were stripped of their sails, and lowered; the loose and standing rigging strapped to the masts; the spars, forebooms, and gaffs unshipped, and secured to the outside of the vessels to avert the danger from splinters, which, in naval actions, is often greater than from the shots themselves. From the main-deck every thing was removed that could obstruct the easy handling of the tremendous mortars; and the men were drilled to skill and alertness in firing the huge engines of death. The work was hastened on the mortar-schooners, because the plan was to rush them into position, and let them harass the Confederates with a steady bombardment, while the ships-of-war were preparing for their part in the coming fight.

The mortar-fleet was under command of Admiral Porter, an able and energetic officer. He soon had his ships ready, and began moving them into position along the banks of the river, out of sight of the forts. To further conceal them from the gunners in the forts, he had the masts and rigging wrapped with green foliage; so that, lying against the dense thickets of willows that skirt that part of the river, they were invisible. Other boats that were in more exposed positions had their hulls covered with grass and reeds, so that they seemed a part of the swamp that bordered the river. After the line of fire had been obtained by a careful mathematical survey, Porter got all his mortar-boats into position, and began his bombardment. The gunners on the mortar-boats could not see the forts; but the range had been calculated for them, and they merely fired mechanically. A lookout, perched on the masthead, could see over the low willow-forest, and watch the course of the shells as they rushed high into the air, and then, falling with a graceful curve, plunged into the forts. The firing was begun on the 16th of April, and was kept up with a will. The twenty huge mortars keeping up a constant fire, made a deafening roar that shook the earth, and could be heard far up the river at New Orleans, where the people poured out into the streets, and gayly predicted defeat for any enemy who should attack "the boys in the forts." The forts were not slow in returning the fire; but as the mortar-vessels were hidden, and did not offer very large marks, their fire was rather ineffective. Parties of Confederates, old swamp-hunters, and skilled riflemen, stole down through the dense thickets, to pick off the crews of the mortar-schooners. They managed to kill a few gunners in this way, but were soon driven away by the point-blank fire of the supporting gunboats. But all this time the shells were falling thick and fast, driving the soldiers to the bomb-proofs, and tearing to pieces every thing unprotected. One shell set fire to some wooden structures that stood on the parade-ground in Fort Jackson; and, as the smoke and flames rose in the air, the gunners down the river thought that the fort was burning, and cheered and fired with renewed vigor. The shells that burst upon the levee soon cut great trenches in it, so that the mighty Mississippi broke through with a rush, and flooded the country all about. But the forts seemed as strong and unconquered as ever.

While the soldiers were crowded together in the bomb-proofs to escape the flying bits of shell, the sailors on the little fleet of Confederate vessels anchored above them were busily engaged in getting ready a fire-raft which was to float down the river, and make havoc among the vessels of the Union fleet. Two such rafts were prepared; one of which, an immense affair, carrying cords of blazing pine-wood, was sent down in the early morning at a time when the vessels were utterly unprepared to defend themselves. Luckily it grounded on a sandbar, and burned and crackled away harmlessly until it was consumed. This warned Commander Porter of the danger in which his mortar-vessels were of a second attack of the same nature; and accordingly he put in readiness one hundred and fifty small boats with picked crews, and well supplied with axes and grapnels, whose duty it was to grapple any future rafts, and tow them into a harmless position. They did not have long to wait. At sundown that night, Commander Porter reviewed his little squadron of row-boats as they lay drawn up in line along the low marshy shores of the mighty river. The sun sank a glowing red ball beneath the line at which the blue waters of the gulf and the blue arch of heaven seemed to meet. The long southern twilight gradually deepened into a black, moonless night. The cries of frogs and seabirds, and the little flashes of the fireflies, were silenced and blotted out by the incessant roar and flash of the tremendous mortars that kept up their deadly work. Suddenly in the distance the sky grows red and lurid. "The fort is burning!" cry the men at the guns; but from the masthead comes the response, "No, the fire is on the river. It is another fire-raft." The alarm was instantly given to all the vessels of the fleet. Bright colored signal-lights blazed on the decks, and the dark, slender cordage stood out against the brilliant red and green fires that flickered strangely upon the dark wooded banks of the river. Rockets rushed high into the air, and, bursting, let fall a shower of party-colored lights that told the watchers far down the river that danger was to be expected. Then the signal-lights went out, and all was dark and silent save where the lurid glare of the great mass of fire could be seen floating in the great curves of the tortuous river toward the crowded ships. It was a time of intense suspense. The little flotilla of fire-boats, organized by Commander Porter that day, was on the alert; and the blue-jackets bent to their oars with a will, and soon had their boats ranged along a bend far above the fleet. Here they waited to catch the fiery monster, and save the ships. The danger came nearer fast. Rapidly the flames increased in volume, until the whole surrounding region was lighted up by the glare; while from the floating fire, a huge black column of smoke arose, and blended with the clouds that glowed as though they themselves were on fire. When the raft came into view around a point, it was seen to be too big for the boats to handle unaided, and two gunboats slipped their cables, and started for the thing of terror. From every side the row-boats dashed at the raft. Some grappled it, and the sailors tugged lustily at their oars, seeking to drag the mass of flames toward the shore. Then the "Westfield," under full head of steam, dashed furiously against the raft, crashing in the timbers and sending great clouds of sparks flying high in the air. From her hose-pipes she poured floods of water on the crackling, roaring, blazing mass; while all the time, with her powerful engines, she was pushing it toward the shore.

In the mean time, the sailors from the fleet of small boats were swarming upon the raft wherever they could find a foot-hold free from flame. Some carrying buckets dashed water upon the flames, some with axes cut loose flaming timbers, and let them float harmlessly down the river. It was a fight in which all the men were on one side; but it was a grand sight, and was eagerly watched by those on the imperilled vessels. The immediate arena of the conflict was bright as day, but all around was gloom. At last the pluck and determination of the men triumph over the flames. The raft, flaming, smouldering, broken, is towed out of the channel, and left to end its life in fitful flashes on a sandy point. The returning boats are greeted with cheers, and soon darkness and silence fall upon the scene. The mortars cease their thunderous work for the night; and ere long the only sounds heard are the rush of the mighty waters,

FIRE-RAFT AT FORTS OF THE MISSISSIPPI.

or the faint cry of the night-birds in the forest. The sentinel pacing the deck peers in vain through the gloom. War gives way for a time to rest.

Hardly had the gray dawn begun to appear, when the roll of the drums on the decks of the ships was heard; and, soon after, the roar of the opening gun was heard from one of the mortar-schooners. Again the bombardment was opened. The twenty boats in the mortar-fleet were divided into three divisions, each of which fired for two hours in succession, and then stopped for a time to allow the great cannon to cool. Thus a continuous bombardment was kept up, and the soldiers in the forts were given no time to repair the damages caused by the bursting shells. Every mortar was fired once in five minutes; so that one shell was hurled towards the fort about every minute, while sometimes three shells would be seen sweeping with majestic curves through the air at the same time. The shells weighed two hundred and fifteen pounds; and when they were hurled into the air by the explosion of twenty pounds of powder, the boat bearing the mortar was driven down into the water six or eight inches, and the light railings and woodwork of buildings at the Balize, thirty miles away, were shattered by the concussion. The shells rose high in the air, with an unearthly shriek, and after a curve of a mile and a half fell into or near the forts, and, bursting, threw their deadly fragments in all directions. Day after day, and night after night, this went on. If the men on the mortar-schooners showed bravery and endurance in keeping up so exhausting a fire so steadily, what shall we say for the men in the forts who bore up against it so nobly? Before noon of the first day of the bombardment, the soldiers of Fort Jackson saw their barracks burned, with their clothing, bedding, and several days' rations. Shells were pouring in upon them from vessels that they could not see. The smooth-bore guns mounted in the embrasures would hardly send a shot to the nearest of the hostile gunboats. Then the river broke through its banks, and half the fort was transformed into a morass. An officer in Fort Jackson said, after the surrender, that in two hours over one hundred shells had fallen upon the parade-ground of that work, tearing it up terribly. For six days this terrible fire was endured;

and during the latter half of the bombardment the water stood knee deep on the gun-platforms, and the gunners worked at their guns until their shoes, soaked for days and days, fairly fell from their feet. For bed and bedding they had the wet earth, for rations raw meat and mouldy bread. If there were glory and victory for the Union sailors, let there at least be honor and credit granted the soldiers of the gray for the dogged courage with which they bore the terrible bombardment from Porter's flotilla.

While the mortars were pounding away through those six long days and nights, Farragut was getting ready to take his ships past the forts. Union scouts and spies had travelled over every foot of land and water about the forts; and the exact strength of the Confederates, and the difficulties to be overcome, were clearly known to the Federal admiral. One of the chief obstructions was a chain of rafts and old hulks that stretched across the channel by which the fleet would be obliged to ascend the river. Under cover of a tremendous fire from all the mortars, two gunboats were sent up to remove this obstruction. The night was dark and favorable to the enterprise, and the vessels reached the chain before they were discovered. Then, under a fierce cannonade from the forts, Lieut. Caldwell put off in a row-boat from his vessel, boarded one of the hulks, and managed to break the chain. The string of hulks was quickly swept ashore by the swift current, and the channel was open for the ascent of the Union fleet.

On the 23d of April, Farragut determined that his fleet should make the attempt to get past the forts the following day. He knew that the enemy must be exhausted with the terrible strain of Porter's bombardment, and he felt that the opportunity had arrived for him to make a successful dash for the upper river. The fleet was all prepared for a desperate struggle. Many of the captains had daubed the sides of their vessels with the river mud, that they might be less prominent marks for the Confederate gunners. The chain cables of all the vessels were coiled about vulnerable parts, or draped over the sides amidships to protect the boilers. Knowing that it was to be a night action, the gun-decks had been whitewashed; so that even by the dim, uncertain light of the battle lanterns, the gunners could see plainly all objects about them. Hammocks and nettings were stretched

BREAKING THE CHAIN.

above the decks to catch flying splinters from the spars overhead. Late at night the admiral in his longboat was pulled from ship to ship to view the preparations made, and see that each captain fully understood his orders.

It was two o'clock on the morning of the 24th of April, when the Confederates on the parapets of their forts might have heard the shrill notes of fifes, the steady tramp of men, the sharp clicking of capstans, and the grating of chain cables passing through the hawse-holes on the ships below. Indeed, it is probable that these sounds were heard at the forts, and were understood, for the Confederates were on the alert when the ships came steaming up the river.

They formed in a stately line of battle, headed by the "Cayuga." As they came up the stream, the gunners in the forts could see the mastheads over the low willow thickets that bordered the banks of the stream. The line of obstructions was reached and passed, and then the whole furious fire of both forts fell upon the advancing ships. Gallantly they kept on their way, firing thunderous broadsides from each side. And, while the ships were under the direct fire of the forts, the enemy's fleet came dashing down the river to dispute the way. This was more to the taste of Farragut and his boys in blue. They were tired of fighting stone walls. In the van of the Confederate squadron was the ram "Manassas," that had created such a panic among the blockading squadron a month before. She plunged desperately into the fight. The great frigate "Brooklyn" was a prominent vessel in the Union line, and at her the ram dashed. The bold hearts on the grand old frigate did not seek to avoid the conflict, and the two vessels rushed together. The ram struck the "Brooklyn" a glancing blow; and the shot from her one gun was returned by a hail of cannon-balls from the frigate's tremendous broadside, many of which broke through the iron plating. Nothing daunted, the ram backed off and rushed at the frigate again. This time she struck full on the frigate's side. The shock was terrible. Men on the gun-deck of the ram were hurled to the deck, with the blood streaming from their nostrils. The frigate keeled over farther and farther, until all thought that she would be borne beneath the

RAM "TENNESSEE" AT MOBILE BAY.

water by the pressure of the ram. All the time the spiteful bow-gun of the iron monster was hurling its bolts into her hull. But the blow of the ram had done no damage, for she had struck one of the coils of chain that had been hung down the "Brooklyn's" side. The two vessels slowly swung apart; and, after a final broadside from the "Brooklyn," the "Manassas" drifted away in the pitchy darkness to seek for new adversaries. She was not long in finding one; for as the gray dawn was breaking she suddenly found herself under the very bows of the "Mississippi," which was bearing down upon her and seemed sure to run her down. The captain of the "Manassas" was an able steersman, and neatly dodged the blow; but in this quick movement he ran his vessel ashore, and she lay there under the guns of the "Mississippi," and unable to bring any of her own guns to bear. The captain of the frigate was not slow in taking advantage of this chance to be revenged for all the trouble she had given the Union fleet; and he took up a good position, and pounded away with his heavy guns at the iron monster. The heavy shots crashed through the iron plating and came plunging in the portholes, seeking every nook and cranny about the vessel. It was too much for men to stand, and the crew of the "Manassas" fled to the woods; while their vessel was soon set on fire with red-hot shots, and blew up with a tremendous report soon after.

In the mean time, the ships of the Union fleet were doing daring work, and meeting a determined resistance. The flag-ship "Hartford" was met by a tug which pushed a huge burning fire-raft against her sides. There the flaming thing lay right up against the port-holes, the flames catching the tarred rigging, and running up the masts. Farragut walked his quarter-deck as coolly as though the ship was on parade. "Don't flinch from that fire, boys," he sang out, as the flames rushed in the port-holes, and drove the men from their guns. "There's a hotter fire than that for those who don't do their duty. Give that rascally little tug a shot, and don't let her go off with a whole coat." But the tug did get away, after all; and no one can feel sorry that men plucky enough to take an unarmed tug into a terrible fight of frigates and ironclads should escape with their lives. The men on the "Hartford" fought the flames with hose and buckets, and at last got rid of their dangerous neighbor. Then they saw a steamer crowded with men rushing toward the flag-ship without firing a shot, and evidently intending to board. Capt. Broome, with a crew of marines, was working a bow-gun on the "Hartford." Carefully he trained the huge piece upon the approaching steamer. He stepped back, stooped for a last glance along the sights, then with a quick pull of the lanyard the great gun went off with a roar, followed instantly by a louder explosion from the attacking steamer. When the smoke cleared away, all looked eagerly for the enemy; but she had vanished as if by magic. That single shot, striking her magazine, had blown her up with all on board.

Much of the hardest fighting was done by the smaller vessels on either side. The little Confederate "cotton-clad" "Governor Moore" made a desperate fight, dashing through the Union fleet, taking and giving broadsides in every direction. The Union vessel "Varuna" also did daring work, and naturally these two ships met in desperate conflict. After exchanging broadsides, the "Governor Moore" rammed her adversary, and, while bearing down on her, received a severe raking fire from the "Varuna." The "Governor Moore" was in such a position that none of her guns could be brought to bear; but her captain suddenly depressed the muzzle of his bow-gun, and sent a shot crashing through *his own* deck and side, and deep into the hull of the "Varuna." The vessels soon parted, but the "Varuna" had received her death-wound, and sank in shallow water. The "Governor Moore" kept on her way, but was knocked to pieces by the fire from the heavy guns of the frigates shortly after.

And so the battle raged for five hours. To recount in full the deeds of valor done, would be to tell the story of each ship engaged, and would require volumes. Witnesses who saw the fight from the start were deeply impressed by the majesty of the scene. It was like a grand panorama. "From almost perfect silence, — the steamers moving through the water like phantom ships, — one incessant roar of heavy cannon commenced, the Confederate forts and gunboats opening together on the head of our line as it came within range. The Union vessels returned the fire as they came up, and soon the hundred and seventy guns of our fleet joined in the thunder which seemed to shake the very earth. A lurid glare was thrown over the scene by the burning rafts; and, as the bombshells crossed each other and exploded in the air, it seemed as if a battle were taking place in the heavens as well as on the earth. It all ended as suddenly as it commenced."

While this gigantic contest was going on in the river abreast of the forts, the people of New Orleans were thronging the streets, listening to the unceasing roar of the great guns, and discussing, with pale faces and anxious hearts, the outcome of the fight. "Farragut can never pass our forts. His wooden ships will be blown to pieces by their fire, or dashed into atoms by the 'Manassas,'" people said. But many listened in silence: they had husbands, sons, or brothers in that fearful fight, and who could tell that they would return alive? By and by the firing ceased. Only an occasional shot broke the stillness of the morning. Then came the suspense. Had the fleet been beaten back, or was it above the forts, and even now sullenly steaming up to the city? Everybody rushed for the housetops to look to the southward, over the low land through which the Mississippi winds. An hour's waiting, and they see curls of smoke rising above the trees, then slender dark lines moving along above the treetops. "Are they our ships?" every one cries; and no one answers until the dark lines are seen to be crossed by others at right angles. They are masts with yard-arms, masts of sea-going vessels, the masts of the invader's fleet. A cry of grief, of fear, of rage, goes up from the housetops. "To the levee!" cry the men, and soon the streets resound with the rush of many feet toward the river. "The river is crooked, and its current swift. It will be hours before the Yankees can arrive: let us burn, destroy, that they may find no booty." Let one who was in the sorrowful city that terrible April day tell the story. "I went to the river-side. There, until far into the night, I saw hundreds of drays carrying cotton out of the presses and yards to the wharves, where it was fired. The glare of those sinuous miles of flame set men and women weeping and wailing thirty miles away, on the farther shore of Lake Pontchartrain. But the next day was the day of terrors. During the night, fear, wrath, and sense of betrayal, had run through the people as the fire had run through the cotton. You have seen, perhaps, a family fleeing, with lamentations and wringing of hands, out of a burning house; multiply it by thousands upon thousands: that was New Orleans, though the houses were not burning. The firemen were out; but they cast fire on the waters, putting the torch to the empty ships and cutting them loose to float down the river.

"Whoever could go was going. The great mass that had no place to go to, or means to go with, was beside itself. 'Betrayed! bètrayed!' it cried, and ran in throngs from street to street, seeking some vent, some victim for its wrath. I saw a crowd catch a poor fellow at the corner of Magazine and Common Streets, whose crime was that he looked like a stranger and might be a spy. He was the palest living man I ever saw. They swung him to a neighboring lamp-post; but the Foreign Legion was patroling the town in strong squads, and one of its lieutenants, all green and gold, leaped with drawn sword, cut the rope, and saved the man. This was one occurrence; there were many like it. I stood in the rear door of our store, Canal Street, soon after re-opening it. The junior of the firm was within. I called him to look toward the river. The masts of the cutter 'Washington' were slowly tipping, declining, sinking — down she went. The gunboat moored next her began to smoke all over and then to blaze. My employers lifted up their heels and left the city, left their goods and their affairs in the hands of one mere lad — no stranger would have thought I had reached fourteen — and one big German porter. I closed the doors, sent the porter to his place in the Foreign Legion, and ran to the levee to see the sights.

"What a gathering! — the riff-raff of the wharves, the town, the gutters. Such women! such wrecks of women! and all the juvenile rag-tag. The lower steamboat-landing, well covered with sugar, rice, and molasses, was being rifled. The men smashed; the women scooped up the smashings. The river was overflowing the top of the levee. A rain-storm began to threaten. 'Are the Yankee ships in sight?' I asked of an idler. He pointed out the tops of their naked masts as they showed up across the huge bend of the river. They were engaging the batteries at Camp

NEW ORLEANS ON THE APPROACH OF THE FLEET.

Chalmette, the old field of Jackson's renown. Presently that was over. Ah, me! I see them now as they come slowly round Slaughterhouse Point, into full view: silent, so grim and terrible, black with men, heavy with deadly portent, the long banished stars and stripes flying against the frowning sky. Oh for the 'Mississippi,' the 'Mississippi!' Just then she came down upon them. But how? Drifting helplessly, a mass of flames.

"The crowds on the levee howled and screamed with rage. The swarming decks answered never a word; but one old tar on the 'Hartford,' standing with lanyard in hand, beside a great pivot-gun, so plain to view that you could see him smile, silently patted its big black breech and blandly grinned."

As the masts of the fleet came up the river, a young man stepped out upon the roof of the City Hall, and swiftly hoisted the flag of the State of Louisiana. When the ships came up, two officers were sent ashore to demand the surrender of the city; and shoulder to shoulder the two old sailors marched through a howling, cursing mob to the City Hall. The mayor refused to surrender the city, saying that Farragut already had captured it. The officers went back to their ships, and the flag still floated. Two days later the officers, with a hundred sailors and marines, returned and demanded that the flag be hauled down. No one in the city would tear it down, and the Federals went up to the roof to lower it themselves. The street and surrounding housetops were crowded with a hostile people, all armed. No one could tell that the fall of the flag would not be followed by a volley from the undisciplined populace. The marines in front of the building stood grouped about two loaded howitzers that bore upon the darkly muttering crowd. Violence was in the air. As the two officers rose to go to the roof, the mayor, a young Creole, left the room and descended the stairs. Quietly he stepped out into the street, and without a word stood before one of the howitzers, his arms folded, eying the gunner, who stood with lanyard in hand, ready to fire at the word of command. The flag fell slowly from the staff. Not a sound arose from the crowd. All were watching the mayor, who stood coldly looking on death. The

Federal officers came down carrying the flag. A few sharp commands, and the marines tramped away down the street, with the howitzers clanking behind them. The crowd cheered for Mayor Monroe and dispersed, and New Orleans became again a city of the United States.

CHAPTER XIV.

ALONG THE MISSISSIPPI. — FORTS JACKSON AND ST. PHILIP SURRENDER. — THE BATTLE AT ST. CHARLES. — THE RAM "ARKANSAS." — BOMBARDMENT AND CAPTURE OF PORT HUDSON.

WHILE New Orleans was thus excited over the capture of the city, the soldiers in the forts below were debating as to the course they should adopt. They had not surrendered; and although the great bastions were pounded out of shape by the heavy guns of the fleet, yet they were still formidable defences, giving perfect security to the men in the bomb-proofs. But their case was hopeless: for Farragut was at New Orleans, and could cut off their supplies; while Porter, with his mortar-boats, was below them, putting escape out of the question. Every now and then a big shell would drop on the parade, and its flying pieces would remind the garrison that their enemies were getting impatient. After waiting a day or two, Porter sent a lieutenant with a flag of truce to the fort, calling upon the Confederate commander to surrender the two forts and the shattered remnant of the Confederate navy. He complimented the Confederates upon their gallant defence, but warned them, that, should they refuse to surrender, he would recommence his bombardment with new vigor. The Confederates refused to surrender until they heard from New Orleans; and the next day the monotonous thunder of the heavy mortars began again, and again the heavy shells began falling thick and fast upon the forts. Wearily the gray-coated soldiers settled down to continue what they felt must be a useless defence. The officers did their best to inspirit the men; but all knew that a surrender must come before long, and at last the men mutinously left their guns, and said they would fight no longer. They had borne without flinching a terrible bombardment, and now they felt that to fight longer would be a foolish sacrifice of life. Many left the forts, and plunged into the woods to escape the terrible shells. Gen. Duncan saw that all was lost, and on the night of the 28th of April sent an officer to the fleet announcing the surrender. On the following day Porter proceeded up-stream with his squadron, and anchored off the fort. A boat, manned by six trim sailors in dress uniforms, put off, and soon returned, bringing the commander of the defeated forces and two or three officers. They were received on the "Harriet Lane," and Commodore Porter had made great preparations for the meeting. The crews of all the vessels were dressed in snow-white mustering-suits, and the officers in brass-buttoned blue coats and white trousers. The decks were scrubbed, and all traces of the fight cleared away. As the Confederate officers came up to the fleet, one of them, a former lieutenant in the Union navy, said, "Look at the old navy. I feel proud when I see them. There are no half-breeds there: they are the simon-pure." As the Confederates came over the side, Porter stood, with his officers, ready to receive them. The greatest politeness was observed on either side; and Porter writes, "Their bearing was that of men who had gained a victory, instead of undergoing defeat." While the papers of capitulation were being signed, a message came from the deck that the huge Confederate ironclad "Louisiana" was drifting down upon them, a mass of flames, and there was great danger that she would blow up in the midst of the Union fleet. "This is sharp practice, gentlemen," said Porter, "and some of us will perhaps be blown up; but I know what to do. If you can stand what is coming, we can; but I will make it lively for those people if anybody in the flotilla is injured."

"I told Lieut. Wainwright to hail the steamer next him," writes Capt. Porter, "and tell her captain to pass the word for the others to veer out all their riding-chains to the bitter end, and stand by to sheer clear of the burning ironclad as she drifted down. I then sat down to the table, and said, 'Gentlemen, we will proceed to sign the capitulation.' I handed the paper to Gen. Duncan, and looked at the Confederate officers to see how they would behave under the circumstances of a great ironclad dropping down on them, all in flames, with twenty thousand pounds of powder in her magazines. For myself, I hoped the fire would not reach the powder until the ship had drifted some distance below us. My greatest fear was that she would run foul of some of the steamers.

"While I was thinking this over, the officers were sitting as coolly as if at tea-table among their friends.

"Just then there was a stir on deck, a kind of swaying of the vessel to and fro, a rumbling in the air, then an explosion which seemed to shake the heavens. The 'Harriet Lane' was thrown two streaks over, and every thing in the cabin was jostled from side to side ; but not a man left his seat, or showed any intention of doing so.

"I was glad that I had signed before the explosion took place, as I would not have liked to have my autograph look shaky."

The destruction of the "Louisiana" was a bit of trickery on the part of the Confederate naval officers, which Farragut punished by sending them North as close prisoners, while the army officers were granted freedom under parol. So ended the Confederate control over the mouth of the Mississippi ; and Porter, after waiting long enough to see a blue-coat garrison in Forts St. Philip and Jackson, started up the river to rejoin his chief in New Orleans.

But, on reaching the city, he found that the energetic admiral had already started out to clear the river of the Confederate batteries that lined it on either side as far up as Vicksburg. This was a service of no little danger, and one bringing but little satisfaction ; for no sooner had the gunboats left one point, from which by hard firing they had driven the Confederates, than the latter would return in force, build up again their shattered earthworks, mount new guns, and be once more ready for battle. But more powerful than these little one or two gun-batteries were the Confederate works at Port Hudson, the destruction of which was absolutely necessary for further Union successes on the great river. Between Port Hudson and Vicksburg, the river was completely under the control of the Confederates; and it was a powerful gunboat that could hope to navigate that stretch of water unharmed. Farragut determined to attack Port Hudson, and set the 14th of March, 1863, as the date for the action.

Port Hudson batteries were perched on a high bluff that overlooks one of those abrupt curves around which the current of the Mississippi River sweeps with such terrific force. The heavy guns bore down upon a point at which the ships would almost inevitably be swept out of their course by the swift stream, and where the river was filled with treacherous shifting shoals. Naval officers all agreed that to pass those batteries was a more difficult task than had been the passage of the forts below New Orleans; yet Farragut, eager to get at the stronghold of the foe in Vicksburg, determined to make the attempt. The mortar-vessels were stationed below to drive the enemy from his guns with well-directed bombs; while the fleet, led by the stanch old "Hartford," should make a bold dash up the river.

Night fell upon the scene; and the ships weighed anchor, and started upon their perilous voyage. To the side of each man-of-war was bound a gunboat to tow the great vessel out of danger in case of disaster. Silently the long string of vessels swept upward towards the batteries; but, as the "Hartford" came into range, the watchful Confederates gave the alarm, and the nearest battery at once opened fire. Then from Porter's mortar-schooners far down the river came an answering roar; and, as ship after ship came up into range, she opened with shot and shell upon the works. On the dark river-banks great alarm fires were kindled, lighting up the water with a lurid glare, and making the ships clearly visible to the Confederate gunners. But soon the smoke of battle settled down over all; and gunners, whether on shore or on the ships, fired at random. The "Hartford" led the way, and picked out the course; and the other vessels followed carefully in her wake. In the mizzen-top of the flag-ship was stationed a cool old river pilot, who had guided many a huge river steamer, freighted with precious lives, through the mazy channels of the Mississippi. There, high above the battle-smoke, heedless of the grape-shot and bits of flying shell whistling around him, he stood at his post, calmly giving his orders through a speaking-tube that led to the wheel-room. Now and then the admiral on the deck below would call up, asking about the pilot's safety, and was always answered with a cheery hail. But though the "Hartford" went by the batteries, heedless of the storm and lead poured upon her, she found herself alone, when, after firing a last gun, she swept into the clear air and tranquil water out of range of the enemy's guns. She waited some time for the other ships to come up, while all on board watched eagerly, save those who lay moaning on the surgeon's tables in the cockpit below. The night wore on, and all on board were consumed with anxiety for the fate of the vessels that had dropped behind. The lookout in the tops reported that he could see far down the river a bright red light that could only be caused by a burning vessel. It proved to be the steamer "Mississippi," that had grounded under the guns of the batteries, and had been fired and abandoned by her crew. But of this the admiral knew nothing; and when, after an hour or two, he heard the dull, heavy boom of an explosion, he went sadly to his cabin, fearing that the lives of many valiant sailors had been sacrificed. There was no way to communicate with the fleet below, and it was not until days afterward that the admiral learned how his fleet had been beaten back by the heavy guns of the Confederates and the swift current of the river. The "Richmond" grounded at a point within easy range of the batteries, and her crew fought desperately while shell after shell went crashing through her hull. They saw the other vessels of the fleet go drifting by helpless in the mighty current of the river, but they faltered not in their brave defence until they saw their ship a wreck and in flames. Then leaving their dead comrades with the "Richmond" for a funeral pyre, they escaped to the shore, and threaded their way through miles of morasses and dense thickets until they came to the mortar-boats, where they found refuge and rest. And so that first attack on Port Hudson ended with Farragut above the batteries, and his ships below. It had only served to prove, that, safe in their heavy earthworks, the Confederates could defy any attack by ships alone. This fact was clear to the Union authorities, and they began massing troops about the hostile works. Two months later, Porter's mortar-boats, the frigates and gunboats, and the batteries and muskets of an immense body of troops, opened on the works. While the heavy fire was being kept up, the Union armies were closing in, digging trenches, and surrounding the Confederates on all sides. The firing came to be short-range work and very deadly. "To show you what cool and desperate fighting it was," says a Confederate, "I had at least twenty-five shots at Federals not two hundred feet away. In one instance I fired upon a lieutenant who was urging on his men. I wounded him in his left arm. He fired at me with his revolver, and sent a bullet through my cap. Next time I hit him in the hip, and he fell; but, while I was reloading, he raised himself up, and shot the man next to me through the head. The officer was so close to me that I could tell the color of his eyes, and detect a small scar on his face."

This sort of work continued for weeks, with occasional charges by the Federals. Farragut's fleet kept up its bombardment, but did little damage. One of the Confederate soldiers said, some time after the war, "One can get used to almost any thing. After the first two or three days, we took the bombardment as part of the regular routine. Pieces of shell were continually flying about, and it was the regular thing for a bomb to drop down among us at intervals. I have seen them come down within fifty feet of a sentinel, and throw up a wagon-load of dirt, without his even turning his head. We had but few men hurt by the artillery-fire. I do not believe we averaged one man hit for every thousand pounds of metal thrown. I remember that one day I counted thirteen shells and bombs hurled at the spot where I was posted before we had a man hurt, and he was only slightly wounded." Naturally, such work as this could not drive the Confederates from their trenches; and the fleet soon concluded to leave the army to capture Port Hudson, while the ships steamed on up the river toward Vicksburg. The army kept up the siege for weeks, until the Confederates, hearing of the fall of Vicksburg, surrendered.

While the Union fleet was thus fighting its way up to Vicksburg, the Confederates were working away at a great ram that they were building in a secluded spot far up the Yazoo River. Work on the ram was being pushed with the greatest energy; and the Union sailors, in their ships on the Mississippi, listened daily to the stories of escaping negroes, and wondered when the big ship would come down and give them a tussle. The crew of the ram were no less impatient for the fray; for they were tired of being hidden away up a little river, plagued by mosquitoes and gnats. The dark shades of the heavy forests were seldom brightened by a ray of sun. The stream was full of alligators, that lay lazily on the banks all day, and bellowed dismally all night. The chirp of a bird was rarely heard. In its place were the discordant screams of cranes, or hisses of the moccasins or cotton-mouths. When at last the carpenters' clatter had ceased, and the ram, ready for action, lay in the little river, the crew were mustered on the deck, and told that the new boat had been built to clear the Union vessels from the Mississippi, and that purpose should be carried out. No white flag was to flutter from that flag-staff; and she should sink with all her crew before she would surrender. Any sailor who feared to enter upon such a service might leave the ship at once. No one left; and the "Arkansas" started down the river to look for an enemy. She was not long in finding one. At the mouth of the Yazoo floated three Union gunboats, — the "Carondelet," the "Tyler," and the "Queen of the West." As the ram came down into sight, her men heard the roll of the drums on the decks of the hostile vessels. The gunboats quickly opened fire, which was as promptly returned by the "Arkansas;" and, as she came swiftly rushing down the stream, the three vessels fled before her. The men on the ram were all new recruits, and made awkward work of the firing; but as she came to close quarters she sent her shells crashing into the Union ships, while the shot she received in return rattled harmlessly off her steel-mailed sides. The "Carondelet" was the first vessel to come to grief. She had hardly fired four shots when a heavy solid shot crashed through her side, and rattled against the most delicate part of the engine. She was helpless at once; and hardly had this damage been reported when a second shot came with a burst into an open port, killed five men, and broke its way out the other side. In ten minutes her decks were slippery with blood, and thick strewn with wounded and dead men. The current of the river drifted her upon a sandbar; and she lay there helplessly, now and again answering the galling fire of her foe with a feeble shot. Pouring in a last broadside, the "Arkansas" steamed past her, and, disregarding the other two vessels, headed for Vicksburg, where she knew her aid was sorely needed.

The news of her coming preceded her; and, when she came within sight

THE "ARKANSAS" UNDER FIRE.

of the steeples of the city, at least ten thousand people were watching her progress, and wondering whether she could pass by the Federal batteries and through the Federal fleet. The Federal fleet was all ready for her, and prepared such a gauntlet for the "Arkansas" as had never been run by any vessel. As she came within range, every Union gun that could be brought to bear opened; and shot and shell rained from shore-batteries and marine guns upon the tough hide of the ram. As she sped by the vessels, they gave her their broadsides, and the effect was tremendous. As the huge iron balls struck the ship, she keeled far over; and to her crew inside, it seemed as though she was being lifted bodily out of the water. Not a shot broke through the armor; but the terrible concussions knocked men down, and made blood come pouring from their nostrils. For new men, her crew fought well and bravely; though two fell flat on their faces, afraid to lift their heads, lest they be taken off by a shell.

When it was seen that the "Arkansas" was likely to pass through the lines unscathed, the Federals tried to blockade her way; but she deviated not an inch from her path. The vessel that stood before her had to move aside, or take the chances of a blow from her terrible iron beak. She came straight to the centre of the fleet before opening fire; and when her port-holes were opened, and the big guns peered out, they found plenty of targets. Her first volley knocked a gunboat to pieces; and in another minute she had crashed into the side of a Union ram, sending that unlucky craft ashore for repairs. But the storm of solid shot was too much for her; and she was forced to seek shelter under the bluffs, where the heavy guns of the Confederate shore-batteries compelled the Union ships to keep a respectful distance. Here she lay for several weeks, beating off every assault of the Federals, and making a valuable addition to the defences of the city. But, in an evil hour, the Confederate authorities decided to send her down the river to recapture Baton Rouge. When her journey was but half completed, she was pounced upon by several United States vessels, with the "Essex" in the lead. Her engines breaking down, she drifted upon a sand-bank; and the attacking ships pounded her at their leisure, until, with the fire bursting from her port-holes, she was abandoned by her crew, and blazed away until her career was ended by the explosion of her magazine. She had given the Federal fleet some hard tussles, but beyond that had done nothing of the work the Confederates so fondly hoped of her.

While the flotilla of gunboats, led by the "Essex," were planning for the destruction of the "Arkansas," a small naval expedition, consisting of three gunboats, was threading its way up the narrow channel of the White River in search of some Confederate batteries said to be on the banks. Within twelve hours from the start, the sailors learned from a ragged negro, whom they captured on the shore, that the Confederates had powerful batteries only five miles farther up, and that the river channel was obstructed by sunken vessels. Anchor was cast for the night; and in the morning the troops accompanying the expedition were landed, and plunged into the forest with the plan of taking the fort by a rush from the rear. The gunboats began a slow advance up the river, throwing shells into the woods ahead of them. The blue-jackets kept carefully under cover; for, though they could see no foe, yet the constant singing of rifle-bullets about the ships proved that somewhere in those bushes were concealed sharp-shooters whose powder was good and whose aim was true. The "Mound City" was leading the gunboats, and had advanced within six hundred yards of the enemy's guns, when a single shot, fired from a masked battery high up the bluffs, rang out sharply amid the rattle of small-arms. It was the first cannon-shot fired by the Confederates in that engagement, and it was probably the most horribly deadly shot fired in the war. It entered the port-casemate forward, killed three men standing at the gun, and plunged into the boiler. In an instant the scalding steam came hissing out, filling the ship from stem to stern, and horribly scalding every one upon the gun-deck. The deck was covered with writhing forms, and screams of agony rang out above the harsh noise of the escaping steam and the roar of battle outside. Many were blown overboard; more crawled out of the port-holes, and dropped into the river to escape the scalding steam, and struggling in the water were killed by rifle-balls or the fragments of the shells that were bursting all around. The helpless gunboat turned round and round in the stream, and drifted away, carrying a crew of dead and dying men. So great was the horror of the scene, that one of the officers, himself unhurt, who saw his comrades thus tortured all about him, went insane.

While this scene was going on before the fort, the Union troops had come up behind it, and with a cheer rushed over the breastworks, and drove the garrison to surrender. The Confederate banner fell from the staff, and the stars and stripes went up in its place. But how great was the price that the Federals had to pay for that victory! That night, with muffled drums, and arms reversed, the blue-jackets carried to the grave fifty-nine of their comrades, who twelve hours before were active men. With three volleys of musketry the simple rites over the sailors' graves were ended; and those who were left alive, only said with a sigh, "It is the fortune of war."

CHAPTER XV.

ON TO VICKSBURG.—BOMBARDMENT OF THE CONFEDERATE STRONGHOLD.—PORTER'S CRUISE IN THE FORESTS.

WHILE the smaller gunboats were thus making dashes into the enemy's country, destroying batteries and unfinished war-vessels, and burning salt-works, the heavier vessels of the fleet were being massed about Vicksburg, and were preparing to aid the army in reducing that city to subjection. We need not describe the way in which Gen. Grant had been rushing his troops toward that point, how for weeks his engineers had been planning trenches and approaches to the Confederate works, until toward the middle part of June, 1863, the people in that city found themselves hemmed in by a huge girdle of trenches, batteries, and military camps. Gen. Pemberton, with his army of Confederate soldiers, had been forced backward from point after point, until at last he found himself in Vicksburg, with the prospect of a long siege before him, and no way to get past the inexorable lines of blue that surrounded him. It is true that he had a wonderfully strong position, and many were the tongues that said Vicksburg could never be taken. But though stronger than Sebastopol, stronger than the Rock of Gibraltar, Vicksburg was destined to fall before that mighty army that encircled it, and was slowly starving the city into subjection.

But the Union soldiers, looking from their camps toward the Confederate citadel, saw that they had before them some severe work before that flag that flaunted over the city should be replaced by the stars and stripes. The city stands on a towering bluff high above the eastern bank of the Mississippi River. On that frowning height the busy hands of Pemberton's soldiers had reared mighty batteries, that commanded the Mississippi for miles up and down stream. To think of carrying the works by assault, was madness. Sherman had tried, and was beaten back with terrible loss. Then Grant, with nearly twenty thousand men, and with the co-operation of the river-flotilla, came upon the stage, and determined to take the city though it kept him at bay for months.

All imaginable plans were tried to get the army below the city; for Grant's command had come down from Cairo, and were at the northern and most impregnable side of the enemy's works. As at Island No. 10, a sharp bend in the river made a long peninsula right under the Confederates' guns. Grant, remembering the plan adopted before, set to work to cut a canal through the peninsula, so that the gunboats and transports might get below the forts. Twelve hundred negroes worked with a will upon this ditch for weeks. Then came a terrible rain-storm: the swollen, muddy torrent of the river broke in upon the unfinished canal, and that work was wasted. Then a new plan was suggested, this time by Commodore David Porter, who all through the war showed the greatest delight in taking his big gunboats into ditches where nothing larger than a frog or musk-rat could hope to navigate, and then bringing them out again safe after all.

The country back of Vicksburg was fairly honeycombed with shallow lakes, creeks, and those sluggish black streams called in the South bayous. Porter had been looking over this aqueous territory for some time, and had sent one of his lieutenants off in a steam-launch to see what could be done in that network of ditches. When the explorer returned, he brought cheering news. He was confident that, with tugs and gangs of axemen clearing the way, the gunboats could be taken up the Yazoo River, then into a wide bayou, and finally through a maze of small water-ways, until they should reach the Mississippi again below the Vicksburg batteries. Then the transports could follow, the troops could march down the other side of the river, be met by the transports, ferried across, and take Vicksburg on the flank. It was a beautiful plan; and Porter went to Grant with it, full of enthusiasm.

Gen. Grant considered the matter for some time, but finally gave his consent, and detailed a number of blue-coated soldiers to aid Porter's blue-jackets in the work. They first cut the levees, and let the mighty tide of the Mississippi sweep in, filling the bayous to the brim, and flooding all the country round about. Then the gunboats plunged in, and were borne along on the rushing tide until they brought up, all standing, against the trunks of trees, or had their smoke-stacks caught by overhanging branches.

Then came the tug of war; and the axemen were called to the front, and set to work. They chopped their way along for some distance; the rapid current from the river banging the vessels against the trees and stumps, until all the standing rigging and light cabins were swept away. After a good deal of work they saw before them a broad river, wide enough for two vessels to steam abreast. Soon they drifted out into it, and the commanding officer sang out cheerily, "On to Vicksburg, boys, and no more trees to saw." And so they steamed on, thinking how neatly they should take the "gray-coats" in the rear, when suddenly a bend in the river showed them, just ahead, a fort in the middle of the river, with the channel blocked on either side. That was a surprise. The works were new, and the water was still muddy about the sunken steamers. Clearly the wily Pemberton had heard of this inland naval expedition, and was determined to check it effectually.

The gunboats backed water, and crowded in confused groups. The gunners in the fort took hurried aim, and pulled the lanyards of their cannon, forgetting that those pieces were not loaded. It was hard to tell which party was the more excited at the unexpected meeting. This gave the blue-jackets a chance to collect their thoughts, and in a minute or two the gunboats opened fire; but they were soon convinced that the fort was too much for them, and they turned and crawled back through the woods to the fleet above Vicksburg. Pemberton scored one point for successful strategy.

But, even while this expedition was working its way back to the station of the vessels on the Mississippi, Porter was starting another through a second chain of water-courses that he had discovered. This time he was so sure of getting into the rear of Vicksburg, that he took four of his big iron-clads, and two light mortar-boats built especially for work in the woods. Gen. Sherman, with a strong army-force, marched overland, keeping up with the gunboats. Admiral Porter, in his Memoirs, gives a graphic picture of this expedition. Back of Vicksburg the country is low, and intersected in every direction by narrow, tortuous bayous, lined on either side by gloomy morasses or majestic forests. Into these little-known watercourses Porter boldly led his ponderous iron-clads; while Sherman, with a detachment of troops, advanced along the shore, keeping as near the flotilla as possible. Seldom have naval vessels been detailed upon so strange a service. For days they steamed on under the spreading branches of trees, that often spanned the bayous in a mighty arch overhead, shutting out all sunlight. For a time this navigation of placid, shady water-ways was pleasant enough; but, as they penetrated farther into the interior, the jackies sighed for the blue waters of the ocean, or even for the turbid current of the Mississippi. The heavy foliage that gave so grateful a shade also harbored all sorts of animals; and coons, rats, mice, and wildcats, that had been driven to the trees for shelter during the prevailing high water, peered down upon the sailors, and often dropped sociably down upon the decks of the vessels gliding beneath.

At some portions of the voyage the flotilla seemed to be steaming through the primeval forest. The bayou was but a few feet wider than the gunboats, and its banks were lined by gnarled and knotted old veterans of the forest, — live oaks, sycamore, and tupelo gum trees that had stood in majestic dignity on the banks of the dark and sullen stream for centuries. Sometimes majestic vistas would open; broad avenues carpeted with velvet turf, and walled in by the massive tree trunks, extending from the banks of the stream far back into the country.

Again, the stately forests would be replaced by fields of waving corn or rice, with the tops of a row of negro cabins or the columned front of a planter's house showing in the distance. Then, as the flotilla steamed on, this fair prospect would disappear, and be replaced by noisome cypress brakes, hung thick with the funereal Spanish moss, and harboring beneath the black water many a noxious reptile.

So through the ever-changing scenery the gunboats moved along, making but little progress, but meeting with no serious obstacle, until one morning there appeared on a bit of high ground, some yards in advance of the leading gunboat, an army officer mounted on an old white horse. It was Gen. Sherman, and his troops were in camp near by. He greeted the naval forces cheerily, and, rallying Porter on the amphibious service into which his gunboats had been forced, warned him that he would soon have not a smoke-stack standing, nor a boat left at the davits.

"So much the better," said the undaunted admiral. "All I want is an engine, guns, and a hull to float them. As to boats, they are very much in the way."

A short time only was spent in consultation, and then Sherman with his forces left the bayou and plunged into the interior, first warning Porter that he would have a hard time getting any farther, even if the enemy did not come down and surround him. But Porter was not the man to abandon the advance, so long as there was water enough to float his gunboats. Besides, he had gained some ideas regarding navigation in the forests, that enabled him to move his fleet forward with more celerity than at first. When a tree blocked the course of the iron-clads, they no longer stopped to clear it away by work with the axes; but, clapping on all steam, the powerful rams dashed at the woody obstruction, and with repeated blows soon knocked it out of the way.

Soon after leaving Sherman, Porter saw that the difficulties he had thus far met and conquered were as nothing to those which he had yet to encounter. The comparatively broad stream up which he had been steaming came to an end, and his further progress must be through Cypress Bayou, a canal just forty-six feet wide. The broadest gunboat was forty-two feet wide, and to enter that narrow stream made retreat out of the question: there could be no turning round to fly. The levees rose on either side of the narrow canal high above the decks of the ironclads, so that the cannon could not be sufficiently elevated to do effective work in case of an attack. But, there were nine feet of water in the great ditch; and that was enough for Porter, who pressed boldly on.

The country into which the combined military and naval expedition was advancing was in truth the granary of Vicksburg. On all other sides of the beleaguered city, the Federal lines were drawn so closely that the wagons laden with farm produce could not hope to pass. But here, back of the city, and far from the camps of Grant's legions, the work of raising produce for the gallant people of Vicksburg was prosecuted with the most untiring vigor. The sight, then, of the advancing gunboats aroused the greatest consternation. From the deck of his vessel Porter could see the people striving to save their property from the advancing enemy. Great droves of cattle were being driven away far into the interior; negroes were skurrying in all directions, driving poultry and pigs to the safe concealment of the forest; wagons groaning under the weight of farm and garden produce could be seen disappearing in the distance. What the inhabitants could not save they destroyed, in order that it might not profit the invaders. A short distance from the mouth of the bayou were six thousand bales of cotton piled up on opposite sides of the stream, ready to be taken aboard a steamer when the war should end. As the gunboats advanced slowly, making little headway against the two-knot current of the bayou, Porter saw two men, carrying lighted pine-knots, dash up to the cotton, and begin to set it afire. The admiral looked on in disgust. "'What fools these mortals be!'" said he to an officer standing at his side; "but I suppose those men have a right to burn their own cotton, especially as we have no way of preventing them."

"I can send a howitzer shell at them, sir," said the officer, "and drive them away."

But to this Porter demurred, saying that he had no desire to kill the men, and that they might do as they liked with their own. Accordingly the officers quietly watched the vandals, until, after twenty minutes' work, the cotton was blazing, and a dense mass of smoke cut off all vision ahead, and rose high in the air. Then Porter began to suspect that he had made a mistake. The difficulties of navigation in the bayou were great enough, without having smoke and fire added to them. Yet to wait for the cotton to burn up might cause a serious delay. On the high bank of the bayou stood a negro begging the sailors to take him aboard.

"Hallo, there, Sambo!" sung out Porter, "how long will it take this cotton to burn up?"

"Two day, massa," responded the contraband; "p'raps tree."

That ended the debate. "Ring the bell to go ahead fast," said the admiral to the pilot; and away went the flotilla at full speed, plunging into the smoke and fire. It was a hot experience for the sailors. The heavy iron-clads made but slow progress, and were scorched and blistered with the heat. The ports were all shut down, and the crews called to fire-quarters, buckets in hand. To remain on deck, was impossible. Porter and his captain made the trial, but had hardly entered the smoke when the scorching heat drove both into the shelter of an iron-covered deck-house. The pilot standing at the wheel seized a flag, and, wrapping it about his face and body, was able to stay at his post. As the flames grew hotter, the sailors below opened the main hatch, and, thrusting up a hose, deluged the deck with floods of water. So, without a man in sight, the huge iron ship moved along between the walls of flame. Suddenly came an enormous crash. The gunboat shivered, and for a moment stood still; then, gathering headway, moved on again, though with much ominous grating beneath her keel. Soon after she passed out of the smoke and heat, and all hands rushed on deck for a whiff of the fresh, cool air. Their first thought was of the cause of the collision; and, looking eagerly astern, they saw a heavy bridge, about fifty feet of which had been demolished by the tremendous power of the ram. This gave Porter a hint as to the force he had at his command; and thereafter bridges were rammed as a matter of course whenever they impeded the progress of the iron-clads. The astonishment of the people along the shore may well be imagined.

The great and formidable obstacles that stood in the path of the squadron were, as a rule, overcome by the exertion of the great powers of the steam-driven, iron-plated vessels; but at last there came a check, that, though it seemed at first insignificant, terminated the sylvan manœuvres of the iron-clad navy. After running the gantlet of the burning cotton, butting down trees, and smashing through bridges, the column entered a stretch of smooth water that seemed to promise fair and unobstructed sailing. But toward the end of this expanse of water a kind of green scum was evident, extending right across the bayou, from bank to bank. Porter's keen eye caught sight of this; and, turning to one of the negroes who had taken refuge on the gunboat, he asked what it was. "It's nuffin' but willows, sah," he replied. "When de water's out of de bayou, den we cuts de willows to make baskets with. You kin go troo dat like a eel."

Satisfied with this explanation, the admiral ordered the tug which led the column to go ahead. Under a full head of steam, the tug dashed into the willows, but began to slow up, until, after going about thirty yards, she stopped, unable to go forward or back. Undaunted by this unexpected resistance, Porter cried out that the "Cincinnati" would push the tug along; and the heavy gunboat, withdrawing a short distance to gain headway, hurled herself forward, and dashed into the willows with a force that would have carried her through any bridge ever built. But the old fable of the lion bound down by the silken net was here re-enacted. The gunboat did not even reach the tug. The slender willow-shoots trailed along the sides, caught in the rough ends of the iron overhang, and held the vessel immovable. Abandoning the attempt to advance, the gunboat strove to back out, but to no avail. Then hooks were rigged over the side to break away the withes, and men slung in ropes alongside vigorously wielded sharp cutlasses and saws; but still the willows retained their grip. Matters were now getting serious; and, to add to Porter's perplexity, reports came in that Confederate troops were coming down upon him. Then he began to lose confidence in his iron-clads, and wish right heartily for Sherman and his soldiers, of whose whereabouts he could gain no knowledge. The enemy did not leave him long in doubts as to their intention, and soon began a vigorous fire of shells from the woods. Porter stopped that promptly by manning his mortars and firing a few shells at a range measured by the sound of the enemy's cannon. The immediate silence of the hostile batteries proved the accuracy of the admiral's calculations, and gave him time to devise means for escaping from his perilous position.

How to do it without aid from Sherman's troops, was a difficult question; and in his perplexity he exclaimed aloud, "Why don't Sherman come on? I'd give ten dollars to get a telegram to him." The admiral was standing at the moment on the bank of the bayou, near a group of negroes; and an athletic-looking contraband stepped forward, and, announcing himself as a "telegram-wire," offered to carry the note "to kingdum kum for half a dollar." After sharply cross-questioning the volunteer, Porter wrote on a scrap of paper, "DEAR SHERMAN, — Hurry up, for Heaven's sake. I never knew how helpless an iron-clad could be, steaming around through the woods without an army to back her."

"Where will you carry this?" asked Porter, handing the despatch to the negro.

"In my calabash kiver, massa," responded the messenger with a grin; and, stowing the paper away in his woolly hair, he darted away.

The telegram being thus despatched, Porter again turned his attention to the willows; and, a fortunate rise in the water having occurred, he was able to extricate his vessels and begin his retreat down the bayou. He was somewhat perplexed by the silence of the Confederates, from whom he had heard nothing since his mortars silenced their masked batteries. The conundrum was solved by the sound of wood-chopping in the forests ahead, and the discovery shortly after of two heavy logs lying athwart the bayou, and stopping the progress of the vessels. An hour's hard work with axe and saw removed this obstruction; and the tug, slipping

PORTER'S FLOTILLA ON THE RED RIVER.

through first, shot ahead to prevent any more tree-felling. The loud reports of her howitzer soon carried back to the fleet the news that she had come up with the enemy, and was disputing with them the right to the bayou.

The difficulties of the retreat were no less great than those of the advance, with the intermittent attacks of the enemy added. The work of removing heavy, soggy logs, half submerged beneath the black waters of the bayou, clearing away standing trees, and breaking up and removing Red-river rafts, wearied the sailors, and left them little spirit to meet the enemy's attacks. The faint sounds of wood-chopping in the distance told too well of the additional impediments yet in store for the adventurous mariners. Scouts sent out reported that the enemy had impressed great gangs of negroes, and were forcing them to do the work of felling the trees that were to hem in Uncle Sam's gunboats, for the benefit of the C.S.A. But the plans of the Confederates to this end were easily defeated. Porter had not only many willing arms at his command, but the powerful aid of steam. When the gunboats came to a tree lying across the bayou, a landing party went ashore and fastened large pulleys to a tree on the bank. Then a rope was passed through the block; and one end having been made fast to the fallen tree, the other was taken aboard a gunboat. The word was then given, "Back the iron-clad hard;" and the fallen monarch of the forest was soon dragged across the bayou and out of the way. So expert did the jackies become in this work, that they were soon able to clear away the trees faster than the enemy could fell them. The tug then went ahead, and for a time put an end to further tree-chopping, and captured several of the negro axemen.

From the captured contrabands Porter learned that the attempt to cut off his retreat was directed by the military authorities at Vicksburg. This was a startling revelation. He had thought that the Confederates were in entire ignorance of his movement; and now it turned out that the wily Pemberton had kept a sharp lookout on the marauding gunboats, and was shrewdly planning for their capture. While Porter was pondering over this new discovery, a party of scouts came in, bringing in four captured Confederates, two of whom were commissioned officers. The commanding officer, a mere boy, was somewhat chagrined at being captured, but felt confident that his friends would recapture him shortly. Porter politely asked him to take a glass of wine and some supper.

"I don't care if I do," responded the youngster; "and I have the less compunction in taking it, as it belongs to us anyhow. In two hours you will be surrounded and bagged. You can't escape. How in the Devil's name you ever got here, is a wonder to me."

Porter smiled pleasantly, and, helping his guests lavishly, proceeded to question them on the numbers and position of the Confederate troops. He learned that a large body of troops had been sent out to surround the iron-clads, and were even then closing in upon the intruders. The danger was imminent, but Porter showed no trepidation.

"How far off are your troops?" he asked.

"About four miles. They will bag you at daylight," was the confident response.

"Well, gentlemen," said the admiral, "Gen. Sherman is now surrounding your forces with ten thousand men, and will capture them all before daylight." And so saying the admiral went on deck, leaving his captives lost in wonder; for the information carried to the Vicksburg authorities had made no mention of troops.

Though Porter had put on so bold a front before his captives, he really felt much anxiety for the fate of his iron-clads. He could hear nothing from Sherman, who might be thirty miles away for all he knew. Accordingly he retraced his course for a few miles, to throw the enemy off the scent, and the next day began again his descent of the bayou, bumping along stern foremost amid snags and standing trees. The enemy soon gave evidence that he was on the watch, and opened fire with his artillery from the rear. At this one gunboat steamed back and silenced the artillery for a time, after which she rejoined her fellows. Sharp-shooters in the thickets along the levee then began to grow troublesome; and the whistle of the rifle-balls, with an occasional *ping* as one struck the smoke-stack, warned the sailors that the deck of a gunboat in a narrow canal was no safe place in time of war. The high levees on either side of the bayou made it impossible to use the guns properly: so Porter turned them into mortars, and, by using very small charges of powder, pitched shells up into the air, dropping them into the bushes back of the levee. This somewhat checked the fire of the sharp-shooters, but the decks were still dangerous places to frequent. A rifle-ball struck Lieut. Wells in the head as he stood talking to Porter; and he fell, apparently dead, upon the deck. The admiral beckoned an officer to come and bear away the body; but the newcomer was also hit, and fell across the body of the first. Porter concluded that the locality was getting rather hot, and gladly stepped behind a heavy plate of sheet-iron, which an old quartermaster brought him with the remark, "There, sir, stand behind that. They've fired at you long enough."

From behind his shield, Porter looked out anxiously at the forces by which he was beleaguered. He could see clearly that the Confederates were increasing in numbers; and, when at last he saw a long gray column come sweeping out of the woods, his heart failed him, and for a moment he thought that the fate of his flotilla was sealed. But at that very moment deliverance was at hand. The Confederates were seen to fall into confusion, waver, and give way before a thin blue line,—the advance guard of Sherman's troops. The negro "telegram-wire" had proved faithful, and Sherman had come on to the rescue.

That ended the difficulties of the flotilla. The enemy, once brought face to face with Sherman's men, departed abruptly; and soon the doughty general, mounted on an old gray horse, came riding down to the edge of the bayou, for a word with Porter. Seeing the admiral on the deck of his gunboat, he shouted out, "Hallo! Porter, what did you get into such an ugly scrape for? So much for you navy fellows getting out of your element. Better send for the soldiers always. My boys will put you through. Here's your little nigger. He came through all right, and I started at once. Your gunboats are enough to scare the crows: they look as if you had got a terrible hammering."

Somewhat crestfallen, Porter remarked, that he "never knew what helpless things iron-clads could become when they got in a ditch, and had no soldiers about." As Sherman declined to come aboard, Porter went below to look after his two prisoners.

"Well, gentlemen," said he, as he entered the cabin, "you were right. We are surrounded by troops."

The two Confederates were greatly exultant, but assured Porter that they would see that he was kindly treated when taken into Vicksburg.

"To Vicksburg!" said he with mock amazement. "Who said any thing of Vicksburg?"

"Why, of course you'll be taken there as a prisoner, now that our men have surrounded you."

"Oh, you are mistaken there!" responded Porter. "The troops by whom I am surrounded are Sherman's boys, six thousand strong." And at this news the chagrined captives subsided, and began to consider the prospects of a trip to the North, and incarceration in one of the military prisons.

Sherman's army soon came up in force, and went into camp along the road that skirted the levee. As night fell, the scene took on a wild and picturesque air. In the narrow bayou lay the gunboats, strung out in single file along a line of half a mile. They bore many signs of the hard knocks they had received in their excursion through the woods. Boats, davits, steam-pipes, and every thing breakable that rose above the level of the deck, had been swept away by the overhanging boughs, or dashed to pieces by falling trees. The smoke-stacks and wheel-houses were riddled by the bullets of the Confederate sharp-shooters. The decks were covered with rubbish of all kinds, and here and there was a fissure that told of the bursting of some Confederate shell. The paint was blistered, and peeling off, from the effects of the cotton-fire through which the fleet had dashed.

On the shore blazed the camp-fires of Sherman's troops; and about the huge flaming piles the weary soldiers threw themselves down to catch a moment's rest, while the company cooks prepared the evening meal. Many of the idle soldiers strolled down to the edge of the bayou, and, forming a line along the levee, began chaffing the sailors on the ludicrous failure of their attempt to perform naval evolutions in a swamp.

"What's gone with your boats, Jack?" sung out one tall fellow in cavalry garb. "Been in dry-dock for repairs?"

"How do you like playing mud-turtle?" said another. "Better stick to salt water after this."

"Don't go bush-whacking again, unless you have the soldiers with you. You look as if your mothers didn't know you were out." And at this a yell of approval went up all along the line, while the badgered sailors growled and tried to make sharp retorts to the stinging ridicule of the landsmen.

So ended this memorable gunboat expedition. It is unparalleled in the history of warfare. The feats performed by the unwieldy iron-clads in the narrow bayous gained for them, from Lincoln, the title of "web-footed" gunboats. They had traversed shallow and tortuous channels; they had cleared their path of trees, snags, and even bridges; they had run the gantlet of flaming cotton-bales and Confederate bullets. After meeting and overcoming so many obstacles, their final stoppage by a thicket of pitiful willow-shoots irritated the blue-jackets and their commander extremely. Porter had penetrated so far into the Yazoo country, that he could see how great damage could be inflicted upon the Confederates, if the expedition could but be carried out successfully. He had definite information to the effect, that, at Yazoo City, the Confederates had a thriving shipyard, at which they were pressing forward the construction of steam-rams with which to sweep the Mississippi. To reach that point and destroy the vessels, would have been a service thoroughly in accord with his tastes; but the willows held him back. However, he was able to console himself with the thought that the rams were not likely to do the Confederates any immediate service; for a truthful contraband, brought in by the Union scouts, informed the admiral that "dey has no bottom in, no sides to 'em, an' no top on to 'em, sah; an' dere injines is in Richmon'."

When the dangers encountered by the gunboats during this expedition are considered, the damage sustained seems surprisingly small. Had the

Confederates acted promptly and vigorously, the intruders would never have escaped from the swamps into which their temerity had led them. A few torpedoes, judiciously planted in the muddy bed of the bayou, would have effectively prevented any farther advance. More than once the Confederates posted their artillery within effective range, and opened a rapid and well-directed fire upon the gunboats, but erred in using explosive shells instead of solid shot. "They were evidently greenhorns," wrote Porter, exulting over his narrow escape, "and failed to understand that we were iron-clad, and did not mind *bursting*-shell. If they had used solid shot, they might have hurt us." The infantry forces of the enemy were ample to have given the marauding gunboats a vast deal of trouble, if the Confederate officers had been enterprising, and had seized upon the opportunities afforded them. Night after night the flotilla lay tied up in the centre of a narrow bayou, with the levees towering so high above the gunboats' ports, that the cannon were useless. At such a time, a determined assault by a body of hostile infantry could hardly have been resisted. Such an attack was the danger which Porter most feared throughout the expedition, and he nightly made preparations for a desperate resistance. The widest part of the bayou was chosen for the anchorage, in order that a strip of water at least four feet wide might separate the gunboats from the shore. The sides of the iron-clads were then greased, and the guns loaded with grape, and elevated as much as possible. Landing parties with howitzers were sent ashore, and posted so as to enfilade any attacking force; scouts were sent out in all directions; and the crews of the gunboats slept at their quarters all night, ready for action at the first alarm. But it is doubtful whether even these elaborate precautions could have saved the flotilla, had the Confederates brought one regiment to the assault. However, the enemy let the golden moment pass; and, after suffering the agonies of suspense for several days, Porter at last saw his gunboats safely anchored by the side of Sherman's protecting regiments.

Sherman and Porter held a consultation that night, and concluded that it was useless to try to get around Vicksburg by hauling the gunboats

DUMMY GUNBOAT PASSING FORTS ON THE MISSISSIPPI.

through the woods; and the following morning the flotilla started back to the Union headquarters on the Mississippi.

Gen. Grant was beginning to get impatient. Weeks had passed away, and there were still no gunboats or transports below the Vicksburg batteries to aid him in carrying out his military plans. He held a long consultation with Porter, the outcome of which was that the admiral decided to run his gunboats and transports right through the fire of the Confederate guns.

But, before sending a vessel through, Porter thought that he would test the accuracy of the Confederate gunners by giving them a dummy to fire at. He took a large flat boat, and built it up with logs and lumber until it looked like a powerful ram. Two huge wheel-houses towered amidships, on each of which was painted, in great, staring letters, "Deluded Rebels, cave in." From the open ports, the muzzles of what appeared to be heavy rifles protruded; though the guns that seemed so formidable were really only logs of wood. Two high smoke-stacks, built of empty pork-barrels, rose from the centre of this strange craft; and at the bottom of each stack was an iron pot, in which was a heap of tar and oakum that sent forth volumes of black smoke when lighted. One dark night the fires in this sham monster were lighted, and she was towed down to the Confederate batteries, and set drifting down the river. She was quickly discovered, and the batteries on the bluffs opened on her with a roar. There was nothing about the dummy to be hurt, however; and it was impossible to sink her. So she sailed majestically through the plunging hail of solid shot, and past the terrible batteries that were thought to be a match for any thing afloat. The Confederates in the trenches looked at each other in astonishment and dismay. Word was sent to Gen. Pemberton that a powerful Yankee ironclad had passed the batteries unhurt, and was speeding down the stream. The General's first thought was of a gunboat, the "Indianola," lately captured from the Federals, and now being converted into an iron-clad ram. She must be saved from recapture, even if it should be necessary to destroy her. Word was hurriedly sent down the river that a formidable ram was bearing down upon the "Indianola;" and, if the latter vessel was not in condition to do battle, she should be blown up. Accordingly, while the dummy ram, caught in an eddy of the river, was whirling helplessly around just below Vicksburg, the Confederates put the torch to their new war-vessel, and she was soon a heap of ashes. Porter's little joke was a good one for the United States.

But all the time that the Union navy was making these futile attempts to get the better of the wily general who held the fort at Vicksburg, a constant bombardment of the city was kept up. From gunboats and land batteries, shells were hurled into the streets of the town, tearing down houses, killing men, women, and children, and driving the inhabitants to their cellars, or to deep caves dug in the hills. The fire from the Union gunboats was most destructive, for they could drop down to an advantageous point, shell the city until tired, then steam back into safety again.

Cave-digging in the city became a regular business; and caves brought from twenty to fifty dollars, according to their size. They generally consisted of two or three rooms, and people lived in them quite cheerfully during the time that the iron hail was falling in the city's streets.

A Northern woman, who was pent up in Vicksburg during the siege, tells graphically the story of the bombardment:—

"For many nights we have had but little sleep, because the Federal gunboats have been running past the batteries. The uproar when this is happening is phenomenal. The first night the thundering artillery burst the bars of sleep, we thought it an attack by the river. To get into garments, and rush up-stairs, was the work of a moment. From the upper gallery we have a fine view of the river; and soon a red glare lit up the scene, and showed a small boat, towing two large barges, gliding by. The Confederates had set fire to a house near the bank. Another night, eight boats ran by, throwing a shower of shot; and two burning houses made the river clear as day. One of the batteries has a remarkable gun they call 'whistling Dick,' because of the screeching, whistling sound it gives; and certainly it does sound like a tortured thing. Added to all this is the indescribable Confederate yell, which is a soul-harrowing sound to hear. I have gained respect for the mechanism of the human ear, which stands it all without injury. The streets are seldom quiet at night: even the dragging about of cannon makes a din in these echoing gullies. The other night we were on the gallery till the last of the eight boats got by. Next day a friend said to H——, 'It was a wonder you didn't have your heads taken off last night. I passed, and saw them stretched over the gallery; and grape-shot were whizzing up the street just on a level with you.' The double roar of batteries and boats was so great, we never noticed the whizzing. Yesterday the 'Cincinnati' attempted to go by in daylight, but was disabled and sunk. It was a pitiful sight: we could not see the *finale*, though we saw her rendered helpless.

"Since that day the regular siege has continued. We are utterly cut off from the world, surrounded by a circle of fire. Would it be wise, like the scorpion, to sting ourselves to death? The fiery shower of shells goes on day and night. H——'s occupation, of course, is gone, his office closed. Every man has to carry a pass in his pocket. People do nothing but eat what they can get, sleep when they can, and dodge the shells. There are three intervals when the shelling stops, — either for the guns to cool, or for the gunners' meals, I suppose, — about eight in the morning, the same in the evening, and at noon. In that time we have to both prepare and eat ours. Clothing cannot be washed, or any thing else done. On the 19th and 22d, when the assaults were made on the lines, I watched the soldiers cooking on the green opposite. The half-spent balls, coming all the way from those lines, were flying so thick that they were obliged to dodge at every turn. At all the caves I could see from my high perch, people were sitting, eating their poor suppers at the cave doors, ready to plunge in again. As the first shell again flew, they dived; and not a human being was visible. The sharp crackle of the musketry-firing was a strong contrast to the scream of the bombs. I think all the dogs and cats must be killed or starved: we don't see any more pitiful animals prowling around. . . . The cellar is so damp and musty, the bedding has to be carried out and laid in the sun every day, with the forecast that it may be demolished at any moment. The confinement is dreadful. To sit and listen as if waiting for death in a horrible manner, would drive me insane. I don't know what others do, but we read when I am not scribbling in this. H—— borrowed somewhere a lot of Dickens's novels, and we re-read them by the dim light in the cellar. When the shelling abates, H—— goes to walk about a little, or get the 'Daily Citizen,' which is still issuing a tiny sheet at twenty-five and fifty cents a copy. It is, of course, but a rehash of speculations which amuses a half-hour. To-day he heard, while out, that expert swimmers are crossing the Mississippi on logs at night, to bring and carry news to Johnston. I am so tired of corn-bread, which I never liked, that I eat it with tears in my eyes. We are lucky to get a quart of milk daily from a family near, who have a cow they hourly expect to be killed. I send five dollars to market each morning, and it buys a small piece of mule-meat. Rice and milk is my main food: I can't eat the mule-meat. We boil the rice, and eat it cold, with milk, for supper. Martha runs the gauntlet to buy the meat and milk once a day in a perfect terror. The shells seem to have many different names. I hear the soldiers say, 'That's a mortar-shell. There goes a Parrott. That's a rifle-shell.' They are all equally terrible. A pair of chimney-swallows have built in the parlor chimney. The concussion of the house often sends down parts of their nest, which they patiently pick up and re-ascend with."

Grant's impassable lines about the beleaguered city soon made starvation more to be feared than even the terrible shells from the cannon of the gunboats. Necessaries of all sorts became wofully scarce in Vicksburg. Five dollars could purchase only a little bit of mule's flesh, hardly enough for a meal for two people. Flour was not to be had at any price. Bread was made of coarse corn-meal or grated peas. The ammunition of the soldiers in the trenches soon began to give out, and the utmost economy was exercised. Many of the soldiers were armed with muskets that required caps, and it was not many days before caps were at a great premium. They were generally smuggled into the city through the Union lines by fleet-footed carriers, who ran a long gauntlet of Union pickets. Many were shot down in the attempt, but more succeeded. One man, who brought in sixteen thousand caps, was nine days travelling thirteen miles, and was fired on more than twenty times.

But, though Grant could have starved the city into subjection by simply

PASSING THE VICKSBURG BATTERIES.

sitting and waiting, he grew tired of this, and determined to force matters to an issue. The first thing to be done was to get the gunboats and transports past the batteries. The transports were put into shape to stand a cannonade by having their weaker parts covered with cotton-bales; and on one dark night in June, the flotilla started down the river, with the iron-clad gunboats in advance. Admiral Porter led in the "Benton." At eleven o'clock the fleet got under way; and, as the "Benton" came abreast of the first batteries, the alarm was given in the Confederate camp, and a fierce cannonade began. Huge fires were lighted on the shores to light up the river, and make the gunboats visible to the Confederate cannoneers. The war-ships swung grandly around the bend, responding with rapid broadsides to the fire of the forts. All the vessels were hit once or oftener. The heavy smoke that accompanies such fierce cannonading hung over the river, cutting off all view of the surroundings from the sailors. The eddying currents of the river caught the steamers, swinging them now this way, now that, until the perplexed pilots knew not which way their vessels were headed. The blue-jackets at the guns worked away cheerily, knowing that enemies were on every side of them, and that, no matter which way their missiles sped, an enemy was to be found. More than one vessel turned completely around; and once, when the rising breeze cleared away the smoke, the pilot of the "Benton" found that he was taking his ship up-stream again, and was in imminent danger of running down a friendly gunboat. But they all passed on without receiving any severe injuries, and at five o'clock in the morning lay anchored far below the city, ready to begin the attack upon the Confederate batteries at Grand Gulf, which were called "the key to Vicksburg."

CHAPTER XVI.

VICKSBURG SURRENDERS, AND THE MISSISSIPPI IS OPENED.—NAVAL EVENTS ALONG THE GULF COAST.

THE first grand step toward the capture of Vicksburg was made when the river-flotilla followed Porter down the Mississippi, and past the guns of the Confederate batteries. Grant, with his army, had followed along the western bank of the great river; and we now find him ready to cross the river, and move upon the Vicksburg batteries from the south. But, before this could be done, the Confederate works at Grand Gulf must be silenced; and it again happened that the navy was to be the chief factor in the contest. For this new battle all the blue-jackets were ready and anxious. Admiral Porter says that "when daylight broke, after the passage of the fleet, I was besieged by the commanding officers of the gunboats, who came to tell me of their mishaps; but, when I intimated that I intended to leave at Carthage any vessel that could not stand the hammering they would be subject to at Grand Gulf, they suddenly discovered that no damage had been done to their vessels, which, if any thing, were better prepared for action than when they started out!"

The Confederate works at Grand Gulf mounted eighteen guns; and, as they stood upon high bluffs overlooking the river, they were most formidable. It was decided by the Federals that the navy alone should undertake the task of reducing the fortifications, — a decision that was of benefit to the Confederates, for their strongest position was along the river-front. Four of the guns held a raking position up and down the long stretch of muddy water that swirled and eddied by with a current of seven miles an hour.

While the fort had the advantage of position, the gunboats were much stronger in their armament; and the contest was looked forward to as one bound to be desperate. The position of every gun in the batteries, and the size of the garrison, were well known to every commander of a Union vessel; and they made the most careful preparations for the assault.

The Confederates knew that the result of that day's battle would decide the ownership of Vicksburg, and they were prepared to offer the most desperate resistance. The orders at every battery were to use shell alone; and the men were instructed to fire carefully, and only after taking deadly aim. In a high tree just outside the fort a lookout was stationed; and at early daylight, on the morning of the 29th of April, 1863, he signalled that the fleet of gunboats was bearing down upon the works.

Men who were in the fort that morning saw a strange panorama. The stillness was most profound on the shore and on the river. The boats moved slowly and grandly down, not a man in sight, and with no sign of life. The trees up the river were black with Federal spectators; and the chirp of birds was all about the men who stood waiting beside the huge cannon.

Porter went at his work with a vim which made the forest tremble and the river bubble. For the first few minutes the Confederates were appalled by the fierceness of the fire, which stands on record as the fastest in the war; but, when the forts did get down to their work, they went in with a roar that almost deafened the Federal soldiers three miles away. Great shells burst over the gunboats, or, falling into the water close by their sides, threw up columns of water that deluged the decks. The vessels found the greatest difficulty in getting good positions for the swift-eddying current. One moment they were bow on, the next headed down stream, or up, or whirling around in circles. Of course this greatly hurt the aim of the gunners, but it likewise made the vessels poor targets for the Confederates.

Three gunboats — the "Benton," "Tuscumbia," and "Lafayette" — engaged the upper battery; and nowhere in naval history is found the record of faster firing than was done by these ships. Their huge shells tore away at the walls of earth, throwing up tons of dirt with each explosion, but not seeming to affect the strength of the fort at all. Not a shot entered an embrasure, though many came near it. One of the Confederate artillerists said after the fight, —

"There was not one single minute in all that five hours in which I did not expect death. We all worked away as if in a nightmare, and we all felt that any moment might be our last. The 'Benton' fired repeatedly at my gun; and as many as twenty of her shells struck the opening, tearing holes in the parapet ten feet back. Twenty times we were almost buried out of sight under the clouds of dirt, and the loose earth was knee deep around our gun when the fight closed. Not one of us was hit hard enough to draw blood, and yet we all felt ten years older for that five hours' work. I sighted the gun, and saw fourteen of my shot hit the 'Benton,' and six plunge into another."

The gunboats fought in a way that showed desperate determination. The first gun from the "Lafayette" was answered by a shell which crashed through her side and exploded in a wardroom, knocking every thing into chips. Three times the carpenter came up and reported to the captain that the ship was sinking; and each time the reply was, "Very well, sir: keep right on firing until the guns are under water." When the ship came out of the fight, she counted up fifty scars.

The long-range firing that was carried on at first did not satisfy the "Mound City." One particular gunner on the Confederate works seemed to cherish a spite against her; and every time the flame leaped from the muzzle of his gun, a solid shot banged against the gunboat's side. This was not to be tamely borne; and the "Mound City" rushed up so close to the bank that her bow stirred up the mud, and from that position opened fast and furiously upon the forts with grape and canister. A hail of rifle-bullets fell upon her decks; but she stuck to her post, and succeeded in driving the enemy to the bomb-proofs.

But, with all their pluck and rapid firing, the gunners of the fleet were making no impression on the works. Gen. Grant, who was watching the engagement from a tug in mid-stream, saw this, and determined to rush his soldiers past the fort in transports, while the navy engaged the enemy's guns. This was done quickly, and towards night the ships returned to their post up the river, leaving the Confederates in possession of the batteries. But the great point had been gained; and Grant's army was moving on Vicksburg, with nothing to interfere with its besieging operations.

Then began that series of attacks and repulses, of building trenches, paralleling, and advancing steadily, until the lines of the Federals and the Confederates were so close together that the men used to shout jokes and taunts over the breastworks. All the Confederates were known as "Johnnies," and all Union soldiers as "Yanks." Often "Johnny" would call out, "Well, Yank, when are you coming into town?" Sometimes the answer was, "We propose to celebrate the Fourth of July there." The "Johnnies" did not believe this; but it was true, nevertheless, for on July 4 Grant's victorious army marched into Vicksburg. A day or two later the Confederate works at Port Hudson and Grand Gulf were surrendered to the Federals, and the Mississippi was again open for commerce throughout its length.

When the fall of Vicksburg had thus left the river clear, Admiral Porter was ordered to take his fleet up the Red River, and clear away any Confederate works that he might find on the banks of that stream. Gen. A. J. Smith, with a strong body of troops, accompanied him; while Gen. Banks was to march his troops overland from Texas, and join the expedition at Shreveport. For several days the gunboats pressed forward up the crooked stream, meeting with no opposition, save from the sharp-shooters who lined the banks on either side, and kept up a constant fire of small-arms.

Shreveport was reached in safety; and, after a short halt, the flotilla started again on their voyage up the river. They had proceeded but a

MANNING THE YARDS.

short distance when a courier came galloping down the river's bank, waving a despatch, which he handed to Admiral Porter.

"The despatch read, 'Gen. Banks badly defeated; return.' Here was a dilemma to be placed in, — a victorious army between us and our own forces; a long, winding, shallow river wherein the vessels were continually grounding; a long string of empty transports, with many doubtful captains, who were constantly making excuses to lie by or to land (in other words, who were trying to put their vessels into the power of the Confederates); and a thousand points on the river where we could be attacked with great advantage by the enemy; and the banks lined with sharp-shooters, by whom every incautious soldier who showed himself was shot."

But, though the admiral clearly saw all the dangers he was exposed to, and which he recounts in the foregoing paragraph, he did not propose to return, but pressed forward. He soon reached the scene of battle, and with the big guns of his boats covered the retreat of the troops; then, having done all there was to be done, started down the river.

But now came the great trouble of the whole expedition. Those Southern rivers are accustomed in summer to fall rapidly until they become mere dry ditches, with a narrow rivulet, hardly deep enough to float a rowboat, flowing down the centre. This was the summer season, and the Red River was falling fast. The banks swarmed with gray-coated soldiery, anxious to be on hand to capture the ships. At Grand Écore the "Eastport" became unmanageable, and was blown up. The fleet continued on its way quietly, until a serious obstacle was met. Admiral Porter writes: —

"One of the 'Cricket's' guns was mounted on the upper deck forward, to command the banks; and a crew of six men were kept stationed at it, ready to fire at any thing hostile.

"We went along at a moderate pace, to keep within supporting distance of each other. I was sitting on the upper deck, reading, with one eye on the book and the other on the bushes, when I saw men's heads, and sang out to the commanding officer, Gorringe, 'Give those fellows in the bushes a two-second shell.' A moment after the shell burst in the midst of the people on the bank.

"'Give them another dose,' I said, when, to my astonishment, there came on board a shower of projectiles that fairly made the little 'Cricket' stagger. Nineteen shells burst on board our vessel at the first volley. It was the gun-battery of which our prisoner had told us. We were going along at this time about six knots an hour; and, before we could fire another gun, we were right under the battery and turning the point, presenting the 'Cricket's' stern to the enemy. They gave us nine shells when we were not more than twenty yards distant from the bank, all of which burst inside of us; and, as the vessel's stern was presented, they poured in ten more shots, which raked us fore and aft.

"Then came the roar of three thousand muskets, which seemed to strike every spot in the vessel. Fortunately her sides were musket-proof.

"The 'Cricket' stopped. I had been expecting it. How, thought I, could all these shells go through a vessel without disabling the machinery? The Rebels gave three cheers, and let us drift on: they were determined to have the whole of us. They opened their guns on the two pump-boats, and sunk them at the first discharge. The poor negroes that could swim tried to reach the shore; but the musketeers picked off those that were in the water or clinging to the wrecks. It was a dreadful spectacle to witness, with no power to prevent it; but it turned out to be the salvation of the 'Cricket.' All this took place in less than five minutes.

"The moment the 'Cricket' received the first discharge of artillery, I went on deck to the pilot-house, saluted by a volley of musketry as I passed along; and, as I opened the pilot-house door, I saw that the pilot, Mr. Drening, had his head cut open by a piece of shell, and the blood was streaming down his cheeks. He still held on to the wheel. 'I am all right, sir,' he said: 'I won't give up the wheel.'

"Gorringe was perfectly cool, and was ringing the engine-room bell to go ahead. In front of the wheel-house, the bodies of the men who manned the howitzer were piled up. A shell had struck the gun, and, exploding, had killed all the crew, — a glorious death for them."

Porter now found himself in a bad fix. His guns could not be elevated enough to bear on the batteries that stood on the crest of the high bluffs.

There was nothing to do but to run by at the best possible rate of speed. Suddenly the engine stopped, and the vessel floated helplessly down the stream. Porter rushed below to discover the trouble. In the engine-room stood the engineer leaning heavily against the throttle. Porter shouted at him, but received no reply; then, putting his hand on the man's shoulder, found him dead. The admiral threw the body aside, pulled open the throttle, and the "Cricket" glided along past the batteries to a safe refuge downstream. The other ships came down safely, although more or less cut up; and the flotilla continued its retreat down the stream. For a day or two all went smoothly as a holiday excursion; then came a sudden reverse, that, for for a time, seemed to make certain the loss of the entire fleet. At Alexandria the Red-river bottom is full of great rocks that make it impassable except at the highest water. When Porter's gunboats arrived, they found themselves caught in a trap from which there seemed to be no hope of escape. The army was encamped along the banks of the river, and the soldiers began again their jokes upon Porter's habit of taking gunboats for an overland journey. The army generals began to get impatient, and advised Porter to blow up his ships, as the troops must soon march on and leave him. Porter was sick in bed, but this suggestion aroused him. "Burn my gunboats!" he cried, springing to his feet. "Never! I'll wait here for high water if I have to wait two years." And, indeed, it began to look as though he would be forced to wait nearly that long.

In this time of suspense, there arose a man equal to the emergency. A certain Lieut.-Col. Bailey, who had been a Wisconsin lumberman, came to Porter, and suggested that a dam should be built to raise the water fourteen feet above the falls. Porter jumped at the suggestion, and eight thousand men were set to work.

"It will take too much time to enter into the details of this truly wonderful work," writes Admiral Porter. "Suffice it to say that the dam had nearly reached completion in eight days' working-time, and the water had risen sufficiently on the upper falls to allow the 'Fort Hindman,' 'Osage,' and 'Neosho' to get down and be ready to pass the dam. In another day it would have been high enough to enable all the other vessels to pass the upper falls. Unfortunately, on the morning of the 9th instant the pressure of water became so great that it swept away two of the stone barges which swung in below the dam on one side. Seeing this unfortunate accident, I jumped on a horse, and rode up to where the upper vessels were anchored, and ordered the 'Lexington' to pass the upper falls if possible, and immedi-

BAILEY'S DAM ON THE RED RIVER.

ately attempt to go through the dam. I thought I might be able to save the four vessels below, not knowing whether the persons employed on the work would ever have the heart to renew their enterprise.

"The 'Lexington' succeeded in getting over the upper falls just in time, the water rapidly falling as she was passing over. She then steered directly for the opening in the dam, through which the water was rushing so furiously that it seemed as if nothing but destruction awaited her. Thousands of beating hearts looked on, anxious for the result. The silence was so great as the 'Lexington' approached the dam, that a pin might almost be heard to fall. She entered the gap with a full head of steam on, pitched down the roaring torrent, made two or three spasmodic rolls, hung for a moment on the rocks below, was then swept into deep water by the current, and rounded to safely into the bank. Thirty thousand voices rose in one deafening cheer, and universal joy seemed to pervade the face of every man present."

After the dam was repaired, the rest of the fleet passed down safely.

With the escape of the Red-river flotilla, the career of Admiral Porter on the rivers ended. Indeed, there was but little work for the river navy remaining. The Mississippi, Tennessee, and Cumberland Rivers were opened; and the Confederate works on the smaller streams were unimportant, and could be left to fall with the fall of the Confederacy, which was near at hand. There was work for fighting sea-captains along the Atlantic coast, and thither Admiral Porter was ordered. He will re-appear at the bombardment of Fort Fisher.

An event which caused the greatest excitement in naval circles at this time, and which for courage and dash has probably never been equalled in the history of the world, was the run of the Confederate privateer "Florida" past the United States fleet blockading the harbor of Mobile. The "Florida" was originally a merchant-ship, known as the "Oreto;" and under that name she sailed from Liverpool, carrying a peaceful cargo, and manned by sailors who had no idea that any thing beyond a peaceable voyage was planned. She was commanded by an English sea-captain; and, although the United States consul at Liverpool looked on her with some suspicion, yet he could find no pretext upon which to oppose her departure.

Hardly had the ship passed the mouth of the Mersey, when her course was shaped for Nassau, the haven of privateers and blockade-runners. At Nassau several officers of the Confederate navy were living; and from the anxiety with which they scanned the horizon day after day, through their telescopes, it would seem that they were watching for some friendly craft. The "Oreto" arrived safely at Nassau; and a young gentleman who had come with her made all possible haste ashore, and delivered to the watchful gentlemen in the town certain letters, which made them first look with the greatest satisfaction at the newly arrived ship, and then begin again their outlook for vessels. The letters were from Capt. Bulloch, the agent in London of the Confederacy;,and by them he notified his brother naval officers that he delivered to them the "Oreto," an admirably built ship, suited for an armed cruiser. "It has been impossible to get the regular battery intended for her on board," wrote Capt. Bulloch; "but I have sent out four seven-inch rifled guns, with all necessary equipments, in the steamship 'Bahama,' bound for Nassau."

So here were the naval officers and their ship, but the guns were yet to come; and, when they did come, some shrewd planning would be necessary to get the guns mounted without alarming the British authorities. By the time the "Bahama" arrived, the plans were all made. As the steamer came up to the dock, a small schooner slipped alongside, and eight or ten heavy cases were transferred from the larger vessel's hold to the deck of the coaster. Then the little vessel sailed over to Green Cay, a desert island about sixty miles from Nassau, where she was soon joined by the "Oreto." There the work of changing the peaceful merchantman "Oreto" into the war-cruiser "Florida" began.

The work of transferring the armament, and mounting the guns, was very laborious. The hot sun of August at the equator poured down upon them. Exposure and general discomforts told heavily upon them; and before long the yellow-fever, that most terrible scourge of the West Indies, broke out among the men. There was no surgeon on board, and the care of the sick fell upon Capt. Maffitt. Two United States men-of-war were hunting through the West Indies for the vessel they knew was fitting out somewhere amid the coral reefs and sandy, desolate keys. But Maffitt kept up his courage, and before long found himself at sea, with a good stanch ship and crew, that, though short-handed, was made up of the very best material. But he had hardly cut loose from civilization, and started out upon his cruise, when he discovered, that, in the worry and haste of his departure, he had put to sea without rammers or sponges for his guns. He was in a desperate plight. Had the smallest United States man-of-war met the "Florida," the Confederate could not have offered the slightest resistance. She could not have even fired a gun. Capt. Maffitt ran his vessel into Havana in the hopes of being allowed to refit there; but the fortunes of the Confederacy were waning fast, and all nations feared to give it aid or comfort. Seeing no hope, Maffitt determined to dare all things, and make a dash for Mobile through the very centre of the blockading-fleet.

When the "Florida" put out from the harbor of Havana, only four or five men were able to be on deck. The rest, with her commander, were below, deathly sick with yellow-fever. Under the command of a young lieutenant, her course was laid for Mobile; and in a few hours the smoke of the blockading-vessels could be seen rising on the clear air. An English ensign was hoisted, and the fleet ship dashed towards the men-o'-war that lay in wait. A blank cartridge was fired to warn her away, but she paid no heed. Then came a solid shot that ploughed up the water before her bow. As this evoked no response, the whole fleet opened fire with shot and shell. "Had they depressed their guns but a little," said Maffitt afterwards, "the career of the 'Florida' would have ended then and there." But, as it was, she sped on, with no signs of damage save the flying ends of cut cordage. She could not respond to the fire, for but three men remained on her deck. So, silently and grimly, she rushed through the fleet, and finally passed the last frigate. Quarter of an hour later she anchored under the guns of Fort Morgan. She had received eight shots in her hull, and her masts were chipped by dozens of fragments of shell. After refitting, the "Florida" waited nearly a month for a chance to get out again. Finally the moment arrived; and she made her escape, though chased for four hours by the blockaders. Once on the open sea, she began the regular career of Confederate cruisers, burned unarmed ships, and avoided war-vessels, until she was run down in a neutral port by a Union man-of-war, whose commander acted in utter defiance of all the rules of modern warfare. In the career of the "Florida," after her escape from Mobile, there was nothing of moment; and her capture, treacherous as it was, brought more discredit upon the Northern arms than did her depredations work injury to the Northern merchant-marine.

CHAPTER XVII.

OPERATIONS ABOUT CHARLESTON.—THE BOMBARDMENT, THE SIEGE, AND THE CAPTURE.

WE have now reached the period at which the rapid decline in the prospects of the Confederacy had become apparent, not only to its enemies, but to its friends. Throughout the South the stars and bars floated over only three strongholds of any importance,— Charleston, Mobile, and Wilmington. One after the other these were destined to fall, and their final overthrow was to be the work of the navy. It was no easy task in any one of the three instances to dislodge the Confederates from their positions; for though beaten in the Middle States, driven from the Mississippi, and with their very citadel at Vicksburg in the hands of the Federals, they still fought with a courage and desperation that for a long time baffled the attacks of the Unionists.

From the very opening of the war, Charleston Harbor had been the scene of naval hostilities. The Confederates, looking upon their mouldering wharves, and vessels tugging idly at their chains, then looking out to sea past Fort Sumter, could see the ships of the blockading-squadron maintaining the watchful guard that was slowly reducing the city to penury. What wonder that the blood of the good people of Charleston boiled, and that they built, and hurled against their hated enemy, weird naval monsters, shapeless torpedo-boats running beneath the water, or huge rams that might even batter in the heavy walls of Fort Sumter!

One attack so made was successful to a certain extent. It was in February, 1864, that an inventive genius in the beleaguered city brought out a steam torpedo-boat. The craft was about twenty-five feet long, shaped like a cigar, built of boiler iron, and propelled by a screw. She had no smoke-stack, and her deck barely rose above the surface of the water. Running out from her bow was a stout spar fifteen feet long, bearing at its end a huge torpedo charged with two hundred pounds of powder. Just before nine o'clock one night, the lookout on the deck of the frigate "Housatonic" saw this strange object approaching the ship. It was a bright night, with no sea on. As yet torpedoes were hardly known, so the lookout took it for a large fish, and simply watched with interest its playful movements. Not until it came so close that no guns could be brought to bear, did any suspicion of danger enter the lookout's mind. Then there was the roll of the alarm-drums; while the men rushed to the side, and poured a fierce fire from small-arms on the mysterious object. The "Housatonic" started her engines, and tried to escape; but, before any headway could be gained, the launch dashed alongside, and a slight jar was felt. Then, with a tremendous roar, a huge column of water was thrown high in air, washing away men and boats from the deck of the war-ship. A hole large enough to drive a horse through was rent in the hull of the ship. Great beams were broken in twain, the heaviest guns were dismounted, and men were hurled fifty feet into the air. In five minutes the ship had gone to the bottom, and boats from other vessels were picking up the crew. The launch escaped in the excitement.

The Union sailor-boys did not let the Confederates outdo them in dash and pluck. One of the cleverest bits of work in the whole war was done by four boat-crews from two men-of-war on the Charleston station. Word had been brought to the blockaders, that, far up a little deep and narrow creek, a large steamship was loading with cotton, expecting to reach the ocean through the labyrinth of inlets that fairly honeycomb the South Carolina coast. Should she once get into that network of water-ways, it

CUTTING OUT A BLOCKADE-RUNNER.

would require a whole fleet to catch her; for there was no telling at what point she might emerge.

It was at once determined to try to capture her as she lay at her deck, and four boats' crews of picked men were sent out on the expedition. It was early evening when they set out; and all through the dark night they pulled away, threading the mazes of the tidal inlets. Just as the eastern horizon was beginning to grow gray with the coming dawn, they came in sight of their destination. Sure enough, there on the bank of the river was a little Southern village, changed into a prosperous town by the blockade-runners that had evidently been making this place a harbor for some time.

All was dark and silent as the grave. Confident in their fancied security, the blockade-runners had all turned in, leaving no one on guard. The steamer was loaded, and ready to sail in the morning; and the thin wreaths of smoke rising from her smoke-stack told that the fires were up. Stealthily the sailors pulled alongside, and clambered on deck. Without a word they stole below, put the crew under guards, and rushed into the engine-room, where they found the engineer dozing on his stool. He was ordered to get under way at once; and, though he looked rather dazed, he obeyed the order. And in fifteen minutes the steamer was speeding down-stream, leaving the old town still asleep.

One man alone of all the townspeople had seen the capture. A negro, hiding behind a pile of lumber on the dock, had watched the whole affair, and, as if struck dumb with astonishment, failed to give the alarm until the steamer was out of sight down the winding stream. The blue-jackets took their capture safely out of the enemy's lines, and the next day it was sent to New York as a prize.

While the navy was keeping the port of Charleston sealed, and every now and then beating back the improvised gunboats that the Confederates sent out in the forlorn hope of breaking through the blockade, the armies of the North were closing in upon the doomed city. All the North cried aloud for the capture of Charleston. It was the city which fired the first gun of the war. Let it be reduced! On every available point of land a

Union battery was built. Far out in the swamps back of the city, where it was thought no living thing save reptiles could exist, the soldiers of the North had raised a battery, mounting one two-hundred-pound gun. When a young lieutenant was ordered to build this battery, he looked the ground over, and reported the thing impossible. "There is no such word as impossible," sternly answered the colonel. "Set to work, and call for whatever you need to secure success."

The next day the lieutenant, who was a bit of a wag, made a requisition on the quartermaster for one hundred men eighteen feet high, to wade through mud sixteen feet deep. Pleasantry is not appreciated in war; and the officer was arrested, but soon secured his release, and built the battery with men of ordinary height.

In April, 1862, Admiral Du Pont had lined his iron-clads and monitors up before the beetling walls of Fort Sumter, and had hurled solid shot for hours, with only the effect of breaking away sharp corners and projecting edges of the fort, but leaving it still as powerful a work of defence as ever. The little monitors exposed to the terrible fire from the guns of Sumter were fairly riddled; and, when the signal was finally made to withdraw from the action, the humblest sailor knew that Charleston would only fall after a siege as protracted and wearisome as that of Vicksburg.

The investment of Charleston lasted from the date of that first attack upon Fort Sumter until 1865. From time to time the war-vessels would throw a few shells into the city, as a reminder to the inhabitants that they were under surveillance. Early in the siege the Swamp Angel, as the big gun back in the swamp was called, began sending hourly messages, in the form of two-hundred-pound shells, into the city. In one quarter, where the shells fell thickest, a severe fire was started, which raged fiercely, driving people from their homes, and reducing whole blocks to ashes; while the deadly shells aided in the work of destruction. But the life of the Swamp Angel, whose shells were the most destructive, was but short; for, after a few days' work, it burst, scattering the sand-bags, of which the battery was built, far and wide over the swamp.

The officers of the army, who were bringing their troops nearer and

CHARLESTON BOMBARDED.

nearer to the city, expected the iron-clad vessels to steam boldly up the harbor, and compel a surrender of the city; but the naval officers dared not,

WAR-SHIPS OFF CHARLESTON HARBOR.

owing to the torpedoes with which the channel was thickly planted. If Sumter could only be captured, the torpedoes could be searched out and easily removed; and, with this thought in mind, a number of bold sailors fitted out an expedition to attack the fort. Thirty boats, filled with armed men, made their way to the base of the shattered walls of the fort. As they came up, not a sign of life was to be seen about the huge black monster that had so long kept the iron-clads at bay. Rapidly and silently the men swarmed from their boats, and, led by three brave officers, began the ascent of the sloping walls. "The Johnnies are asleep," they whispered to each other: "we have the fort this time." But the Johnnies were wide awake, and waiting behind those grim bastions until the proper moment should arrive. Higher and higher climbed the blue-jackets; and they were just about to spring over the last barrier, when there rose before them a wall of men and a deadly fire of musketry, and a storm of hand-grenades cut their ranks to pieces. Around the corner of the fort steamed a small gunboat, which opened fire on the assailants. The carnage was terrible; and the sailors were driven back to their boats, leaving two hundred dead and wounded, and three stands of colors, as trophies for the garrison.

After that grapple with the giant fortress, the Federals did not again try to come to close quarters; but, keeping at a distance, maintained a steady fire upon the fort, which drove its defenders from the guns, and enabled the Union troops to throw up batteries upon all the neighboring islands. The fleet then remained on blockading-service until Feb. 18, 1865, when the Confederates evacuated the city, and left the fort to the victorious Federals. Five years after the date when Major Anderson with his little band of soldiers had marched out of Sumter, leaving the fort to the enemy, the same gallant officer returned, and with his own hand hoisted the same tattered flag over the almost ruined fortress, amid salvos of artillery and the cheers of a victorious army and navy.

CHAPTER XVIII.

THE BATTLE OF MOBILE BAY.

THE last two actions of the United States navy in the civil war were destined to be the grandest successes of a long record of daring and successful exploits. Farragut at Mobile, and Porter at Fort Fisher, added to their wondrous careers the cap-sheaves of two victories wrested from apparently unconquerable adversaries.

It was on a bright August morning in 1864 that Admiral Farragut stood on the deck of his stanch frigate the "Hartford," that had borne him through so many desperate battles. Around the flag-ship were clustered the vessels of the Gulf squadron. There was the battered old "Brooklyn," scarred with the wounds of a dozen fights; the "Richmond" and the "Itasca," that received their baptism of fire at the fight below New Orleans. In all there were fourteen wooden vessels and four iron-clad monitors assembled in front of the strongest combination of harbor defences that war-ships ever yet dared attack. Yet Farragut was there that bright summer morning to enter that bay, and batter the forts of the enemy into subjection. To capture the city was not his purpose, — that he left to the army, — but the harbor forts and the great ram "Tennessee" must strike their colors to the navy.

Before arranging for the attack, the admiral made a reconnoissance, the results of which are thus told by one of his officers: "On the afternoon of the day of our arrival, Admiral Farragut, with the commanding officers of the different vessels, made a reconnoissance on the steam-tender 'Cowslip,' running inside of Sand Island, where the monitors were anchored, and near enough to get a good view of both forts. On the left, some two miles distant, was Fort Gaines, a small brick-and-earth work, mounting a few heavy guns, but too far away from the ship-channel to cause much uneasiness to the fleet. Fort Morgan was on the right, one of the strongest of the old stone forts, and greatly strengthened by immense piles of sand-bags covering every portion of the exposed front. The fort was well equipped with three tiers of heavy guns, some of them of the best English make, imported by the Confederates. In addition, there was in front a battery of eleven powerful guns, at the water's edge on the beach. All the guns, of both fort and water battery, were within point-blank range of the only channel through which the fleet could pass. The Rebels considered the works impregnable, but they did not depend solely upon them. Just around the point of land, behind Fort Morgan, we could see that afternoon three saucy-looking gunboats and the famous ram 'Tennessee.' The latter was then considered the strongest and most powerful iron-clad ever put afloat; looking like a great turtle, with sloping sides covered with iron plates six inches in thickness, thoroughly riveted together, and having a formidable iron beak projecting under the water. Her armament consisted of six heavy guns of English make, sending a solid shot weighing one hundred and ten pounds, — a small affair compared with the heavy guns of the present time, but irresistible then against every thing but the turrets of the monitors. In addition to these means of resistance, the narrow channel in front of the fort had been lined with torpedoes. These were under the water, anchored to the bottom, and were chiefly in the shape of beer-kegs filled with powder, from the sides of which projected numerous little tubes containing fulminate, which it was expected would be exploded by contact with the passing vessels.

"Except for what Farragut had already accomplished on the Mississippi, it would have been considered a foolhardy experiment for wooden vessels to attempt to pass so close to one of the strongest forts on the coast ; but when to the forts were added the knowledge of the strength of the ram, and the supposed deadly character of the torpedoes, it may be imagined that the coming event impressed the person taking his first glimpse of naval warfare as decidedly hazardous and unpleasant. So daring an attempt was never made in any country but this, and was never successfully made by any commander except Farragut, who in this, as in his previous exploits in passing the forts of the Mississippi, proved himself the greatest naval commander the world has ever seen. It was the confidence reposed in him, the recollection that he had never failed in any of his attempts, and his manifest faith in the success of the projected movement, that inspired all around him."

When the reconnoissance was completed, the admiral called a council of his captains in the ward-room of the "Hartford," and announced that the attack would be made early the following morning. The council over, each commander returned to his ship, there to make ready for the dread business of the morrow. The same writer whom we have before quoted tells how the night before a battle is spent by brave men not afraid of death : —

"At sunset the last order had been issued. Every commanding officer knew his duty, and unusual quiet prevailed in the fleet. The waters of the Gulf rested for a time from their customary tumult, a gentle breeze relieved the midsummer heat, and the evening closed upon us as peacefully as if we had been on board a yachting squadron at Newport. During the early part of the night, the stillness was almost oppressive. The officers of the 'Hartford' gathered around the capacious ward-room table, writing what they knew might be their last letters to loved ones far away, or giving to friends messages and instructions in case of death. There were no signs of fear; but, like brave and intelligent men, they recognized the stern possibilities of the morrow, and acted accordingly.

"But this occupied but little time; and then, business over, there followed an hour of unrestrained jollity. Many an old story was retold, and ancient conundrum repeated. Old officers forgot for the moment their customary dignity, and it was evident that all were exhilarated and stimulated by the knowledge of the coming struggle. Capt. Heywood of the marines proposed a final 'walk-around;' Tyson solemnly requested information as to 'Which would you rather do or go by Fort Morgan?' and all agreed they would prefer to 'do.' La Rue Adams repeated the benediction with which the French instructor at the naval academy was wont to greet his boys as they were going into examination: 'Vell, fellows, I hope ve vill do as vell as I hope ve vill do.' Finally, Chief Engineer Williamson suggested an adjournment to the forecastle for a last smoke, and the smoking club went forward; but somehow smoke had lost its customary flavor, and, after a few whiffs, all hands turned in, to enjoy what sleep would come."

When the morning dawned, the men were called to quarters, and the advance upon the forts was begun at once. It was a foggy morning, and the ships looked like phantom vessels as they moved forward in line of battle, with the "Brooklyn" in the van. Second came the "Hartford," with the admiral high up in the rigging, where he could overlook the whole scene.

"Nearly every man had his watch in his hand, and waited for the first shot. To us, ignorant of every thing going on above, every minute seemed an hour; and there was a feeling of great relief when the boom of the first gun was heard. This was from the monitor 'Tecumseh,' at forty-seven minutes past six o'clock. Presently one or two of our forward guns opened, and we could hear the distant sound of the guns of the fort in reply. Soon the cannon-balls began to crash through the deck above us, and then the thunder of our whole broadside of twelve Dahlgren guns kept the vessel in a quiver. But as yet no wounded were sent down, and we knew we were still at comparatively long range. In the intense excitement of the occasion, it seemed that hours had passed; but it was just twenty minutes from the time we went below when an officer shouted down the hatchway: 'Send up an army signal-officer immediately: the 'Brooklyn' is signalling.' In a moment the writer was on deck, where he found the situation as follows: The 'Brooklyn,' directly in front of us, had stopped, and was backing and signalling; the tide was with us, setting strongly through the channel, and the stopping of the 'Brooklyn' threatened to bring the whole fleet into collision and confusion; the advance vessels of the line were trying to back to prevent a catastrophe, but were apparently not able to overcome the force of the current; and there was danger not only of collision, but of being drifted on shore."

While the fleet was thus embarrassed and hampered, the gunners in the forts were pouring in their shot thick and fast. On the decks of the ships the most terrible scenes of death were visible. Along the port side the bodies of the dead were ranged in long rows, while the wounded were carried below, until the surgeon's room was filled to its last corner. One poor fellow on the "Hartford" lost both legs by a cannon-ball, and, falling, threw up both arms just in time to have them carried away also. Strange to say, he recovered from these fearful wounds.

Just as the fight was at its hottest, and the vessels were nearing the line, the passage of which meant victory, there went up a cry from the whole fleet, "The 'Tecumseh!' Look at the 'Tecumseh!'" All eyes were turned on the monitor, and every one saw that she was sinking. She staggered for a moment, and went down with a rush, carrying her brave commander and over a hundred of her crew. A few escaped, the last of whom was the pilot. As the pilot was rushing for the hatchway that led to the open air and to life, he met at the foot of a narrow ladder Commander Craven. Craven stepped back, saying gravely, "After you, pilot;" and the pilot passed out. "There was nothing after me," said he, in relating the story afterwards; "for as I sprang out of the hatchway the water rushed in, carrying all behind me to the bottom."

This terrible sight made the ships stop for a moment in some confusion; but Farragut signalled sternly from his flagship, "Go on," and all advanced again. As the fight grew fiercer, the admiral grew tired of being on the second ship in the line, and ordered the "Hartford" to forge ahead.

"On board a war steamer the engines are directed by the tap of a bell, the wires connected with which lead to the quarter-deck. One stroke of the bell means 'go ahead;' two, 'stop;' three, 'back;' and four, 'go ahead as fast as possible.' Leaning down through the shrouds to the officer on deck at the bell-pull, the admiral shouted, 'Four bells, *eight bells*, SIXTEEN BELLS! Give her all the steam you've got!' The order was instantly transmitted, and the old ship seemed imbued with the admiral's spirit; and running past the "Brooklyn" and the monitors, regardless of fort, ram, gunboats, and the unseen foe beneath, dashed ahead, all alone, save for her gallant consort, the "Metacomet.'"

But by this time the fleet was well abreast of the forts, and now, pouring out broadside after broadside, they swept along past the terrible ramparts. The Confederate gunboats had found the fight too hot for them, and had fled for shelter, with the exception of the dreaded "Tennessee," which seemed to be holding itself in reserve. It was but a short time before the vessels were safely past the fort, and out of range, floating on the smooth waters of the inner bay. Then the crews were piped to breakfast, and all hands began to recount their narrow escapes.

But the end was not yet, for the ram "Tennessee" was now ready to try her mettle with the fleet. Lieut. Kinney of the "Hartford" tells graphically the story of the desperate fight that the ram carried on alone against the whole attacking flotilla.

"We were just beginning to feel the re-action following such a season of extreme peril and excitement, when we were brought to our senses by the sharp, penetrating voice of executive officer Kimberly calling all hands to quarters; and a messenger-boy hurried down to us with the word, 'The ram is coming.' Every man hastened to his post, the writer to the quarter-deck, where the admiral and fleet-captain were standing. The cause of the new excitement was evident at once. The 'Tennessee,' as if ashamed of her failure, had left the fort and was making at full speed directly for the "Hartford," being then perhaps a mile and a half distant. The spectacle was a grand one, and was viewed by the Rebel soldiers in both forts, who were now out of range of our guns, and lined the walls. Few audiences have ever witnessed so imposing a sight. The great ram came on for a single-handed contest with the fleet. She was believed to be invulnerable, and had powerful double engines by which she could be easily handled; while our monitors were so slow-gaited that they were unable to offer any

FIGHT AT MOBILE BAY.

serious obstacle to her approach. Farragut himself seemed to place his chief dependence on his wooden vessels. Doubtless the crowd of Confederate soldiers who watched the fight expected to see the 'Tennessee' sink the Yankee vessels in detail, and the chances seemed in its favor. . .

"Meanwhile, the general signal, 'Attack the enemy,' had gone up to the peak of the 'Hartford;' and there followed a general slipping of cables, and a friendly rivalry to see which could quickest meet the foe. The 'Monongahela,' with her artificial iron prow, was bravely in the lead, and struck the Rebel craft amidships at full speed, doing no damage to the ram, but having her own iron prow destroyed, and being otherwise injured. Next came the 'Lackawanna,' with a like result. The huge iron frame of the 'Tennessee' scarcely felt the shock, while the wooden bow of the Union ship was badly demoralized. For an instant the two vessels swung head and stern alongside of each other. In his official report, Capt. Marchand naïvely remarks:—

"'A few of the enemy were seen through their ports, who were using *most opprobrious* language. Our marines opened on them with muskets: even a spittoon and a holystone were thrown at them from our deck, which drove them away.'

"The 'Tennessee' fired two shots through her bow, and then kept on for the 'Hartford.' The two flag-ships approached each other, bow to bow. The two admirals, Farragut and Buchanan, had entered our navy together as boys, and up to the outbreak of the war had been warm friends. But now each was hoping for the overthrow of the other; and, had Buchanan possessed the grit of Farragut, it is probable that moment would have witnessed the destruction of both vessels. For had the ram struck us square, as it came, bows on, it would have ploughed its way half through the 'Hartford;' and, as we sank, we should have carried it to the bottom, unable to extricate itself. But the Rebel admiral was not desirous of so much glory; and, just as the two vessels were meeting, the course of the 'Tennessee' was slightly changed, enough to strike us only a glancing blow on the port-bow, which left us uninjured, while the two vessels grated past each other. He tried to sink us with a broadside as he went by; but only one of his guns went off, the primers in all the others failing. That gun sent a shell that entered the berth-deck of the 'Hartford,' and killed five men."

But by this time the unequal conflict was becoming too much even for a man of Buchanan's courage. The armor of the ram was penetrated in several places, and at last came a shot that almost fatally wounded her commander. With the controlling mind that guided her course gone, the ram was useless; and in a moment a white flag fluttered from the shattered stump of her flagstaff. And so closed the naval battle that effectually ended Confederate rule on the Gulf coast, and earned for Farragut his proudest laurels.

CHAPTER XIX.

THE FALL OF FORT FISHER. — THE NAVY ENDS ITS WORK.

IN noticing the work of the blockading-fleet, we have spoken of the fine harbor of Wilmington, and the powerful works that defended its entrance. This Confederate stronghold was known as Fort Fisher, and had been for a long time a cause of anxiety and worry to the Northern authorities. The war had gone past Fort Fisher. To the north and to the south of it, the country was under the sway of the Federal authorities; but there in North Carolina stood the formidable bastions over which floated, in defiance of the laws of the Union, the stars and bars of the rapidly dying Confederacy. With its connected batteries, Fort Fisher mounted seventy-five guns, and was stronger than the celebrated Malakoff at Sebastopol.

To reduce this stronghold, a joint naval and military expedition was fitted out; and Gen. Butler was placed in command of the land forces, while Admiral Porter, torn from his beloved Western rivers, was given command of the fleet. Butler introduced a novel feature at the very opening of the siege. He procured an old steamer, and had her packed full of gunpowder. On a dark night this craft was towed close to the walls of the fort and set afire, in the hopes that she might, in blowing up, tear the works to pieces.

But in this the projectors were disappointed; for the explosion, though a terrific one, did absolutely no harm to the Confederate works. When Porter finally did get into the fort, he asked a soldier what he thought of the attempt to blow them up. "It was a mighty mean trick," responded the Southerner satirically. "You woke us all up."

After this fiasco had set all the world laughing, Butler retired voluntarily, and was succeeded by Gen. Terry; and on Christmas Eve of the year 1864 the fleet began the bombardment, although the land forces were not yet prepared for the assault. It was the grandest armada that was ever arrayed against any fortress. The thunder of nearly five hundred guns rent the air on that Christmas Eve, when carols were being sung in Christian churches throughout the world. Tremendous as was the cannonade, the earthworks were almost a match for it. The fort was not a mass of masonry that these enormous guns might batter down and crumble into rubbish, but a huge bank of earth in which the shells might harmlessly bury themselves. But five hundred cannon are more than a match for any fort, and so they soon proved to be in this instance. Earthworks, guns, and men alike went down before them. The iron-clads were stationed about three-quarters of a mile from the fort, a little farther out were the frigates and heavy sloops, and still beyond were the smaller vessels, — all firing to cover themselves; and all along the whole extended line there blazed one almost continuous sheet of flame, while the rolling thunder of the broadsides, and the defiant answering roar from the guns of the forts, shook earth and sea. Clouds of dust went up from the bastions of the fort, and mingled with the floating smoke above. Within the forts, there was a scene of the most terrible confusion: guns were overturned, piles of cannon-balls were knocked to pieces and scattered about, and two magazines were blown up and scattered fragments all over the parade. In one hour and a quarter all the gunners were driven to the bomb-proofs, and the forts were silenced, not returning a single shot.

On Christmas morning Gen. Terry arrived with all his transports, and the attack was recommenced. Early in the morning the ships fell into position and began a slow fire, merely to cover the landing of the troops.

CHARGE OF SAILORS AT FORT FISHER.

Again the garrison was driven to the bomb-proofs; and, indeed, so entirely were they chased from their posts, that a Federal soldier went into the fort and brought off a Confederate flag without ever having been seen by the garrison. All the troops were landed; but for some reason the attack was deferred, much to the disgust of the officers of the fleet, who felt sure that the fort could be taken then by a dash. But the troops returned to their transports or went into camp, and it was not until weeks after that the assault was fairly made. In the mean time, the ships rode out the winter gales at their anchors, doing a little desultory firing to keep the garrison in a state of unrest.

On the 14th of January the heavy bombardment began again, and again the troops were landed. By night it was seen that every gun on the face of the fort was disabled, and it was decided to storm the works the next day. Sixteen hundred sailors and four hundred marines were told off as the storming-party.

Early in the morning the ships began a fierce cannonade, under cover of which the sailors and marines landed, and threw up light breastworks to cover them until the time should be ripe for the charge. The arrangements contemplated a fierce charge by the blue-jackets, armed with their cutlasses and revolvers; while the marines, remaining in the rifle-pits, should cover the advancing party with a hot fire of musketry. The soldiers from the army-camp were to charge the fort on the other side.

At three o'clock came the signal that all was ready. The whistles of the ships rent the air; and the blue-jackets, with ringing cheers, dashed in a compact body up the beach. But in an instant the Confederate ramparts were black with men, and a furious fire of musketry rained down upon the sailors, who were helpless. The marines in the rifle-pits failed to do what was expected of them, and the sailors halted for a moment in surprise.

As they stood, a most destructive fire rained down upon them; and the poor fellows, grasping their useless cutlasses, turned and fled down the beach, leaving great heaps of dead and wounded behind. Then the Confederates, thinking the day was theirs, sprang on the ramparts, and began a vigorous cheer just as the Union soldiers came pouring over the landward face of the fort. Then ensued a fierce hand-to-hand fight that lasted for hours. The blue-jackets, encouraged, rushed back to the fight, and now at close quarters swung their cutlasses with deadly effect, until step by step the Confederates were driven out of the fort. Then the fleet opened upon them, and they fled for dear life while a sailor sprang to the flagstaff and pulled down the Confederate flag. Fort Fisher had fallen. It was a noble victory, and formed a fitting climax to the work of the navy throughout that great war.

With the fall of Fort Fisher, the navy ceased to be a prominent factor in the war. Its work was done. Along the seacoast, and inland as far as navigable rivers extended, the ships of the North had carried the starry banner; and the sailor-boys of the North had defended it. And their opponents, whether on sea or shore, had shown themselves courageous and dashing, and worthy to be numbered as men of the same nation as those who proved the victors. And who can doubt, that, should the need arise, the sons of these men will show that they have in their veins the blood that animated the Blue-Jackets of '61?

www.ingramcontent.com/pod-product-compliance
Lightning Source LLC
Chambersburg PA
CBHW030011240426
43672CB00007B/911